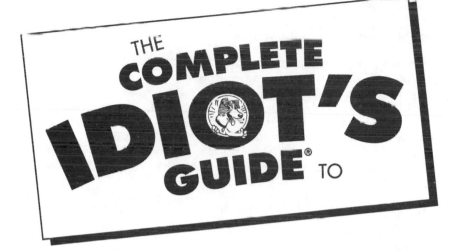

THE COMPLETE IDIOT'S GUIDE® TO

Jack Russell Terriers

by Deborah Britt-Hay

Howell Book House   Alpha Books
Divisions of Macmillan General Reference USA
A Pearson Education Macmillan Company
1633 Broadway, New York NY 10019-6785

Macmillan General Reference books may be purchased for business or sales
promotional use. For information please write: Special Markets Department,
Macmillan Publishing USA, 1633 Broadway, New York, NY 10019-6785.

International Standard Book Number: 1-58245-042-0
Library of Congress Catalog Card Number: 99-10109

01   00   99   8   7   6   5   4   3   2   1

Interpretation of the printing code: The rightmost number of the first
series of numbers is the year of the book's printing; the rightmost
number of the second series of numbers is the number of the book's
printing. For example, a printing code of 99-1 shows that the first
printing occurred in 1999.

Printed in the United States of America

Note: This publication contains the opinions and ideas of its author.
It is intended to provide helpful and informative material on the subject matter covered. It is sold with the understanding that the author
and publisher are not engaged in rendering professional services in
the book. If the reader requires personal assistance or advice, a competent professional should be consulted.

The author and publisher specifically disclaim any responsibility for
any liability, loss or risk, personal or otherwise, which is incurred as a
consequence, directly or indirectly, of the use and application of any
of the contents of this book.

All photography not otherwise acknowledged courtesy of Mark Hay or Randy
Williams and Panache Sport Horses.

Contents at a Glance

Top Tips for Raising Your Jack Russell Terrier Right

1. Choose the puppy or dog that best fits *your* criteria, which should be based on your family's needs, desires and lifestyle.

2. Unless you are positive you want to show or breed your JRT, have it spayed or neutered to prevent an unwanted litter.

3. Remember that many of the odd things your JRT does are normal for the breed. All Jack Russells are all a bit strange!

4. Give your Jack Russell Terrier plenty of room to run and lots of time and exercise with the family. Your JRT needs your attention and won't be happy if left alone in the backyard.

5. Realize that your Jack Russell might take longer to housetrain than other dogs you might have owned. It's not that they aren't as smart; they simply have their own agendas and could take six to eight months to accept your program.

6. Setting the command hierarchy right off the bat is an important part of JRT training. Your terrier needs to know that you are the top dog. Be careful not to antagonize an overly aggressive dog, however, and realize that setting a superior position does not mean intimidating or abusing your terrier.

7. Obedience training is extremely important for a JRT. All Jack Russells should know the basic commands and should perform them consistently.

8. It's easier to prevent bad behaviors from developing than to stop them after they're learned.

9. Puppy-proof your house prior to bringing your JRT home. Many common household items can be dangerous or deadly to your puppy if preventative steps aren't taken.

10. You might encounter some tough discipline problems when training your JRT. Stay calm, keep your temper firmly in check and approach the solution with a clear head and plenty of patience and understanding.

11. Choose your veterinarian with the same care you would use when choosing your family doctor. Don't be afraid to ask questions regarding services and fees. Be sure to take your terrier in for its shots and address any medical concerns with your vet.

12. Select a dog food that is appropriate for your JRT's age and activity level and stick with it. Changing foods can cause digestive upset in your JRT and can lead to allergies or skin conditions.

13. Older terriers and those with special needs require additional attention and care. Be sure to check with your vet if your terrier falls into this category and discuss options to keep it comfortable and healthy.

14. JRTs love to play and need you to be involved in their exercise. Choose fun activities such as beach excursions, terrier trials or agility training to keep your family and your terrier interested and exercised.

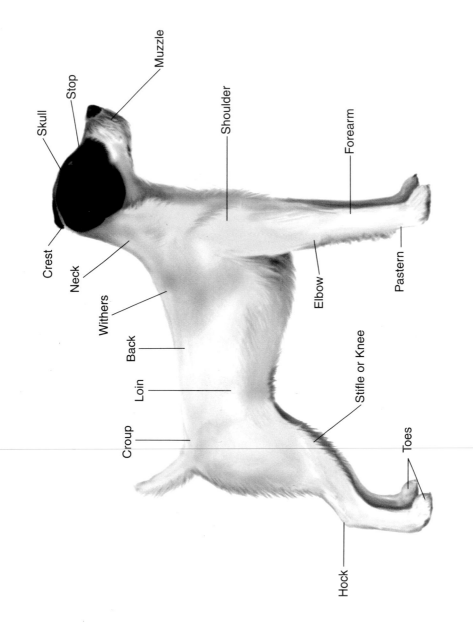

External Features of the Jack Russell Terrier

Contents

Foreword

When I first was approached about writing a foreword for a new Jack Russell Terrier book, I was a little apprehensive. Having been a professional dog trainer for more than twenty-three years and knowing how difficult JRTs can be to train, I wanted to be sure the book would really describe the personality of the breed and would show both its positive and negative traits. When I talked to Deborah, I became excited about the concept: to create a book geared toward new Jack Russell owners who might not know what the breed is all about, to help them decide whether the breed is for them and to help them manage their terrorists after they decide they want to bring one home. That is exactly what has been missing from the bookshelves and is exactly what this book provides.

I own more than forty dogs and have been training Jack Russells specifically for fifteen years. I have had the good fortune to work with some phenomenal trainers including Frank Inn, who trained Benji. I have worked hard to make a name for myself in the animal-acting field, and it's exciting to see my own dogs, such as Wishbone, succeed in their careers.

What you see on the big screen, however, is not real life. I trained Wishbone (a.k.a. Soccer) for more than seven years before I knew he would land a role. I knew he had what it took to succeed, but many long hours of rigorous training and uncertainty preceded his success. I was lucky with Wishbone. Only one out of every ten dogs I work with ever makes it. It is a physically and mentally draining career, and few know the rigorous schedule and demanding tricks these dogs are asked to perform. Training just one of these tricks can take between three days and six months to perfect.

Training any dog, let alone a Jack Russell Terrier, is never easy. You need a lot of patience and an understanding of what makes your own dog tick before you can be successful in your training endeavors. Although the JRT is an incredibly smart breed, these dogs also are opinionated and are more than a little odd. They have quirky behaviors not found in other breeds, which makes training them a bit of a challenge. They are notoriously hard to focus and can be quite stubborn when they want to be. They certainly are not the dogs for everyone.

I was asked to provide some words of advice for you, the potential Jack Russell owner. I first would tell you that, if I had to own just one dog, it would not be a JRT. I love Soccer and the other JRTs I own, but they can be tough. If you decide this is the breed for you, I would urge you to have a solidly fenced yard and to be prepared for a whirlwind of activity. JRTs are NOT couch potatoes. They love to be active, and strong obedience training is a must for this breed. They are good with children and families, and they love to be surrounded by attention. If you are an outdoor person who loves an active lifestyle such as jogging or camping, this might be the perfect breed for you. If you prefer a more sedentary lifestyle, however, and you aren't sure you're ready for the Tasmanian Devil of terriers to enter your home, consider another breed for your doggy options.

If you decide to purchase a Jack Russell, be prepared. You will laugh like you've never laughed before, you will be amazed and frustrated by your dog's intelligence, and you will have a lifelong friend that will probably go to the ends of the earth to try to please you. In other words, you are about to be owned by a Jack Russell Terrier!

Jackie Martin-Kaptan
Owner and trainer of Wishbone

Jackie Martin-Kaptan with Wishbone. Copyright © photographs of Wishbone 1995 Big Feats Entertainment, L.P. All rights reserved. Used with permission.

Introduction

I bet you can't turn on the TV without seeing a commercial or a sit-com showcasing the antics of a little dog with crimped ears, an alert expression and a tail standing at attention.

This saucy little dog has taken the U.S. by storm and is known as the Jack Russell Terrier or, to those who already own one, a Jack Russell Terrorist. Thanks to the popularity of PBS's *Wishbone* and *Frasier's* Eddie, these British imports have become as hot as the Beatles, Earl Grey tea and taxation.

JRTs, as they are commonly called, are not for everyone. It takes time, patience and an unmistakable sense of humor to tolerate their endless antics and their tireless energy. For thousands of dog owners across the country, however, no other breed is worth considering.

If you're contemplating buying a JRT, you must first decide whether the breed truly is the right one for you and your lifestyle. These appealing little terriers have complex and distinctive personalities that are significantly different from the Poodles, Dobermans or Labs with which you might have been raised. This book will help you explore the intricacies—and oddities—of the Jack Russell personality to determine whether you have what it takes to be owned by a Jack Russell Terrier.

After you've made your decision, I will help you along the fun, but often rocky, path of Jack Russell ownership. You'll learn about house-training, health issues, typical behavioral hurdles and how to have lots of fun with your new little soul-mate. Along the way, some funny stories will show that you really are not alone in this endeavor and that your terrier isn't that eccentric when compared to other JRTs.

This book assumes you know nothing about these feisty little dogs. If you have some experience with Jack Russells, you might want to scan the "In This Chapter" sections to determine which chapters relate to your individual situation and interests. If you are considering buying a Jack Russell Terrier, or if you have a new puppy or dog already, this book will take you step-by-step through the fundamentals of raising and training your JRT.

So let's get started!

Extras

One of the extras that makes this book fun and different from other doggy titles is the boxes scattered throughout the book. These boxes focus your attention on interesting facts, important information and safety warnings that can help your training and handling go more smoothly. "The Least You Need to Know" sections at the end of each chapter also are handy references.

Bet You Didn't Know

These boxes offer fun facts I've picked up along the way that highlight what makes these dogs unique and interesting. They're great conversation starters for cocktail parties.

When to Call the Vet

These boxes contain important health precautions that can save your pampered pooch a lot of discomfort and can save you a lot of sleep. Look here if you think something might be harmful to your dog.

Doggy Do's

When you are looking for reinforcements, Doggy Do's can help steer you in the right direction. They offer special tips for training and caring for your dog and provide shortcuts that can save you time and frustration.

Doggy Don'ts

Read these boxes to avoid common pitfalls in training as well as dangerous handling habits that could hurt you or your dog.

Acknowledgments

I want to take a brief moment to thank a few people whose support, encouragement and suggestions were an integral part of this book's success. Thanks to my personal editor, Nicole Bentley, who made sure chapters were as good as they could get prior to sending them to my publisher. Thanks also to my editor at Howell Book House, Amanda Pisani, whose undying belief in my ideas led to this Idiot's Guide and whose remarkable patience kept me sane as I struggled to find a balance between writing and pregnancy. Thanks to the many friends who generously offered pictures, stories and ideas to help make this book unique. And special thanks to my husband, Mark; to my daughter, Taylor; to my own two rotten Russells, Annie and Bubba; and to all my horses and horse-training clients whose needs often took a backseat so I could provide this guide. You are all very special parts of my life.

About the Author

Deborah Britt-Hay has been breeding, training and laughing at Jack Russell Terriers for the past seven years. She received her first JRT as a wedding present from her husband, Mark. As a nationally accomplished trainer of Arabian, Hackney and dressage horses, Deborah found that her spunky Jack Russell fit right in with both her clients and her horses. She enjoyed her female so much that soon a mate was purchased, and the Hay household has never been the same.

Both dogs—Annie and Bubba—travel with Deborah and her horses to various shows across the nation. She rarely is found without one of her trusted terriers by her side. Intent on breeding just a few puppies with good conformation and temperament, Deborah and her husband breed just one litter each year, and most of the puppies end up in her clients' households. "It's great to see them so often, to watch them grow and to know I am providing a few great family dogs that are dearly loved," Deborah says of her litters. "Now we have a whole herd of our Jack Russells at the barn!"

Deborah and her husband live in southern California with their new daughter, Taylor. Her previous book, *Horse Training Basics: An Indispensable Guide to Beginning Trainers,* was published in 1994. She currently is working on a mainstream suspense series with her mother, Nicole Bentley. As Deborah says, "I love to write and I love to teach, so now I have the best of both worlds!"

Part 1

A Match Made in Heaven or Hell?

Are you still considering whether you have what it takes to be owned by a Jack Russell Terrier? If you have it in your mind that the spotted little bundle of joy you pick will grow up to be the next TV star amid the ranks of Wishbone and Eddie, you will be sadly disappointed. Keep in mind that hours upon hours of training have gone into these dogs to make them the trainable little angels they have become.

But that's why you're reading this book, right? This part guides you through the history of the breed, discusses typical breed types, provides insight into the JRT personality and helps you decide between a puppy and an adult dog. It also provides you with insight into the Hollywood world of Jack Russell Terriers, and it shows that what you see on the big screen isn't necessarily representative of the real antics of the Jack Russell Terrier breed. All these factors help determine whether a Jack Russell Terrier is the right dog for you.

If you decide, after reading this part, that the potential pitfalls are out-weighed by the advantages and the JRT is your perfect pooch, then Part 2 shows you how to cope with your new addition and exactly what you'll need to make a new home for your furry friend. It reiterates the space requirements, the lifestyle considerations, and the adjustments you and your children will have to make for all to go smoothly. So let's see if a JRT is right for you!

Where Did These Critters Come From?

> **In This Chapter**
>
> ➤ A brief look at JRTs in England
>
> ➤ The first kennel club
>
> ➤ The Jack Russell Terrier Club of Great Britain
>
> ➤ JRTs' growing popularity in the U.S.
>
> ➤ Differing opinions

The English Jack Russell Terrier

Like many historical beginnings, the breed known as the Jack Russell Terrier began as a quest—in this case, a quest for a better hunting dog. The story began somewhere between 1815 and 1820 with an avid fox hunter, Reverend John Russell, the vicar of Swimbridge in Devon, who decided he wanted a more efficient fox-hunting terrier than those found within the local dog population. Rather than search the world over to find the perfect hunting companion, Parson Jack, as he was affectionately known, decided to take the best dogs he could find in his area and breed exactly the type of terrier he sought. Thus, the first Jack Russell Terriers were born.

The original Jack Russell Terriers were conceived in Devonshire, England in the mid-1800s. The original female (or *bitch*, to use the

3

proper breeding term) was a terrier named Trump. The vicar found Trump in Oxfordshire while attending Exeter College at Oxford. He immediately was struck by her stature and markings and by her resemblance in size to the vixens he so often hunted. Trump was considered the foundation terrier in Reverend Russell's breeding program and has now become a legend in Jack Russell history. In fact, her likeness still adorns the entrance to the Jack Russell Inn, which is near Barnstable in England.

Bet You Didn't Know

Most early–day prints and lithographs depict terriers with rough or broken coats. Today, however, more smooth–coated Jack Russell Terriers are seen.

It is said that Trump was predominantly white, with only a patch of tan over each eye and ear (also called a full mask) and a penny-sized dot at the base of her tail. Her coat was wiry, and her body was strong and sturdy. She was between 13 and 14 inches tall and possessed all the traits Parson Jack had been looking for in a hunting dog. After some tough negotiating, he made a deal with the milkman who owned her, and Parson Jack happily became Trump's new owner.

It is said that Parson Jack preferred mostly white terriers with few markings and strove to produce dogs with these characteristics. In spite of his preference for white coats, however, the first mating is thought to have occurred between Trump and a fine young terrier with a black-and-tan broken coat. The resulting litter created history as the foundation stock for the Jack Russell type of terrier.

By the 1850s, Parson Jack was considered one of the leading breeders of terriers in England. By the time he died at age 88, Reverend John Russell had made a significant mark on fox terrier history. Allegedly, his breeding stock was disbursed upon his death to Squire Nicholas Snow and, eventually, to Arthur Heinemann, who continued to produce quality terriers in the type and style of Parson Jack's dogs.

The JRT was named after Parson John Russell, who bred white terriers that were rugged and energetic.

Although Parson Jack's terriers were primarily fox terriers in their makeup, they began to take on a different look as Reverend Russell bred for his preferences. He clearly wanted a tough, working dog with a good length of leg and vigorous stamina that would allow it to keep up with the running hounds. He also needed a small dog that easily could penetrate the fox's hole and a strong tail that could be used as a handle to pull it out after the hunt master arrived. Lastly, he needed terriers with a strong instinct to go to ground should the need arise.

Because of the risk of breeding a terrier with bull terrier blood, Parson Jack leaned toward the wire-haired type. He felt the bull terrier cross might make his terriers too aggressive with the foxes, although plenty of smooth-coated terriers were born as a result of his breeding program. His primary goal was to create a terrier that would chase the fox out of the hole to make it accessible to the hunters or that would hold the quarry until called off by the hunt master. He also wanted a terrier he could set to the fox without worrying that the fox would be maimed or killed.

Trump, Parson Jack's foundation bitch, was purchased from a milkman.

No dog with a proclivity toward over-aggressiveness ever became part of Parson Jack's breeding program. Likewise, all dogs produced that did not like to hunt were culled as working terriers and lived their days as pets in the homes of friends and acquaintances who were not interested in hunting. Only dogs with an instinct for earth work, a fierce love of hunting and the conformation and stamina to face the rigors of hunting were allowed to breed and perpetuate the bloodline. Perhaps the success of the breed is the direct result of Reverend Russell's fierce culling process and his determined quest for the best working dog possible.

Bet You Didn't Know

Jack Russell Terriers and their ancestors sometimes were carried on small platforms on their grooms' backs when they went on fox hunts to avoid wearing of the dogs' pads during the chase.

The First Kennel Club

In 1862, England held its first dog show, and Parson Jack won his first honors with one of his dogs. Afterward, Parson Jack became a

Bet You Didn't Know

The word *terrier* is derived from the Latin word *terra*, which means earth. This seems quite appropriate because the terrier is bred to go to ground after its prey, staying there for days if necessary to complete the kill (when hunting a rodent) or until its master pulls it out (when hunting a fox).

dog-show judge with a special eye toward preserving working terriers. When the Kennel Club of Great Britain was formed in 1873, Parson Jack was welcomed as a founding member. The first Kennel Club Stud Book was issued in 1874, and the founders began to look toward the future for their breeding stock. A breed standard was formed, and a rule was established that any dog shown at a show not sanctioned by the Kennel Club rules would be permanently barred from registry.

Despite these restrictions, Reverend Russell held firm to his own beliefs in breed standard and form to function. At the risk of being shunned or even banned, Parson Jack continued to maintain his own breeding stock, pedigrees and standards. He refused to show his dogs in the conformation classes, preferring instead to focus on the working aspects of the dog.

Though he maintained his membership until death, he eventually moved away from the type decreed by the Kennel Club as the ideal hunting dog, the fox terrier, in favor of a hardier working terrier that soon would become known as the Jack Russell Terrier.

Although the fox terrier has moved away from its original purpose as a functional hunting dog towards a loftier, more beautiful show-ring type, Jack Russell breeders have adhered to Parson Jack's quest for the perfect working terrier and have, in essence, created the truest fox-hunting terrier.

To this day, breeders have their own opinions about what characteristics epitomize the Jack Russell breed, and heated discussions have ensued on the subject between Kennel Club members and members of working Jack Russell Terrier clubs worldwide. Although some prefer a longer, leaner terrier and others prefer a shorter, stockier dog, the fundamental hunting instincts remain paramount to all Jack Russell breeders.

Like Reverend Russell, many JRT proponents shun the show ring in favor of working-class competitions. They feel these tests of ability more effectively portray the dog's original purpose. These owners also disagree with the registration process adopted by the Kennel Club of England and the American Kennel Club in the United States. They disagree with these clubs' focus on show-ring terriers and their blanket registration of litters from registered terriers regardless of inherited defects or conformational flaws.

The Jack Russell Terrier Club of Great Britain

The Jack Russell Terrier Club of Great Britain (JRTCGB) was founded in 1975 by Mrs. Romayne Moore, a long-time advocate of the working Jack Russell Terrier and a former founder of the Midland Working Terrier Club. After several false starts and misdirected ambitions, the JRTCGB became the governing body for Jack Russell Terriers in England. It is responsible for drawing up breed standards, by-laws and rules, and it must keep a complete and accurate registry of all eligible Jack Russells in England. It also is responsible for overseeing the future of the breed, including its primary goal of preserving it first and foremost as a hunting dog.

Bet You Didn't Know

Early British terriers were bred for endurance and hard work, not for good looks.

Under this governing umbrella, smaller regional clubs servicing the Isle of Wight, North and South Wales, Thames Valley, Border Counties, Midlands, Southeast and Southwest offer services to their individual areas and make sure JRT owners have the information and support necessary to stay current on the workings of the main registry. In addition, these clubs offer activities, shows, newsletters and advice for members and their dogs. By getting owners involved in activities that take advantage of their terriers' natural hunting instincts and traits, these clubs strive to preserve the working Jack Russell Terrier. Through their registries, they hope to prevent the breed from developing into something different from the sound working terrier that has been in existence for so long.

Jack Russell Terriers Take Over the U.S.A.

Though a select few terriers might have made their way to the United States earlier, the most significant import occurred when Mrs. Slater offered the gift of a JRT puppy to her friend, Mrs. Crawford, in New Jersey in the 1960s. So taken was Mrs. Crawford with her new dog, named Rare, that she wanted to learn everything there was to know about this curious little dog, such as where the breed originated and how to start a breeding program for them in the United States.

She set off for England to educate herself about the breed and its history. She learned that the Jack Russell Terrier originally was bred as a fox hunter. She also learned that they are very efficient rat hunters and are responsible for keeping rodents of all types out of barns, outbuildings and chicken coops. Finally, she learned the different body conformations, coat types and temperaments of the Jack Russell breed.

Armed with this information, Mrs. Crawford contacted as many experts as possible and purchased several terriers to begin her own breeding kennel in the United States, Hamilton Farm Jack Russell Terriers. Between the early 1960s and 1978, Mrs. Crawford produced some of the top Jack Russell Terriers in the country and made a solid name for herself as one of the foremost breeders of Jack Russell Terriers in the United States.

In 1976, Mrs. Crawford founded the Jack Russell Terrier Club of America. Until recently, the JRTCA was the only registry available in the United States to register Jack Russell Terriers. She also became a judge and is known as the foremost defender of the Jack Russell Terrier as a working dog rather than as a show dog, with all its required characteristics.

Bet You Didn't Know

Jack Russell Terriers not only are found in Great Britain and the United States, they also can be found in Australia, Canada, Japan, Malaysia, the Cayman Islands and Singapore.

As the breed increases in popularity, so does the concern of responsible breeders who are eager to maintain the working qualities of the dog. Many litters now are being produced simply to increase the number of JRTs in the U.S. and ostensibly to turn over a quick dollar. The increased visibility of the breed through commercials, television programs and movies has piqued the interest of Americans and has led to a huge demand for this capricious little dog.

In the past several years, the number of JRTs in the United States has grown from several hundred registered with JRTCA to several thousand, and the numbers continue to grow rapidly. Not all of these dogs have been carefully bred to rigorous standards. Many are the result of uninformed breeders and people anxious to capitalize on the rising popularity of the breed. It is important for you to be aware of this trend so you can avoid the pitfalls you might encounter when contacting a less-than-knowledgeable breeder as a source for your new terrier.

Both the British and U.S. registries operate under the same principles, and both are adamant in their duties to maintain accurate bloodline records, strict policies against inbreeding and stringent standards for registration. In addition, both continue to focus their efforts on a strong, working terrier rather than on a purely cosmetic dog more suitable for the show ring than for the hunt.

Differing Opinions

In recent history, there has been dissension even between breeders in the United States. For years the JRTCA and the JRTGB allowed a wide range of height and body style standards to allow for the different types of Jack Russell Terriers, although favoring the longer-legged dogs more similar to the originals Reverend Parson bred. In fact, at least two clubs—the Jack Russell Terrier Breeder's Association (JRTBA) and the Parson Jack Russell Club in England—have splintered off from the original registries. Not only do these clubs strongly favor the longer-legged dogs, they also welcome recognition by the American Kennel Club and the English Kennel Club. They are quite pleased by the recent acceptance of Jack Russell Terriers into both kennel clubs, and they are continuing their efforts to build strong relationships with their all-breed cousins.

Because JRTCA and JRTCGB members are adamantly opposed to the Kennel Club affiliations, it isn't hard to imagine the rift between the two factions. To further muddy the waters, the English Jack Russell Terrier Club of America (EJRTCA) is fighting to uphold the short-legged Jack Russell Terriers and is beginning its own registry for just this type of dog. Now all the registries are preventing cross-registry of any type, creating a serious fragmentation of Jack Russell breeders across the United States and England.

Although there is no doubt that members of all these organizations are sincerely interested in preserving and protecting their vision of the perfect Jack Russell Terrier, and although all believe they have the best interest of the breed at heart, who is truly "right" in this battle remains to be seen. Regardless of the controversy, they all agree that this is a special little dog that deserves to be carefully propagated and cherished by its owners. Like the terriers themselves, their owners differ in attitude, opinions and motivations, but they all fiercely defend their Jack Russells and continue to work toward their own ideals and beliefs.

Doggy Do's

Take all conflicting information from different sources with a grain of salt. All are well-meaning Jack Russell owners with their own ideas of what is correct for the JRT. None of these ideas should be considered gospel, and you should not feel demeaned if your opinions differ from some of theirs.

As the battle rages on, the breed continues to grow in popularity both with specialty groups such as horse owners and with the general public, which has an almost cult-like fascination with these dogs.

Producers are beginning to recognize the natural charisma and charm of these little characters, and more and more JRTs are popping up on television and movie screens across the nation. The more exposure they receive, the more their popularity grows.

As demand increases, so does the chance of overpopulation and unintentional abuse in the hands of the misinformed. With a breed that has remained so unchanged for so long, it would be a shame to see it deteriorate because of its own popularity. Only through education will the breed survive and prosper within homes that love and understand the true heart and nature of the JRT. It is the only way to continue to preserve the breed's uniqueness.

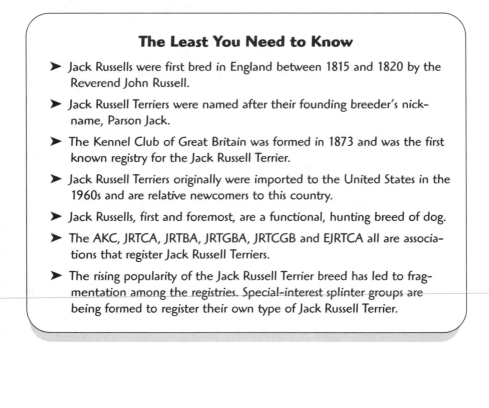

The Least You Need to Know

➤ Jack Russells were first bred in England between 1815 and 1820 by the Reverend John Russell.

➤ Jack Russell Terriers were named after their founding breeder's nickname, Parson Jack.

➤ The Kennel Club of Great Britain was formed in 1873 and was the first known registry for the Jack Russell Terrier.

➤ Jack Russell Terriers originally were imported to the United States in the 1960s and are relative newcomers to this country.

➤ Jack Russells, first and foremost, are a functional, hunting breed of dog.

➤ The AKC, JRTCA, JRTBA, JRTGBA, JRTCGB and EJRTCA all are associations that register Jack Russell Terriers.

➤ The rising popularity of the Jack Russell Terrier breed has led to fragmentation among the registries. Special-interest splinter groups are being formed to register their own type of Jack Russell Terrier.

Chapter 2

What Should a Jack Russell Terrier Look Like?

In This Chapter

➤ Current accepted breed standard

➤ Variations of body type and height

➤ Smooth, furry or somewhere in between?

➤ Common faults

To determine what is "correct" in terms of conformation, you first must understand the characteristics that are considered "accepted breed standard." This question is harder to answer than you might think. Because of the split between the AKC, the JRTCA and the JRTBA, and because of the further addition of the EJRTCA, the matter of "standard" becomes somewhat blurred because each registry holds its own specifications as to desired type. Because the AKC is not currently accepting applications for new registrations and because the EJRTCA focuses only on the newer, short-legged type of dog, this chapter examines the JRTCA standard and how it might apply to your dog search. For more information about the differences in the registries and their individual preferences and requirements, refer to Chapter 1 and the chapters in Part 6.

General Characteristics

Before examining the specific physical characteristics that makes this dog unique, let's look at the overall appearance that a JRT should present. First, the terrier must appear to be alert and energetic. It also should appear to be quick witted, should be eager to join the fray, and should be confident in its actions. The dog should appear balanced and square, even at first glance, and should give the appearance of strength and good health. The tear card in the front of this book shows you the body parts of the Jack Russell.

Because the Jack Russell Terrier was bred to be a hunting dog, it must appear ready for action and excitement and should present a picture of a friendly, outgoing dog with a bright look and a cheerful expression. If you've seen even one Jack Russell Terrier, I'm sure you've noticed that quick, eager-to-pounce look in its eyes, especially if you pick up a ball or another toy. This is the quality that the standard talks about.

Bet You Didn't Know

Jack Russell Terriers often have been described as having the personality of a leprechaun.

Basic Temperament

Although a JRT always should be game for a good hunt, it should not have a hair-trigger bark, should not yap at anything that passes by and should not appear anxious or nervous. A dog that feels the need to bark at the slightest perceived threat usually is timid by nature, a definite fault in the Jack Russell breed. Any inclination towards cowering, timidity or nervousness also is undesirable. Even as a pet, it is easy to see why these traits are frowned upon. Because the JRT's bark is quite loud and distinct, you really don't want to be awakened ten times during night because your JRT *thinks* it might possibly hear something as far as 10 blocks away.

Although the Jack Russell should be confident in its actions, over-aggressiveness—especially toward humans—is not a desired trait. The JRT is bred to be confident in its job as a hunter and to either flush quarry out of its den or hold the quarry in the hole until its master comes and calls it off. Except for its job as a rat hunter, the dog is not asked to attack the quarry, and any such tendencies are seriously frowned upon. As a hunting dog, the JRT should work alongside its master, holding when asked and relinquishing its prey when commanded. It should happily comply with its owner's wishes and should be neither encouraged to display aggression nor punished for being bold.

Doggy Don'ts

Don't confuse nervousness with high energy. A Jack Russell Terrier always is on the move, hunting and exploring its surroundings. An anxious dog—one that routinely paces or is easily upset by changes in its surroundings—is not considered to be of ideal JRT temperament.

Intelligence

Along with its alert, energetic appearance, the JRT also should exude intelligence, which it often does to a maddening degree. The dog is quick to solve problems and is eager to find ways around perceived barriers. All this quick thinking makes the dog delightful to be around and humorous to watch. But be careful. Many a Jack Russell has been known to outsmart its owner!

Charming and playful, the JRT is happiest in the company of its owner, either snuggled up on a bed or curled up at your feet, but always on the lookout for a good game of ball. Remember, however, that the Jack Russell Terrier is far from a couch potato. It needs regular play periods throughout the day to be truly content. When at a loss for a playmate, the JRT is likely to create its own entertainment, either by tearing through the house at break-neck speed like a drag racer, by teaching itself to sit like a gopher to get your attention or by barking at you and then running off to try to entice you to play. The bottom line is, if you don't have a sense of humor, you won't appreciate a Jack Russell Terrier.

Bet You Didn't Know

In sixteenth-century Germany, terriers often were offered as gifts among royalty.

General Appearance

A Jack Russell should range in height from 10 to 15 inches at the withers (the point between the dog's shoulder blades), and its legs should be roughly the same length as its body. As I mentioned in the preceding chapter, there has been much controversy over this wide range of acceptable JRT heights. Such a range was deemed necessary, however, to accommodate the needs of all hunters with varying quarry.

With the exception of the EJRTCA, none of the governing bodies condone the short-legged JRT because of this dog's inability to easily keep up with horses on the hunt. Opponents also cite another drawback to this style of dog, pointing out that the short-legged dogs are stocky in build, which prevents the dog from easily going to ground. Because the quarry these dogs seek often lives in dens deep within the earth and because the openings to these dens often are quite small, any dog that would have trouble penetrating these holes is considered more hindrance than help.

Because the dogs were bred to be working dogs, it is understood by all registries than any scars or injuries as the result of work or an accident should never be penalized unless they interfere with the dog's movement, utility or ability to reproduce. Such scars often are seen on Jack Russell Terrier champions and are the result of either controlled hunting or the dog's own hunting excursions.

When showing Jack Russell Terriers, two groups take into account the wide range in acceptable heights. The smaller class features dogs from 10 to 12½ inches. The taller class allows dogs from 12½ inches up to the maximum of 15 inches in height. Any dog under 12 inches or over 15 inches is not allowed to compete in conformation classes.

This picture shows two dogs at each end of the "acceptable" height standard for JRTCA. JRTs that are considered short-legged are much stockier and appear a bit stubby in relation to the length of their bodies.

Body Fundamentals

The dog's body should be in proportion to its height, creating the appearance of squareness. Its trunk and legs should be well muscled and solidly fit. Sturdy and tough are words often used to describe a Jack Russell's body type, and the overall appearance should be balanced. In male dogs, both testicles must be fully formed and descended to be eligible for competition.

The chest should be narrow, and there should not be excessive distance between the front legs. The overall look should be lean, like the body of a competitive diver or an endurance runner. This characteristic enables the Jack Russell to enter the holes of its prey without getting stuck, an important attribute because many dens are quite long and deep. It is very difficult to dig out a JRT that gets caught within the depths of a fox hole. An age-old guideline is that the circumference of the chest behind the withers can be encircled by average-sized hands when the terrier is in hunting condition. A barrel-chested dog is not able to easily go to ground and is considered less than ideal.

Tops and Tails

The head of a Jack Russell Terrier should be in proportion to its body and should be well muscled through the jaw and the cheeks. It should be moderately wide and should narrow to a clean, fine muzzle. The dog should not have an excessively long nose nor should it appear pug-nosed. The skull should be large enough to enclose a rather large brain, at least in dog terms, but it should not appear coarse or heavy. The eyes should be bright and full of life and always should be watching and taking in the dog's surroundings. The eyes usually are dark in color.

The ears should be small and should present a V-shaped appearance when held at attention. They should not stand straight up away from the head (prick-eared) nor should they droop or fall heavily from the top. The ears should be relatively thin and well shaped and should not be fleshy or thick in appearance. They should look like little triangular flaps that fall evenly over the ear opening.

Bet You Didn't Know

Level bite occurs when the incisors meet one another instead of the top overlapping the bottom. Overbite is an excess of space between the top and bottom teeth, causing the top teeth to protrude away from the bottom teeth.

The bite should slightly overlap in a scissor bite and should be strong and well formed. If the dog has a pug-nosed appearance, it could be the result of an incorrect bite. Likewise, a dog that looks bucktoothed probably has an overbite.

The neck should appear muscular but clean and should taper well into the shoulder, which should be well-laid back and sloping. When looking at the dog from the side, you should be able to see clean, long lines. The angles of the shoulder should look proportional to the angles of the leg, creating a strong, functional front end. There also should be a good angle from the point of the shoulder (the point that sticks out in front of the dog's chest) to the withers (the point where the two shoulders meet behind the dog's neck).

The terrier's front legs should be straight and strong without any deviation as the leg falls from the shoulder. The hindquarters should appear muscular and should show good angulation for drive and impulsion. Again, either look or feel with your fingers to be sure the angles of the hind legs have good slope and are easy to flex. A dog with hind legs that are too straight will not have enough impulsion to keep up with running horses and hounds, and its movements will appear more labored.

The tail should be set high and carried gaily. It should be docked long enough to serve as a handle, which is used to pull the dog from the dens it was bred to find. One of the most common mistakes made by veterinarians in the United States is to dock the JRT's tail too short. A good rule of thumb is that the tail should be docked to two-thirds of its original length. If there is a question, the vet should err on the side of leaving it too long. A properly docked tail should look more like a handle than a stub. When shown, however, a dog is not penalized for having too short a tail, provided it is set well onto its body.

Coat Types and Colors

Although everyone agrees the Jack Russell Terrier should be predominantly white, there has been much debate over which coat type should be considered desirable. Currently, there are three accepted coat types: smooth, rough and broken. If smooth, the coat should be thick and dense for protection against the elements and brush, and it should not feel silky to the touch. If rough or broken, the coat must not be woolly. Rough-coat dogs often appear wiry, and broken-coat dogs look like a blend of the other two. Both broken-coat and rough-coat dogs have longer hair on the jaw, creating a fuzzy-faced appearance. The rough-coat dog requires regular stripping to maintain a neat

Doggy Do's

Groom your dog regularly. All Jack Russell coat types shed. The more brushing you do, the less likely it is that your dog's hair will wind up sprinkled on your clothes and carpet or in your family car.

appearance, although all coat types require some degree of brushing and grooming to stay healthy and neat.

Many people claim the shorthaired Jack Russells shed more, but that could be because their coats are a little more dense and there is more hair to lose. In addition, the shorter hair seems to work its way more easily into the fibers of your clothes, especially whenever you choose to wear black. The best solution is a good brush that gets used often and a good vacuum cleaner.

Although white is the primary color of the Jack Russell Terrier, black, brown and tan markings are acceptable as long as the coat is at least 51 percent white. Most markings come in the form of masks (dark patches around one or both eyes) and body spots. Some JRTs are marked more brightly, however, similar to the markings you see on a cow. All are acceptable, provided the markings don't overpower the basic white coat color. Too much coat coloring (more than 50 percent) and brindle markings (layers of black pigment in regions of lighter color) are unacceptable.

Bet You Didn't Know

A liver nose is a deep reddish-brown color that will disqualify a Jack Russell Terrier from the show ring. (But it won't disqualify a dog from being a great companion!)

Less Than Perfect

Like it or not, no dog (or dog owner for that matter) is perfect—all have one fault or another. In Jack Russell Terrier terms, several characteristics are considered breeding faults and will be penalized in show competition. Any dog displaying shyness, over-aggressiveness or disinterest is penalized. It's hard to be a big game hunter when your dog is snoring under a bush or attacking the other dogs! Likewise, a dog that runs at the sight of a fox hardly is considered an asset.

Hunting Faults

Physically, the list of faults is quite long, and any trait considered weak for hunting is penalized. These necessary physical characteristics are crucial because a dog's success during the hunt depends on its ability to maneuver and to physically perform the tasks asked of it. The terrier must be able to be heard when below ground, so a strong voice is important. Without it, the dog could be hidden in a hole while its owner searches futilely to find it. Although the bark should be easily heard, it should not be high pitched or shrill. You will recognize this fault right away the first time you hear it. A shrill voice penetrates your skull in much the same way as fingernails on a chalkboard. Your only goal in life becomes to find some way to shut it up!

Specific Physical Flaws

The dog must be in fit condition without physical characteristics to hinder it in its work. To this end, the following are considered to be extensive physical faults:

➤ Weak or under-muscled jaws

➤ Incorrect bites

➤ Thick or fat ears

➤ Shoulder blades that are not well formed or that dip down significantly behind the base of the neck

➤ Narrow or weak hips that could lead to hip dysplasia

➤ Ribs that are too sprung, causing a barrel-like appearance

➤ Legs that bow out at the knees (bull-legged)

➤ Legs that are too straight between the top of the hind leg and the hock (the knee-type joint on the back legs)

➤ Small or weak feet

➤ Sluggish or unsound movement

➤ Toeing out or toeing in, which prevents the leg from swinging in a straight line when the dog walks

21

➤ Flipping of the feet either in or out while walking or running

➤ Silky or woolly coats

➤ Shrill or weak voices

➤ Lack of muscle tone or skin tone

➤ Lack of stamina or lung reserve

➤ Any evidence of foreign blood

Quite a list to say the least! Does this mean that a dog with any of these traits is totally unacceptable? No. It simply means the dog would be considered less than ideal in the conformation or breeding class if you were to present it to a licensed Jack Russell Terrier judge for inspection. Most of these factors wouldn't strongly affect a dog that's just a pet, although some could lead to future physical limitations and others, such as the shrill bark, could be quite annoying. This is where your personal goals and ideals come into play.

Bet You Didn't Know

The appearance of the Jack Russell Terrier has changed little over the past hundred years to allow it to continue as a fox-hunting breed.

Your Personal Choice

Most JRTs make wonderful pets, but not all make wonderful show dogs. It is much easier to find a dog of pet quality than it is to find a dog of breeding or show quality. Keep in mind that only dogs presented in AKC, JRTCA or JRTBA conformation trials are judged by these standards, and only dogs that are shown are penalized for these weaknesses. Judge your individual dog by the use you intend for it, and forgive its minor faults if its function is to serve as your companion and lap warmer. Last I checked, JRTCA and AKC had no classes for bed pillows or slipper retrievers.

In the end, it is important to buy from a reputable breeder and to buy the healthiest dog you can find that best fits the criteria *you* have selected as important. Unless you are planning to show your terrier in conformation classes, you should forgive weaknesses that are unimportant to you, provided they don't jeopardize the health and future of your pet. Personality, temperament and appeal are the most important qualities you should consider, and you should resolve to have your dog spayed or neutered as soon as your vet says it's feasible. Don't fall into the lure of breeding a pet-quality dog just to raise a few bucks. It won't pay off in the long run, and you will be adding to the problems the breed already faces—overpopulation and indiscriminate breeding.

Doggy Don'ts

Don't allow a breeder to dissuade you from a dog you are drawn to in favor of a more expensive show-quality dog unless you are seriously planning to breed or show your dog. Although the other dog might be more conformationally correct, the most important feature in a pet is personality. Allow your temperament and preference to be your guide.

If you *do* plan to show your dog, specifically in conformation classes (remember, working class dogs are judged on their performance, *not* their conformation), or if you are considering breeding your dog in the future, you should buy the best dog you can afford with well-known registered parents and from the most prestigious breeder you can find. If you plan to breed your dog, you have to be even more careful about temperament and have to seek even higher standards in conformation and pedigree. Can you see now why it's so important for you to decide ahead of time exactly what you want in a dog?

The Least You Need to Know

➤ Jack Russell Terriers should be sturdy, fit dogs with bright, attentive eyes and an energetic, happy nature.

➤ JRTs have three different coat types: smooth, rough and broken. All coat types require grooming, though the smooth-coat seems to shed more. In addition, all rough-coat and some broken-coat dogs must be stripped on a regular basis.

➤ Any characteristic that would inhibit the dog's usefulness for hunting should be considered a breeding and conformation flaw; however, it won't necessarily hinder your dog's job as a pet.

➤ Each registry differs in its interpretation of the ideal terrier, and the list of registries is growing daily. Approach the registries that most interest you and that fit most closely with your personal goals for you and your dog.

➤ Evaluation of your own hierarchy of requirements is as important as the breed standard when evaluating and choosing a dog.

➤ If you decide on a pet-quality dog, be sure to have it spayed or neutered to prevent any temptation toward indiscriminate breeding.

Chapter 3

A Star Is Born!

In This Chapter

> ➤ JRTs take on Hollywood
>
> ➤ Famous firsts
>
> ➤ *Wishbone*
>
> ➤ *Frasier*
>
> ➤ Other hairy heartthrobs

JRTs Take on Hollywood

With their spunky personalities, endless energy and remarkable intelligence, it's no wonder that Jack Russell Terriers have become a favorite among producers. From television ads to blockbuster hits, the JRT is making its mark on viewers across the nation. Hollywood and Madison Avenue can't seem to get enough of the Jack Russell Terrier.

More and more JRTs are popping up in the most interesting places—Nissan commercials, ads for the Travel Channel, sitcoms such as *Frasier* and even a show called *Wishbone* in which the big star is, what else, a Jack Russell Terrier. We see JRTs alongside such film greats as Jim Carrey in *The Mask* and Gene Hackman in *Crimson Tide*, and these little white dynamos are holding their own in the acting department.

Bet You Didn't Know

Performing comes naturally to Jack Russell Terriers whether on TV, in the movies or in your own home. They love to show off their strange and quirky personalities, and they have more than their share of fun while entertaining you and themselves.

Famous Firsts

The use of terriers in advertising began in the late 1880s when Nipper, a bull/fox terrier mix, became widely known as the RCA dog in the United States. After the death of the terrier's master, he came to live with Mark and Francis Barraud. As a photographer, Francis Barraud recognized the potential in the little dog. At Francis Barraud's studio, Nipper would listen to the old phonograph, cocking his head and appearing fascinated by the pleasant music emanating from the odd machine. It occurred to Mr. Barraud that perhaps Nipper was waiting to hear his master's voice amidst the music. He decided to paint Nipper's portrait and to try to capture his quizzical look as he sat next to the gramophone. The result was the oil painting titled *His Master's Voice.*

Dissatisfied with the painting, which he considered too dark, Barraud visited the Gramophone Company in London and borrowed a brass horn to brighten up the picture. Gramophone executives became interested in the painting, but only if Barraud agreed to replace the Edison Bell cylinder phonograph originally used in the painting with the company's new disc-style gramophone. Thus, a star was born.

The company originally used the portrait under its 1900 English trademark and named the painting *Dog and Trumpet.* Emile Berliner, the inventor of the disc gramophone, saw the painting. Upon his return to the United States, he began using the trademarked image, which he registered in the States as *Nipper and the Gramophone.* A corporate trademark for more than a century, Nipper appears on literally millions of RCA-Victor products. A replica is displayed at the Capitol Records Building in Hollywood, California.

Nipper also was the model for a statue that has become a famous landmark in Albany, New York. Because the statue is so tall, it sports an aircraft beacon on its right ear to ward off possible collisions. Millions of Nipper replicas in rubber, plastic and ceramic have become collectibles for enthusiasts across the nation, and Nipper has become the RCA dog in the minds and hearts of countless of admirers.

In 1990, Nipper was joined by a new puppy companion named Chipper, who represents RCA's semiconductor-based digital products. To portray a youthful image, Chipper is replaced regularly with younger counterparts to retain the puppy look. Regardless of age, the poster children for the RCA Company are undeniably Jack Russell Terriers in all their bright-eyed glory.

Bet You Didn't Know

Several agencies, such as All Tame Animals, Animals in Advertising, Dawn Animal Agency and Media K9, specialize in booking dogs for TV, films and advertising. Many famous dog owners, however, act as the owner, trainer and agent for their dogs.

Wishbone

Perhaps one of the most widely recognized Jack Russell Terriers on television today is Jackie Martin-Kaptan's Soccer, who landed the role of PBS's *Wishbone* after beating out more than one hundred other dogs for the part. Although the part wasn't specifically written for a Jack Russell, *Wishbone* producer Rick Duffield recognized in Soccer the look and attitude that personified the quirky little dog depicted in the show. Soccer doesn't have to act. He really is Wishbone, and he loves to show people just how smart he is.

Soccer's success did not come easily. Ms. Kaptan bought the playful little bundle at 8 weeks of age, hoping he would have what it takes to make it big. She put seven long years of training into him before he ever got his big break. The production schedule and publicity demands for the role keep both her and Soccer hopping—so much so

Soccer, better
known as
Wishbone, dressed
as Odysseus in
"Homer Sweet
Homer."
Copyright ©
photographs of
Wishbone 1995
Big Feats
Entertainment,
L.P. All rights
reserved. Used
with permission.

Doggy Don'ts

In real life, Jack Russells are *not* as they are portrayed in the movies or on television. Don't buy a JRT because you think they are cute or because your children want their own Eddie or Wishbone. In real life, JRTs are nothing like the well-mannered, well-trained stars you see for a few minutes strutting their stuff on television.

that Ms. Kaptan has purchased two other JRTs that share Soccer's unique markings and temperament, just so he can have a weekly break from his show biz schedule.

Although a vast majority of the tricks and most of the show are shot with Soccer, some of the more demanding tricks and many of the print shoots are performed by Soccer stand-ins. Because Soccer is now more than 10 years old, Jackie is understandably protective of her superstar pet. He is still, after all, her own pet and buddy. She is careful to look after both his health and his interests.

The schedule that Soccer and Ms. Martin keep is nothing short of exhausting. Jackie does all the training of all three dogs, and she and her two set assistants are busy with screen blocking, new tricks and wardrobe concerns, not to mention weekend publicity shoots. Because the show is filmed weekly, both she and Soccer have only weekends to learn and perfect new tricks for the upcoming week's show. Most of the tricks Soccer knows took between three days and six months to learn, although Soccer's trademark back-flip took more than ten months of careful training to perfect. It is his most difficult trick, and Jackie meticulously makes sure all important safety factors are in place before shooting this trick for the show.

As if the tricks and staging weren't enough to ask of the rambunctious Jack Russell, he also had to learn to manage the costumes and hats that are so much a part of the Wishbone character. Performing a back-flip attired in a hat and coat can't be easy—especially when the shot must be perfect, with the costume and hat straight and unaffected after the jump. Not only that, Soccer has to make it look fresh and energetic, even if the trick has been performed a number of times. Jackie credits costume designer Stephen Chudej and Wishbone's wardrobe wizard Barbara Baker for making this potentially frustrating aspect of the show run smoothly for both her and her little terrier. It's easy to see, however, why so few trainers succeed in this demanding business.

Soccer Off-Screen

What is Soccer like off-screen? Is he the perfect little terrier that all JRT owners long for? Hardly. Soccer, like all Jack Russells, is a little terror. Smart and playful, he always is looking for ways to amuse himself including hunting imaginary bugs and playing with rocks and water buckets. Having a well-trained Jack Russell Terrier, however, has even more hazards than one would guess.

Bet You Didn't Know

Because Soccer has an abundance of energy and a mischievous streak, he sleeps in a crate at night so Jackie can rest easy that the house will be in one piece come daybreak.

One day Jackie was playing ball with Soccer as she sat on the couch watching TV, something she rarely gets to do. She threw the ball down the hall and it ricocheted off the walls while Soccer gleefully bounced after it, fetching and returning it to her for another throw. After one such throw, Soccer didn't return immediately. Thinking that the ball had bounced into the bathroom or around a corner where Soccer would have to search for it, Jackie smiled to herself and took advantage of the extra few moments of peace while Soccer hunted for his toy.

Her moment of peace was short-lived. After a few minutes, Jackie heard the toilet magically flush, and she knew immediately what had happened. Running into the bathroom and hoping she was wrong, she found her darling little terrier happily watching the swirling water suck the ball down into her home's plumbing. After a repair bill of several hundred dollars, Soccer no longer is allowed in the bathroom.

Soccer is now retired and lives out his days with Jackie and her forty other companions. I'm sure he will have a life filled with balls, rocks and lots of imaginary bugs to hunt. Jackie says she will bring him back if his talents truly are needed for a particular shot; otherwise, the younger terriers now have their moment of doggy stardom. I'm sure Wishbone will continue to be remembered fondly through his show and in the hearts of children across the nation.

Trainer of the Doggy Stars

Jackie is proud of her work with Soccer and other canine screen stars, and she now is recognized as one of the foremost dog trainers in Hollywood. She had the good fortune to work with Frank Inn, trainer of the famous Benji, and has since gone on to work with the canine stars of *True Lies, Look Who's Talking, Shiloh*—both the original and the sequel—and, of course, *Wishbone*.

Bet You Didn't Know

It is because of programs such as *Wishbone* and *Frasier* that the popularity of the breed has grown so fast. They're so cute and smart that everyone wants one. But not everyone should own a JRT!

Moose, known to
Frasier *lovers as*
Eddie.
Photograph of
"Eddie" from
FRASIER ® *courtesy*
of Paramount
Pictures ® & ©
Paramount Pictures
Corporation. All
Rights Reserved.

Eddie

As you undoubtedly know, the cast of the critically acclaimed sitcom *Frasier*, from Paramount Network Television, includes a Jack Russell Terrier. The show made television history by being the only show ever to win five Emmy Awards for Outstanding Comedy Series, and it is one of the most popular series on television.

Known to the world as Eddie, Martin Crane's adoring little companion, the role is played by a spunky little Jack Russell named, of all things, Moose. Not only does Moose add charm and humor to the cast of talented actors, he also allows Martin's character to show a softer side that belies his sarcastic exterior. His appearance on the show has prompted such memorable lines as "Don't stare at me, Eddie. I'm a humane man, but right now I could kick a kitten through an electric fan," which was uttered by Frasier after having a particularly bad day.

Moose's official resumé lists him as an overnight success. He was born in Florida and was chosen from a litter of ten Jack Russell puppies. He is a purported graduate of Orlando University with a bachelor's degree in obedience and has taught sign language at Canine Corral. His first audition was with Universal Studios in Orlando, Florida, where he successfully landed a starring role in their *Animal Actors' Showcase*.

31

From there, Moose won the role of Eddie on *Frasier*. His fuzzy-faced appeal on the sitcom interested a number of editors and ad managers. As a result, his image has graced the cover of *Life*, *TV Guide*, *Entertainment Weekly*, and *Seattle Cigar Lifestyle*. Not to be outdone by the likes of Cindy Crawford and Kathy Ireland, Moose also has his own calendar. It might not be as sexy, but its sales prove that it is just as popular!

Moose divides his time between homes in California and Florida. Moose is represented by Birds and Animals in California and receives considerable fan mail through NBC's studio in Hollywood, California.

Bet You Didn't Know

Even the Internet isn't immune to these furry little terrorists. A sprightly little Jack Russell Terrier named Lucy the Wonder Dog boasts her own Web page featuring Lucy's Store.

Other Hairy Heartthrobs
Jacks in Film

As well known as Wishbone and Eddie are, they aren't the only famous JRTs to hit Hollywood and beyond. A capricious canine named Milo starred alongside Jim Carrey in the movie *The Mask* and added undeniable humor and appeal to the zany comic's role. The JRT provided some amusing moments—and let's face it, it isn't easy to compete with Jim Carrey!

Another big-screen Jack Russell named Barclay has been in increasing demand as a movie addition. He appeared in *Clean Slate*, *Ernest Goes To Jail* and *Volcano*, in which his coat was accidentally singed by fire during one of the eruption scenes. To round out his experience, Barclay also has appeared in a Tide laundry-detergent commercial and a Round-Up weed-killer ad.

Russells Sell!

As Barclay's resumé shows, television producers recognize the ad appeal of the zippy little white dog with the mischievous look and the perky tail. You would be hard pressed to turn on the TV and not see an ad featuring these lovable little terriers.

I'm sure you would recognize Hagis from the Nissan car commercials and Pixie from the Kodak ads. Numerous others, who remain nameless but no less appealing, are featured in Pillsbury Toaster Strudel, T.G.I. Friday's restaurants, Little Caesar's Pizza and U.S. West Direct Yellow Pages ads, just to name a few. They've even teamed up with Tim McGraw to sell beer! How's that for well rounded? Let's not forget the Jacuzzi-operating JRT that won the $100,000 jackpot for his owners in the *America's Funniest Home Videos* giveaway. Now that's making Jack Russell ownership pay off in spades!

Terrier Take-Off

Believe it or not, JRT mania has spread even to outer space. After much research, I found that the first dog in space was an 11 pound terrier named Laika who accompanied cosmonauts during the Sputnik 2 mission launched on November 3, 1957. Although originally thought to be a mutt, NASA sources confirm that Laika most likely was a Jack Russell Terrier. Unfortunately, Laika died during the flight due to inadequate preparations for doggy needs in space, causing a furor in Russia. His picture appears on many Russian stamps, and he was nicknamed Muttnick by astronauts here in the United States.

Doggy Don'ts

Although a number of videos and books are available that offer advice about getting your dog into show business, don't quit your day job just yet. Remember Jackie Martin-Kaptan's warning—show biz is demanding and tiring work, and only a small number will succeed.

Well-Known Owners

Aside from the JRTs that have made names for themselves, many famous people own Jack Russell Terriers. Prince Charles has one, as does Olympic diver Greg Louganis. It also is rumored that George

Patton owned a JRT. A young pitcher, Orlando "El Duque" Hernandez, got his big break in the major leagues when New York Yankees pitcher David Cone was bitten on the finger by his mother's 4-month-old Jack Russell puppy and was unable to start.

The Least You Need to Know

➤ The trademarked RCA dog is a terrier named Nipper. His younger, more recent counterpart is named Chipper.

➤ Soccer's owner (who also is his trainer and his agent) trained him for more than seven years before he landed the part of Wishbone.

➤ *Frasier's* Eddie is played by a JRT named Moose who was born in Florida.

➤ Laika was the first dog on a space flight and was thought to be a Jack Russell Terrier.

➤ Training a Jack Russell for work on television or the big screen is not as easy as it seems. It requires long hours and tireless training to be successful.

You Mean This Is Normal?

In This Chapter

➤ Typical energy levels and how to cope

➤ Inherited personality quirks

➤ Some odd but common behaviors

➤ The little dog complex

➤ Amazing feats

Turbo JRTs

If you ever have spent any time in the company of a Jack Russell Terrier, you instantly know that this little dog is a bit different than any other breed you've encountered. People are drawn to them because they typically are very funny to watch and are amusing to be around. Other pets often are puzzled by them because of their bound-less energy and their ability to be a hundred places at the same time.

One of the most amusing and common behaviors of JRTs is their pro-clivity for rapid and continuous movement. This can take the form of running at full speed around the house or the yard; through door-ways; up and over furniture, human beings and other pets; and back the other way like on a make-shift raceway. After a minute or two, they usually stop, grin at you and then take off again in the other direction. I affectionately call this the "Jack Russell Turbo."

As I've already mentioned, a JRT is a high-energy, high-maintenance dog. This energy and exuberance for life can manifest itself in many ways, and "turboing" is just one of them. Rest assured, yours is not the only household that has been turned into the Indy 500. Jack Russell owners across the nation also are befuddled and amused by this sudden burst of terrier energy. If you can get beyond the irritation of being used as part of a pinball machine, you will find this habit rather endearing. If nothing else, it is certain to bring a smile to your face. That alone is worth the irritation. As an added benefit, unwanted house guests will be quick to change their mind when they get stuck in the middle of the Jack Russell Turbo, leaving you and your family to the relative peace of your home. Granted, you will have to take care that *wanted* house guests are protected from this particular terrier habit.

Even regular exercise will not remove this amusing behavior from your terrier's repertoire, though it might temper it a bit causing the dog to be a little less rambunctious. If the thought of a little white bullet rocketing through your house at a high rate of speed bothers you, you will be sorely disappointed in your choice of breeds. Like digging, barking and hunting, turboing is very much a part of the breed. It is seen in virtually all JRTs and in all different bloodlines.

Doggy Don'ts

Don't leave your puppy alone for extended periods of time unless you want to return home to a demolition derby. Being alone is stressful to your dog.

The Oddball

Although turboing can be amusing, other behaviors can be downright frustrating. Many can be explained by understanding the history of the dog and the traits that were inbred for hunting. Others behaviors are just plain bizarre and can only be described as slightly obsessive or neurotic. Rest assured, *all* JRTs have some odd behavior or another. Let's look at a few of the more readily understandable behaviors before exploring those that are more eccentric.

Forms of Aggression

Although we normally think of aggression as attacking other pets, dogs or people (and some terriers can go overboard in this area), the JRT also can exhibit aggression in other, more amusing ways. I know of one dog that attacks the electric garage door every time it is activated. Although this is hilarious to observe the first few times, it can be scary when the little demon forgets to let go and almost gets carried up into the mechanisms of the door. To make matters worse, the dog attacks not only the owner's garage door but any electric door in the vicinity. How do you explain to a neighbor that your dog is defending you from the garage door?

Another story I've heard is about a male JRT that lives on a farm. His favorite pastime is attacking the family's tractor whenever there is work to be done, much to the frustration of the tractor's operator. He growls and attacks the bucket at the front of the tractor, biting the edge and refusing to let go. When that doesn't work, he works his way around to the wheels of the tractor and hangs onto the lug nuts, going round and round like a slow motion ferris wheel as the giant tires turn. He does this for hours, obviously convinced in his own mind that he is saving his owners from a ferocious metal beast.

Children often assume that, because these terriers are relatively small, they should be friendly and easy to hold. And because these types of JRT behavior often are quite funny, your children will be drawn to the dog and will want to interact with it. If you notice that your terrier or someone else's is involved in these alternate aggressive behaviors, you should not allow your children to approach the dog or try to pick it up. The terrier has become somewhat fixated with the object of its attention and, if startled, could snap out reflexively at the child. The dog does not intend to hurt the child, but it is not making the distinction between the child and the object it is attacking, and it should not be punished if it reacts this way. To the dog, the big bad object would simply be biting back!

Doggy Don'ts

When a Jack Russell is having an "attack" attack, don't allow children to interfere. The dog is, rationally or not, busy keeping the vacuum at bay. In its determination, it may not distinguish between the bad vacuum and the innocent child.

Other aggressive behaviors might take the form of attacking a vacuum, mop or broom, which can make housecleaning a bit more of a chore than it already is. Some dogs go as far as to actually pounce on the machine and hang on as you try to vacuum, or they grab the bristles of the broom and shake their heads vigorously in an attempt to kill it. Socks and clothes also can fall prey to the ferocious Jack Russell, especially when you are trying to get dressed in the morning and already are fifteen minutes late for work. How on earth they know you are late and need this distraction like you need a hole in the head is anyone's guess, but somehow they manage to choose these times to play. If you can manage it, look at your dog's behavior as a sign to lighten up and enjoy the day in spite of your tardiness.

Hunting Behaviors

Like aggression, the hunting instinct is strongly bred into the Jack Russell, and no amount of training will rid this little dog of its desire to seek out the nearest quarry. Although some terriers are honest-to-goodness rodent hunters and will rid your home, barn or yard of anything that remotely resembles a rat, others use their hunting instincts in a more amusing way. Hunting bugs is not at all uncommon; neither is hunting rocks.

Bet You Didn't Know

The hunting instinct, like the need to dig, cannot be bred or trained out of your JRT.

Not only will your JRT hunt odd things, it will spend hours doing so. Sometimes, it will hunt absolutely nothing at all. One of our best breeding bitches will stare at a hole, a corner or even someone's foot for hours on end, getting up only to feebly scratch at the corner in question and then sit down and stare again. I call this "gremlin hunting" because only she can see what she's after. At least I know our home is totally free of gremlins!

Another of our pet dogs hunts bugs on a regular basis. Flies, spiders, mosquitoes—it doesn't matter. He jumps on tables, on couches, in bathtubs, anywhere to gain an advantage over his insect prey. After he catches the bug, he ferociously kills it (which really doesn't take much) and then proudly leaves it there for all to see and goes on to his next victim. He stares at the ceiling, the lamps and the corners of the room to be sure no killer bug has invaded his sanctum. Heaven help the insect that strays into the home of a bug hunter!

Bet You Didn't Know

Horses and Jack Russells get along well because of the dogs' natural hunting background and their ability to sense where the horses' feet will fall as they move about their stalls or in their work. Nonetheless, when around horses, you still should keep an eye on your dog to make sure it doesn't get kicked.

Are you convinced yet that JRTs are a little different? If not, read on and I'll tell you some stories that will really have you scratching your head and laughing. But remember, if you choose to continue on your search for a JRT, you too will have to live with these odd little quirks.

I Swear, It's Nuts!

If turboing and hunting bugs, gremlins and garage doors aren't bad enough, other even stranger behaviors are considered common within the Jack Russell Terrier breed. Some of these behaviors stem from boredom, others from an over-abundance of energy. All, however, seem to portray the intensity and often obsessiveness of the JRT.

Catching Rays

One JRT goes crazy when the children in the family bring out a flashlight. His favorite game is to play "chase the beam of light." The family turns off all the lights in the room, and the dog goes crazy trying to catch the light spot. Another dog, the product of our own breeding program, goes crazy when his "light saber" (of *Star Wars* fame) is brought out. He runs throughout the house, jumping several feet off the ground to try to catch the light saber. Another variation of this is the dog that sits by the window every morning waiting for the sun to come up. When it does, it casts shadows on the wall, and the dog spends the next hour or so jumping on the wall to catch the shadows. Sometimes these dogs get so worked up that they have to be put in their crate just to be calmed down!

Doggy Do's

A JRT is not a couch potato. You need to supply your JRT with activities such as chasing a ball or a Frisbee or just going for a walk. You also should be tolerant of its own attempts at amusement such as hunting bugs, either real or imaginary. If you don't keep your dog busy, it will get into trouble—at least from your point of view.

Rock Dogs

Rocks also are fascinating to many JRTs. Some will carry a rock around for hours and will play "go fetch" with a rock just as they would a ball. Others enjoy chewing or licking rocks or even stalking them. After all, some rocks can be hard to catch! Although this habit often is amusing, it is best not to let your JRT get too involved in rock chewing. It can prematurely wear down its teeth, or even worse, it could crack a tooth resulting in a pretty hefty vet bill to repair the damage.

Some dogs choose very large rocks and make digging them out of the ground and rolling them around an all day project. Again, the danger exists that your little white terror could get *too* involved in its digging and end up with a leg or foot injury that could require veterinary attention. Although permitting your terrier to indulge in these activities allows it to burn off pent up energy, try to limit such physically demanding activities. If you find that your terrier is getting too involved, change its focus by giving it another toy to play with or another activity to divert its attention.

If you find that your terrier is indeed a "rock hound," you need to keep an eye on its dental hygiene to make sure that it is not severely wearing down the tooth surfaces and that no burrs or debris get

Why do so many Jack Russells like to play with rocks? Why not?

caught in the gum, causing possible infection. If you know your dog has had a recent bout of rock wrestling, hold it on your lap and thoroughly check the inside of its mouth—including the inside and outside of the gum surfaces—for abrasions or foreign matter that might have become imbedded. If you find such debris, remove it with a syringe filled with water or with tweezers, much as you would a splinter. Keep an eye on the affected area for a few days to make sure it does not become infected.

Of course, a terrier's taste for rocks doesn't always take the form of digging or carrying them. Some Jack Russells prefer to combine their love of rocks with their love of water, making their antics even more amusing. Remember that a JRT is always thinking—some would even say scheming—to find ways to make life more fun and more interesting. What

When to Call the Vet

If you notice that your dog is limping significantly after coming in from outside, check its legs and paws for obvious injuries. If the limping gets worse, if your dog refuses to put any weight on the limb or if it yelps when the leg is touched, call your vet. It is possible that the dog caused a hairline fracture in its leg from digging.

41

better way is there to amuse themselves than with their two favorite toys?

Water Sports

I have been told many stories, with many variations in theme, about JRTs, rocks and water. One of the funniest was from a woman about her buddy, Scooter. Scooter loved water and would jump in and swim in the family pool whenever given the chance. One afternoon, after playing with a family member in the yard, Scooter carried the rock he had been playing with into the pool area. There he accidentally dropped the rock into the pool. As his owners looked on, Scooter leaned all the way over the pool's edge, putting his head under water to try to get his rock back. When this failed, he ran back and forth along the pool's edge barking, trying to will the rock back up to the surface. After several minutes of futile barking, Scooter tried another plan. He took several steps back away from the pool's edge and jumped headfirst into the pool. Ducking his head under water, he literally dove to the bottom of the pool and retrieved his favorite rock. After he taught himself how to do it, this "rock diving" became a favorite pastime. Now he often amuses himself for hours by tossing in a rock and then going to retrieve it.

Bet You Didn't Know

Bet you didn't know that JRTs, like all dogs, can open their eyes under water and can hold their breath long enough to do some pretty deep dives. Most dogs naturally love water, though others opt for higher, dryer fun.

Pools aren't the only water sports that JRTs enjoy. My own female, Annie, is a sprinkler fanatic, and this special pleasure is passed down from generation to generation of her puppies. I try to warn new JRT owners about this particular penchant for water, though some fail to realize the extent of the fascination until they experience it for themselves. Many Jack Russells will attack yard sprinklers or any human being with a hose in their hand, and try to bite the stream of water that comes out. Some will jump several feet off the ground to grab the water, snapping their jaws in a futile attempt to capture the elusive sprays. The best part is the dreamy look on their faces as they smile at you, soaked from head to toe and panting heavily. How could life get any better?

Problem Solving

Jack Russells are almost uncanny in their ability to problem solve, not only with rocks and water but with life in general. I can't tell you the number of stories I've been told about JRTs finding ways to get to the most amazing places, simply to retrieve a morsel of food or a favorite toy. Many owners underestimate the jumping ability of their Jack Russell Terriers and are amazed when they find out their dog jumped onto the kitchen counter to retrieve a steak left out to thaw or a cookie out of the cookie bin. They also are clever about finding their way into backpacks, duffel bags and drawers, especially if their keen noses pick up something that smells delectable. I have known JRTs to unzip zippers with their teeth, to open drawers with their front paws, and to undo seemingly impossible clasps to get to the desired treat. If you own a JRT, take a word of advice—never underestimate the tenacity of a Jack Russell!

Tasting the Furniture

Another odd behavior common to JRTs is the desire to lick a certain piece of furniture whenever the dog becomes excited. The object might be the corner of a bookcase or the side of a bathtub. Why they do it is anyone's guess, but like all their obsessions, they focus on the object with fierce determination and will literally lick the finish off of the furniture.

I know from personal experience that hot sauce, cayenne pepper and the like are not deterrents when a terrier sets its mind, or in this case its tongue, to a task. The only way to stop the behavior is to catch the dog every time you see it licking the furniture and tell it "No!" Usually the dog is stimulated by your presence, such as when you first come home, so it will only exhibit this behavior in front of you. Obviously, the fact that you are there to watch makes it easy to modify the behavior. Other behaviors, such as digging or hunting rocks, usually are done for the dog's own amusement while you are away; however, they are no less frustrating.

43

If you don't have a sense of humor about such things, you'd better not purchase a Jack Russell Terrier. Like the changing weather and the tides, some things just can't be stopped, and a terrier's odd behavior is one of them. You might be able to get your dog to decrease the frequency of some of its less-desirable idiosyncrasies, but some always will remain.

Doggy Do's

Try to keep a sense of humor if you decide to purchase a JRT. They truly are odd little dogs with extremely quirky personalities, and they often do things that are simply inexplicable. Try not to take their behaviors too seriously.

Break-Dancing

That Jack Russell Terriers love to sleep on their backs with all four feet in the air is pretty common knowledge, but did you know they also incorporate this position into another quirky behavior I affectionately call "break-dancing?" It's true. One day an unsuspecting JRT owner will walk in and see his little white terrorist on its back dancing across the floor. Some seem to do it as a form of scratching the itch on their backs. Others do it when they're excited, such as when their owners get home after an absence. Whatever the reason, the first time you see it, you undoubtedly will do a double take. If you have a shorthaired Jack Russell Terrier, you also will find a nice patch of white hair on your carpet when your funny friend is done dancing.

Some dogs wiggle up and down, back and forth like a sidewinder rattlesnake. Others stand with their rears in the air and their tails wagging as they rub their heads all over the carpet before blissfully throwing themselves to the ground and rubbing their whole body on it. Either way, it looks rather odd. What's even funnier is hearing embarrassed owners trying to explain their dog's behavior to their houseguests. Of course, anyone who owns a JRT soon gets used to this kind of embarrassment.

The Little Napoleon Complex

Perhaps one of the most prevalent oddities of the Jack Russell breed is the dogs' seeming obliviousness to their size. Any Jack Russell owner will tell you that their tiny terrorists view themselves as bigger than a Rottweiler and twice as mean. Though "feisty" is one of the most common words used to describe a Jack Russell Terrier, no one really knows the true accuracy of this description until they have spent some time in the company of a JRT when it's around a larger dog. The comedy is revealed when, inevitably, the larger dog backs down in the face of the ferocious white whirlwind.

Bet You Didn't Know

Jack Russell Terriers often are referred to as "the big dog in a small dog's body." Ironically, JRTs get along much better with larger dogs than they do with smaller ones, perhaps because of their inflated self-image.

Although many novices assume upon first glance that this bravado is a bluff to get the larger dog to back down, those that know the breed understand that nothing could be further from the truth. The JRT truly believes it is as large as and twice as mean as the dog it is approaching. Although many times this ferociousness takes the larger dog off guard, causing it to flee rather than to fight, many Jack Russells have gotten themselves into serious trouble by picking a fight with a larger, meaner dog and not knowing when to quit. Being no real match for a dog the size of a Rottweiler, the JRT can quickly end up on the losing side of the battle. Worse yet, it refuses to give up until it is virtually torn to pieces.

You need to be your JRT's true guardian in these circumstances and not allow it to be overmatched to the point of being injured. If you know that another dog is likely to be aggressive or will defend itself rather than back down, protect your terrier from its own bravado. Either pick your dog up until safely out of the other dog's reach or give the other dog a very wide berth. The saying is true—a JRT often is its own worst enemy.

Amazing Feats

Although Jack Russell Terriers undeniably behave oddly at times, they also possess an almost uncanny ability to notify their owners when something is amiss. Countless stories have been told about JRTs that either have saved a child or another pet from injury or have alerted their owners to a dangerous situation.

One such instance was related to me by the owner of a JRT that had been raised from puppyhood with a cat he considered to be a friend. One day, after moving to a new home, the owner came home to find the cat missing and the back door ajar. The owner searched around the back of the house to no avail. During her search, her JRT named Max kept running up to her, putting his front paws on her legs and then running in front of her and looking back. Irritated by the distraction, the owner kept chasing the terrier away and calling the cat's name.

Finally, she gave up and went back in the house. She sat down by the phone, intending to call some friends to help her search for her cat. The moment she sat down, Max jumped onto her lap and then immediately off again, took several steps away and looked back at her. This happened several times before she finally decided to follow him and see what he wanted. Max dutifully led her into the woods to a large, gnarled stump about 400 feet from her house. She looked inside the opening, only to find her cat bloody and glassy-eyed staring back at her. After dodging some flying claws and coercing the cat out, she realized the cat had been hit by a car. Max had been trying to tell her that his buddy needed help. She rushed the kitty to the vet, who said that, had she waited much longer, he would not have been able to save the cat.

Bet You Didn't Know

A dog resembling a Jack Russell Terrier appears on an eighteenth-century Marseille tarot card. Its companion is The Fool, and the dog looks like it's trying to tell him something important.

Another amazing story also involves a JRT and her kitty pal. Shilo and her cat buddy, Boots, were out on the driveway sunning themselves on a particularly warm fall day. When the sun got too hot, Boots decided to curl up under the shade of the family's car. Unbeknownst to the family, the cat climbed into the car's undercarriage and fell asleep. When the owner came out to run to the store, the cat was stuck under the car. Rather than let her little friend become mincemeat, Shilo barked and ran behind the car, preventing the owner from backing out of the driveway. When the owner got out to see what the fuss was about, he realized that the cat was stuck under the car and couldn't get out. After some wiggling and twisting, Boots was freed unharmed. Who says JRTs and cats can't get along?

If, after reading this chapter, you truly are convinced you are ready to take on this little dynamo, the next step is to decide which JRT is right for you. If you still are doubtful after these stories of antics and heroics, do yourself a favor and explore some other breeds. You must be 100 percent sure of your decision if the relationship is going to work. If there is any doubt in your mind, either spend some time around a Jack Russell Terrier to see whether you have what it takes to be owned by one or pass for now until you're ready to take on the responsibility. They are not easy dogs to live with, although they do make very amusing housemates.

The Least You Need to Know

➤ Don't judge the Jack Russell Terrier's "normalcy" against any other breed. JRTs simply live by their own set of rules.

➤ A sense of humor is a must if you own a Jack Russell Terrier.

➤ JRTs have an obsessive and sometimes neurotic side to their personalities. It can't be changed, so you might as well accept it.

➤ JRTs typically love water and will use almost any excuse to get wet.

➤ Rocks can be favorite toys for your JRT, but care must be exercised so your dog doesn't wear down its teeth.

➤ JRTs have an inflated self-image that can get them in trouble with larger, more aggressive dogs. They often need your help to keep them out of trouble.

➤ Jack Russells are loyal by nature to both their human and pet friends. Acts of courage and selflessness are common within the breed.

Decisions, Decisions

If you've decided you're ready to take the Jack Russell Terrier plunge, you need to decide which type of dog will best suit you and your family. Although a bouncing puppy is undeniably adorable, will it be the best match for your individual situation? Do you have very young children in your home that could be intimidated by the lightning speed and boundless energy that Jack Russell puppies characteristically exhibit? Do you have the available time to spend teaching a puppy basic house rules? Or would an adult dog be easier to handle?

All these questions and many more should be answered before you go looking for a JRT. Until you have a clear picture in your mind of what you want, it will be hard to find just the right dog. It would be like going on a road trip to an unknown destination with no map.

One additional word of warning—if you have any doubts at all, please wait to purchase a JRT. I cannot stress often enough that this breed is not right for everyone. It isn't even right for most people. That said, let's move on to choosing a dog.

Pet or Show Piece?

Right off the bat, you need to determine whether you are interested in a show dog or just a family pet. Your criteria will be very different depending on your answer. Conscientious breeders produce dogs that most closely fit their idea of the ideal Jack Russell Terrier. But is this ideal the same as yours? Although a particular breeder might have his eye on the next national title, you might be looking for a loyal pal and an amusing pet. It is important to decide whether you eventually want to breed your dog or if you simply are looking for a pet that will fit in with your household and your family.

Bet You Didn't Know

Under JRTCA guidelines, a Jack Russell Terrier cannot be registered until it is at least 1 year old.

Selecting a Show Dog

If you are looking for a dog that eventually will be used for breeding, you need to pay close attention to the structure, size, coat condition, health records and conformation requirements for the breed organization you are interested in, and you should buy the dog that most closely fits that ideal. Your dog must be able to stand up to the rigorous testing of both the registering organization and the show ring judges, so you should take special care to seek out and select the most perfect conformational specimen that is available and within your budget. Chances are, you will need to go to a well-known breeder to find this terrier, and you undoubtedly will pay a premium for your selected show dog and pet.

You should consider which breed affiliation you want to be involved in because their standards for what is correct can be quite different.

Both the AKC and the JRTCA are discussed extensively in later chapters, and you should be well informed as to their requirements and preferences before purchasing a puppy. If you are looking to make a decision regarding which club most closely fits your own opinions and ideals, read the relevant chapters of this book before making an educated decision. You then should purchase your puppy based on that registry's requirements.

The paperwork you receive under each registry will be different as well. If you are purchasing an AKC-registered dog for future breeding, it is crucial that you secure the dog's papers and pedigree prior to taking your puppy home. If you are purchasing a puppy or dog under JRTCA standards, you must obtain from the breeder a Certificate of Registration if the dog is 1 year or older, or you can submit a five-generation pedigree and an original stud certificate with the registration application after the dog reaches 1 year of age. If you go the latter route, check the dog's pedigree carefully before you purchase to make sure the dog is not closely inbred. The dog will not be accepted for registry if close inbreeding is present in the pedigree.

It is helpful if you bring the guidelines for the registry under which you will be working when you go to look for your dog or puppy. This way, you can refer to those standards as you examine the puppy, paying attention to each and every conformational requirement. Remember, if you are going to breed or show in accredited competitions, this dog must match the ideal as closely as possible. Don't allow yourself to be swayed away from "perfect" by a cute face or great markings. These are not a strong foundation for a breeding program. Although straight legs, strong hindquarters and a correct bite might not win the hearts of friends and relatives, they go a long way towards producing sound, functional and correct puppies.

Bet You Didn't Know

There has been much controversy over registering the Jack Russell Terrier as a breed because some people consider the dogs to be a strain of terrier rather than an individual breed.

Whether you buy a show dog or a pet-quality JRT, you've got a super friend.
(photo by Mary Bloom)

If showing isn't in your blood and you have no major maternal urges to produce litter after litter of spotted bundles, a pet-quality dog should be your goal. Please note that in no way should a pet-quality JRT be looked upon as inferior. They simply have physical characteristics that would make them less appealing for breeding or showing. These characteristics might include too much coat color, ears that are too large or that don't set properly or legs that are a little too short. None of these characteristics should affect the dog's desirability as a pet.

In your quest for the ideal JRT, you might find a puppy with the perfect personality for your family but that possesses some of these physical "flaws." Don't hesitate to purchase this dog simply because it doesn't fit the breed standard as ideal. Chances are, you will be buying a fabulous friend that will go to the ends of the earth to please you. You soon will see these physical differences as charming and unique rather than as flawed.

Choosing the Perfect Pet

If you are looking to add a pet to your family rather than a show piece, pay very close attention to the personality of the dog you are considering. Is it aggressive? Or is it content to sit back and let the other dogs go first? Do you like its markings? Is it a good size for your family and your surroundings? Is it boisterous and rambunctious or pleasantly friendly? Most importantly, which of the available dogs appeals to you the most, for whatever reason?

Sometimes you simply will be drawn to a particular dog but will be at a loss to explain why. That's perfectly normal! Spend a little more time with this dog to see whether you still like it. Then spend some time with the other dogs you can choose from to see whether you are still drawn back to the first dog. Trust your instincts. You know what you like, and you know what you don't. Don't let someone talk you into a dog or a puppy that you feel just isn't right for you.

Bet You Didn't Know

As a result of TV programs such as *Frasier* and *Wishbone*, the popularity of the Jack Russell Terrier has grown tenfold.

If you decide that you will not be showing or breeding your dog, it makes sense to pay attention to characteristics that will be important to your family. These might include funny or distinct markings, a more feisty or more laid-back temperament and a charming personality. Let yourself be led by your emotions. This is a dog you will have for a long time, so you must be comfortable with it right from the beginning. Being owned by a JRT for life is challenging enough, you should at least really like the dog who owns you.

Remember that what might be right for the breeder's personality or that of an interested friend might not be right for you or your family. Every family's makeup is unique and distinct, just as every terrier has its own personality. Don't let anyone talk you out of a dog you feel is perfect unless they have strong reasons why you should not buy that particular puppy, such as a noticeable structural problem.

This is a pet you will share many years of your life with, and you should make your decision in much the same way you would choose your best friend. First and foremost you must enjoy each other, and you should be able to get along with each other for long periods at a time. Remember that a dog's personality rarely changes dramatically after it reaches 8 or 9 weeks of age. What you see is what you get. Keep this in mind when making your choice.

Youth or Wisdom?

Now it's time to decide whether a puppy or an adult dog better fits your lifestyle.

Pros and Cons of Puppies

There can be little doubt that a cute puppy is hard to resist. When you bring a puppy into your home, you get the opportunity to train it to be the companion you want, and you don't have to "undo" any bad habits an older dog might have developed. Although a puppy certainly will get more attention from your friends and neighbors, it is important to honestly evaluate whether you have the time and the facilities to effectively manage life with a puppy. Puppies can't be left alone to amuse themselves during the day, or you're likely to come home to a house that has been significantly redecorated! Likewise, your housetraining will go smoothly only if you have the patience, time and consistency to produce results.

Doggy Do's

Purchase a puppy or an older dog based on good health and temperament. Pick the personality that fits best with your lifestyle, usually the most friendly but not the most aggressive.

Keep your living arrangements in mind as well. If you live very close to the house next to you, a whining or barking puppy in the middle of the night will not endear you to your neighbors. Remember that any puppy will experience a period of adjustment, and some need a longer time than others. Even when the dog is grown, it still will bark at passing cars and at loud noises. If yours is the only dog on the street, you might want to consider an older dog from the start to break the neighborhood in, so to speak. If you start out with a puppy and have problems, you are likely to find an angry neighbor on your doorstep when you return home from work one day.

As previously mentioned, young children might be more comfortable with a more mature addition to the household. Not only will an older dog be a bit more forgiving of a child's exuberance, it also will be less likely to knock down a small child out of excitement and its moods will be more easily controlled. In addition, you won't have to worry about your young child accidentally stumbling upon one of your puppy's mistakes, creating a messy situation for everyone.

Pros and Cons of Adult Dogs

Adult dogs can be a good choice, especially if they have been spayed or neutered. They already have gone through their terrible teens and are more likely to fit into a subdued lifestyle with a minimum of fuss. They are also more likely to amicably "duke it out" with a dog that is already part of the family without becoming panicked or intimidated. Remember that you want your new addition to be a joy not a hassle. Sometimes this means choosing a dog that is either fully or partially grown and that already has some of the basics in place for you to build on.

Keep in mind, however, that a more mature dog might be a bit more set in its ways. If its previous handling has been good, this shouldn't be a problem. But if its previous owners had trouble with training, you might be inheriting someone else's problems. In this case, an older puppy—say 6 or 7 months old—might be a good compromise. It will still be young enough to accept change, yet it is old enough to control itself and to understand right from the beginning what the ground rules should be.

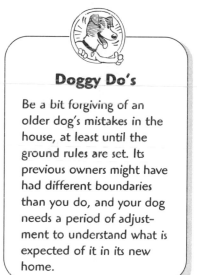

Doggy Do's

Be a bit forgiving of an older dog's mistakes in the house, at least until the ground rules are set. Its previous owners might have had different boundaries than you do, and your dog needs a period of adjustment to understand what is expected of it in its new home.

Environmental Considerations

When making your decision, make sure to consider your individual housing limitations. If you live in a home with a large backyard and have the room and ability to make a dog run—or at least a yard that is adequately fenced—you should be able to consider a dog or a puppy without too much concern. If, however, you are living in an apartment and you would have to time your puppy's potty breaks to when you are available to take it out, and if you have limited space to devote to a puppy play area, an older puppy or dog would be your best bet.

Keep in mind that JRTs have boundless energy. If they are not given plenty of exercise, they will create their own diversions, usually the destruction of something important to you. A young puppy with no supervision and no outlet for its energy will be an unhappy puppy. Apartment training is best reserved for older dogs or for dogs with someone home most of the day who is willing to commit to a regular exercise regime. *All* JRTs, young and old, need plenty of companionship and exercise. If your circumstances don't currently allow for this, you might want to consider postponing your purchase of a JRT until your living conditions change.

Aside from boundless energy, Jack Russell Terriers are curious by nature, always wanting to explore their surroundings and constantly on the lookout for new games with which to amuse themselves. If they are not allowed to go outside for these diversions, each and every nook and cranny in your home becomes fair game for the industrious little terriers. Some JRTs become so destructive that they have to be crated when left at home alone. Others can be trusted (to some extent), provided they receive lots of playtime when their owner is home. The smaller the space to roam, the more likely it is you will have a destruction problem.

I was told by one terrier owner about a time when he inadvertently locked his dog inside his den prior to leaving home. When he returned, the terrier had not only chewed holes in the arms of the couch, it had literally pulled the phone lines out of the walls and the carpet off the floor! Although the owner was not amused, the JRT was proud of its redecorating job and was eager for the next time it would be left in the den. It only takes one such experience to learn the lesson. These little dogs take to destruction with the same obsession they take to playing ball. They can do serious damage to a house and its furnishings in a remarkably short amount of time.

If you have the physical space necessary to house and train a Jack Russell
Terrier, you need to plan where your
puppy or dog will live and what you
will do with it when you are away
from home. Ideally, you will be able
to devote enough time to its training that you will feel confident
when leaving your house that it will
be in one piece when you return. If
you do not have this confidence,
leaving your Jack Russell outside
when you are away is your best bet.

Doggy Do's

Jack Russell Terriers love to
chew and will chew on
almost everything. Make
sure there are no loose
hanging electric cords in
your home and provide
plenty of play toys such as
balls, rawhide bones and
old socks for your terrier to
play with.

The Great Outdoors?

You should know, however, that leaving your JRT outside during an
extended absence is not necessarily a perfect solution. A JRT can be
a persistent and innovative little creature. If you leave your terrier
outside with only a screen door separating it from the inside of your
cozy home, you might come home to find your terrier happily doz-
ing on your couch with a very large hole in your screen door.
Similarly, if you leave your terrier outside for long periods of time
without distractions or supervision, you are likely to return home to
find each and every bulb you've planted dug up and strewn across
your yard or to discover a very large hole beneath the fence that sep-
arates your home from your neighbor's backyard.

JRTs do well outside, provided they have plenty of food and water to
satisfy them for the length of time you will be gone, a cozy bed to
sleep in and lots of toys to amuse them. If the space is too small to
allow running off some energy, you could be setting yourself up for a
persistent digging problem. Take that into consideration when you
plan your run. Also remember that your terrier needs some protection from the elements. If the forecaster is predicting rain, make sure
that your dog can easily go inside a doghouse or under a shelter to
stay dry. If it's going to be very hot outside, make sure to provide
shade as a relief from the sun.

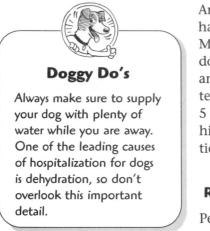

Doggy Do's

Always make sure to supply your dog with plenty of water while you are away. One of the leading causes of hospitalization for dogs is dehydration, so don't overlook this important detail.

Another thing to consider is that JRTs have remarkable jumping ability. Make sure the fence around your doggy run is high enough to prevent an unintended escape. With most terriers, this means a minimum of 5 to 6 feet high. It might need to be higher, however, if your terrier is particularly tenacious or athletic.

Room for Two?

Perhaps one of the hardest things for an owner to remember and understand is that, just because your Jack Russell has been outside in its run all day while you are at work or out shopping, this doesn't mean your terrier has been playing all day. When you finally come home, your JRT will be anxious for your attention and likely will want to play with you.

Doggy Don'ts

Don't relegate your puppy or dog to an enclosed corner of your yard all the time. Your dog wants and needs to be included in your family activities.

Unless your Jack Russell has another dog as a companion that has an energy capacity similar to its own, you can bet your dog has spent a bit of time playing and a lot of time sleeping. It will be revved up and ready to go after its long, relaxing nap, and it's important for you to understand that your dog isn't being bad by wanting your attention. It simply needs your company after a long day of solitude. If you ignore your dog, it is likely to drive you crazy trying to get your attention. You will be in a much better position and frame of mind if you resolve yourself to spending some time playing with your dog when you get home from work or after a long day away from home. You then can unwind in peace, and your JRT will know that it has been acknowledged.

Jack Russell Rescue: An Option?

Rescuing a JRT that has fallen on hard times might be an option to consider when adopting your terrier. It is a wonderful feeling to know that, not only are you adding to your family, you also are helping save a life that would not have such a rosy future if no suitable home were found for it. Just because a dog is coming from the rescue does not mean it is defective or inferior in any way. Most of these dogs simply have ended up in situations where they were misunderstood or abandoned.

Some dogs end up in rescue facilities because their owners develop financial problems or have to make a change in their living arrangements that prevents them from taking along their dog. Some dogs are given up by people who, unlike you, didn't do their research before purchasing a dog and ended up with more than they bargained for. Many of these dogs can be adopted and readily taken into families, provided the new family is willing and able to properly care for them.

As I've mentioned before, a JRT is not the breed for everyone. In reality, few people and families are dedicated to this type of "special needs" pet. If not handled properly, their destructive nature can drive away even the most understanding owner, and their odd behaviors can scare off even the most grounded personality. A sense of humor is an important trait in a Jack Russell owner, as is a solid savings account for unexpected home repairs.

Even though the warnings are repeated relentlessly to new JRT owners, few truly understand what "high energy" means until they have brought home their bundle of joy. Few have experienced the frustrations of trying to bend a terrier's personality to their own will. It complicates matters even more when you consider the extreme intelligence of these sturdy little dogs because no owner likes to be outsmarted by their dog! The owners of the rescue terriers didn't necessarily fail, they simply underestimated the personality of the JRT and overestimated their abilities to manage it.

The benefit of adopting a rescue dog is that they usually are spayed or neutered prior to placement, relieving you of that financial burden. Also, most of these dogs have received some professional handling during their temporary rescue placement. This enables you to get accurate feedback about the dog's personality and quirks. All prospective homes are screened to make sure the terrier does not end up in a bad situation again. This is why it is important to consider all the factors involved and to make an educated decision whether this breed is right for you prior to committing to a dog.

The handlers at Russell Rescue are apt to ask you a long list of questions to determine whether you truly are serious in your commitment to a JRT. They want to know whether you are prepared to handle the energy level, personality quirks and sometimes-aggressive tendencies in the dog. They will inquire about your living arrangements and the facilities available for the dog. They also will ask whether you have children and, if so, what their ages are.

These questions are not meant to be intrusive; the rescue staff simply is trying to make sure the terrier is going to someone fully educated about the benefits and drawbacks of the breed and someone who has a home that satisfies the spatial requirements of the dog. It is the staff's job to make sure the rescued JRT does not end up in a poorly prepared home or with an unsuspecting family. They take their jobs quite seriously. All who have worked with this breed have a true affinity for these dogs and feel quite protective of their future. They simply are trying to find the best home for each dog's unique needs, and they want to make sure the potential owners are fully educated and ready to accept the terrier challenge.

Bet You Didn't Know

A growing number of JRTs have been abandoned by owners who shouldn't have purchased them in the first place and who never inquired about the downside of choosing a JRT. Many rescue organizations such as Russell Rescue, the JRTCA placement service for displaced Jack Russells, have come of age as a result. They use proceeds from donations to locate temporary housing and to pay for neutering, vet fees and so on to keep the programs afloat.

Keep in mind that you might not want to get involved in some cases. Some of these dogs have been abused prior to placement at the rescue, and some need special emotional and physical care as a result of their misfortune. Caring for a healthy, unabused JRT is one thing, but caring for a dog with a significant negative history is quite another. I would venture to say that few first-time terrier owners truly can understand the magnitude of this situation. Many of the previously discussed quirks and traits will be magnified in an abused dog, truly creating a Jack Russell terror. If you are not totally committed to providing this care, you should pass on that particular dog, especially if this is your first terrier.

Most of the time, the JRT's only sin was acting like a terrier with owners who were unprepared for this behavior. Many people see the charming little dog on the television screen and have fantasies of owning the perfect dog just like Wishbone. Although they certainly are charming, Jack Russells are far from perfect, and they often can be frustrating. Remember that years of training have gone into making these perfect little screen actors. As you read in Chapter 3, even Wishbone is not an angel off-screen, and he's had ten years of professional training! Even after a decade, a terrier will still be a terrier, and a JRT will never have the same personality as a Labrador Retriever or a St. Bernard.

The Least You Need to Know

➤ It is important for you to decide whether a puppy or an older dog is best for your situation before beginning your dog search.

➤ You will spend more for a dog that is show quality than for one that is pet quality. Deciding which is important to you can save you a few dollars.

➤ Puppies are far more time consuming and require a more structured environment than adult or juvenile dogs.

➤ Remember to consider your neighbors when deciding whether a puppy would be best for your environment.

➤ Young children often fare better with an older dog.

➤ JRTs can be very destructive when left to their own devices. They should be provided with plenty of toys and opportunities for energy outlets.

➤ No matter how many toys are provided, some JRTs must be crated to curb their destructive nature.

➤ Leaving your Jack Russell outside usually is preferable to leaving it locked in the house, provided you have an adequate facility to do so and are sure to leave it plenty of food and water.

➤ Jack Russell Rescue can provide you with a perfectly suitable dog for a very reasonable price and can give a down-on-its-luck Jack Russell a new start.

➤ Some rescued JRTs might not be suitable for first-time terrier owners.

Part 2

Adapting to a Baby in the House

You think you have decided on a Jack Russell Terrier, but you still need to make some hard decisions—not only about the perfect puppy for you and your family but how (and if) you can provide an adequate environment for that puppy. Jack Russell Terriers require a unique combination of space and exercise to be happy and content little dogs. You need to do some serious thinking to determine whether you and your family are prepared to provide this type of environment.

This part helps guide you through selecting a puppy and a breeder. It helps you evaluate your individual house and lifestyle to make absolutely sure you are willing and able to provide for this breed. You'll get advice about how to introduce your new dog or puppy to existing family members, both two-legged and four-legged, and you'll get housetraining and other training tips. If you still are unsure whether you are really sold on this breed, read this section before making your decision. It's not easy being owned by a JRT, but it sure is fun!

Chapter 6

In Search of Perfection

In This Chapter

➤ Where, oh where, is that perfect puppy?

➤ Questions, questions and more questions

➤ All those adorable faces!

Shopping for a new car, a new home or new furniture can be overwhelming with hundreds of color, size and design choices. The same can be said for shopping for a new JRT puppy. Not only do you have gender and coat types to decide on, you also have a huge variety of colorings, leg lengths and personalities that makes each individual puppy unique. And they're all so cute! Just like shopping for a car, however, it's easy to be swayed away from your original goal by a cute face and smooth-talking breeder.

This is why, after careful consideration and long talks with all family members involved, it is crucial for you to record your preferences in writing before you begin puppy hunting. By committing this wish list in writing, you are less likely to take a wrong turn and end up with something different from what you really want. Have a particular type of puppy in mind and then go looking for the puppy that most closely fits your criteria.

Where, oh Where, Is That Perfect Puppy?

Without question, the best place to get a puppy is from a reputable breeder's establishment. Good breeders work to produce healthy, well-adjusted dogs, and they are honest in their representations of their dogs' assets and less desirable qualities. A good breeder is fully aware of the Jack Russell's needs and quirks and can be very helpful in working with you to select the right puppy for you. In fact, a reputable breeder will try to dissuade you from buying a puppy from him if he feels none of his particular pups would fit into your lifestyle or if he feels a Jack Russell simply is not a good match for you and your family.

As you already have been told—and will continue to be told—the Jack Russell is not for everyone and requires a special family for both parties to be happy. When you purchase a puppy from a concerned breeder, you will be provided with breed-specific information, information about the puppy's parents and information about its upbringing. You also will receive records of the puppy's vaccinations and the documentation necessary to register your dog with any of the registries, unless the dog already comes with AKC accreditation.

Rather than risk the chance of an unhealthy puppy or a puppy that cannot be registered in the future if you so desire, it is best to seek out a known JRT breeder in your area and view the puppies available for purchase. These breeders can be found through the classifieds in the newspaper, through local pet stores or even through a veterinarian's office. If you don't have any luck with these sources, you can contact the AKC and the JRTCA directly to ask for the names of breeders in your area. Keep in mind that prices and types of dogs vary widely from breeder to breeder and from location to location.

Cost Is Only One Factor

When looking through ads and talking to breeders, keep in mind that the cheapest puppy is not always your best buy, and your choice should not be based on price alone. If possible, make price your least important factor (within reason, of course) to avoid making a mistake. Focus instead on the puppy's personality, temperament, markings and breeding to make your decision. Finding a puppy within your budget is important, but try to be a little flexible to get the right terrier for your family.

Doggy Do's

You, as a prospective JRT owner, should spend lots of time shopping for your future pet and should be prepared to ask lots of questions. Not only will you take advantage of the vast knowledge breeders have about JRTs, you also will be able to determine which breeder and which specific puppy will be right for your family.

The Take-Back Policy

As important as it is to find the right puppy, it is equally important for you to be comfortable with the breeder you select. Not all breeders are created equal, and their policies on litters can vary widely. Most reputable breeders have a take-back policy on all their puppies. This means that if, for whatever reason, the puppy doesn't work out for you or your family, the breeder will take back the puppy and place it in another home. You also have the option to try to sell the puppy on your own first, but a take-back policy is a good option if you do not have time to sell the puppy yourself or if your efforts have failed. Although you lose the money you paid for the dog, you do not have to put it in the pound or place it with Russell Rescue. You can be fairly sure the puppy will be placed in a loving home.

Most breeders genuinely are concerned about their puppies and want to find the best homes for them. They would rather take the puppy back and go through the trouble of finding it another home than see the dog go to a home in which its future would be questionable. No breeder likes to see one of his terriers end up in Russell Rescue. A take-back policy proves that the breeder is concerned about both the short-term and long-term welfare of the puppies he produces and that he is not just out to make a quick buck.

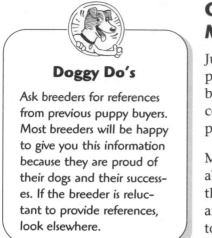

Questions, Questions and More Questions

Just as you are evaluating the puppies presented to you, you also should be evaluating the honesty and the concern of the breeder doing the presenting.

Doggy Do's

Ask breeders for references from previous puppy buyers. Most breeders will be happy to give you this information because they are proud of their dogs and their successes. If the breeder is reluctant to provide references, look elsewhere.

Most breeders are very happy to talk about the puppies they've produced, the homes in which they were placed and almost anything and everything to do with their dogs. Sometimes they talk too much about their dogs! However irritating this might be, it's a good sign. It shows they are educated about their dogs and are willing to share that knowledge with you, the new owner.

Use Your Breeder as a Resource

Breeders who are reluctant to share information and stories about their dogs either are likely to be hiding something in their background or are out of touch with their dogs and the dogs' personalities. Either way, you are not likely to get the solid information you need to make your decision. The breeder is the best source available for learning which puppy has which personality. After talking with you and your family, the breeder should be able to point you in the right direction toward a particular pup.

From birth, puppies—like people—have distinct and individual personalities. Some are more playful, some are more reserved, some are more aggressive, and some are more timid. These traits are unlikely to change much as the puppy grows into adulthood and, therefore, are a good indicator as to whether the dog will fit in with your family and your lifestyle.

Most breeders can easily give you details about their puppies' personalities, and it is important for you to ask them straight out which puppy fits the requirements you are looking for. If they suggest a puppy you are not naturally drawn to, ask them why they feel this

A reputable breeder will want to share information about his puppies and will let you meet the dam (and sire, if he is on the premises). (photo by Laurie Mercer)

puppy is right for you. They might have very good reasons for their choice, and you would do well to keep an open mind. Remember that the breeder has lived with these pups for several weeks and has had the opportunity to view them in a variety of situations. He knows the puppies' personalities better than anyone else and should be able to give you concrete examples of each puppy's typical behavior.

Don't be afraid to ask a breeder about the type of person he feels the breed is best suited for. If he tells you that JRTs will fit in anywhere and that they get along with almost everyone, he clearly is out of touch with his dogs or wants to make a sale at any cost. If he tells you that terriers are eccentric, that they need tons of exercise, that they might not do well with extremely young children and that they are likely to pick a fight with every Rottweiler on the block, you can rest assured you are probably getting some straightforward answers.

Bet You Didn't Know

Your puppy's dewclaws (nails on the back of the dog's legs) should be removed early (ideally at 3 days of age) because they might become torn when it hunts or plays. Ask the puppy's breeder whether this minor surgery already has been performed on the litter.

69

Health Hints

Don't forget to ask about the puppy's vaccination record, whether its dewclaws have been removed, when its next shots are due and when its tail was docked. Most breeders will volunteer this type of information in writing, but some get so busy visiting that they forget to provide this to you. You also should ask whether the breeder provides either a Certificate of Registration from the AKC or a complete, five-generation pedigree of the puppy and a Stud Certificate for JRTCA so that you can register your puppy when it's old enough. All this paperwork should accompany the puppy when you take it home.

The breeder also should provide the name of the puppy food that the puppies have been started on and, ideally, should give you a small supply of food to get you started until you can go to the pet store to buy your own. It is important that you feed your puppy the same brand and type of food it has been eating to minimize the stomach upset and illness that can accompany the stresses of a new home and environment. If that brand is unavailable in your area, ask what the primary ingredients are in the dog food so you can match it closely with another brand.

Get Ready to Get Grilled

Another good sign is if the breeder asks you lots of questions, such as whether you've ever been around Jack Russell Terriers before and what type of home you have. He is not trying to be nosy; he's just concerned about whether you know what you are getting into by purchasing a JRT. Jack Russells are high-energy dogs with unique and odd personalities and clearly are not for everyone. A good breeder will be well aware of this fact and might even try to sway you away from the breed in favor of something more docile. He will want to hear that you have carefully thought your decision through and are well aware of the peculiarities of the breed. He also will want to hear that you are aware of the exercise and environmental needs of the breed and have researched your decision thoroughly.

Perfect Parents?

If possible, you should spend some time with the puppy's sire and dam (or at the very least the dam, or mother) of the litter. The personalities of the litter's parents will give you a good idea of what the puppies' temperaments will be like. Two very aggressive dogs are likely to produce aggressive puppies, and two hyper dogs are likely to produce an extremely active litter.

Bet You Didn't Know

Jack Russell Terriers must be 1 year old before they are eligible for registration with the JRTCA, and they require a five-generation pedigree, a Stud Certificate, and an examination by a licensed veterinarian to be submitted. The AKC, on the other hand, requires the litter be by registered stock and issues registration to the resulting litter shortly after birth.

When evaluating the puppy's parents, keep in mind that you are a stranger to their home, and they are apt to be more active, inquisitive and protective than usual. Give them some leeway to account for this disruption in their routine and take it into account when evaluating their personalities. Ideally, you will find two friendly and energetic dogs that will try to engage you in play or mooch for attention. They should be active without appearing out of control, and they should be likeable and approachable. If a parent is intimidated by your presence or seems overly hostile, it is a sign that these tendencies might run throughout the litter. You might want to pass on this group of pups.

Maturity Milestones

Beware of any breeder who is willing to let his puppies leave their home at younger than 8 weeks of age. Some breeders will make an exception of a week or so if they know the new owners extremely well and are assured they have the appropriate knowledge to care for a puppy this young. As a rule, however, the puppy should not leave prior to the 8-week-old mark. This ensures that the puppy is both physically mature and emotionally secure enough to handle the separation from both its mother and its littermates.

All Those Adorable Faces!

When you are satisfied that you have found a breeder you are comfortable with and breeding stock that fits your idea of worthy parents, it's time to move on to the individual puppies within the litter. Be careful about getting to this step prior to the other evaluations. You could find yourself inextricably wrapped around a furry little paw and make a poor decision regardless of logic or reason!

Watch the Puppies Interact

Assuming you have escaped this trap, look carefully at the puppies in the litter, especially those that fit your gender requirements. Does one immediately catch your eye? If so, focus more on that puppy and notice how it interacts with its littermates. Is it playful and energetic? Or is it timid or listless? Does it seem to be the attacker or the attackee? Does it interact with any toys or chewies in its surroundings? Or is it more interested in either the other puppies or you, the stranger? All these behaviors will give you clues about the puppy's personality.

Check Out Your Choice

After you have watched the puppy interact, ask to have it taken out of the kennel or to an area away from the rest of the litter. Does the puppy appear to be intimidated? Or is it happy to amuse itself with your attentions? Are you able to engage the puppy in play? Does it appear to be timid or a little feisty? Note these personality traits and compare them to the list of desired characteristics you made prior to setting out on your puppy-hunting expedition.

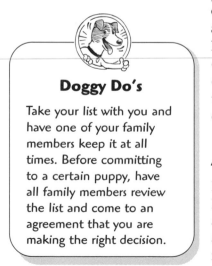

Doggy Do's

Take your list with you and have one of your family members keep it at all times. Before committing to a certain puppy, have all family members review the list and come to an agreement that you are making the right decision.

Assessing Temperament

Pick up the puppy and handle it. Does the puppy wriggle and try to get away? Or does it sit quietly in your arms, perhaps trying to lick your nose? Is the puppy content to be with you? Or is it constantly trying to get back to the pack? Are you able to put the puppy on its back without a major battle? Is the puppy interested in what you are doing? Does it try to attack your finger or is it more curious about your actions?

Most puppies don't like being held on their backs but will accept the position after a bit of coercion. This is a good test to see whether the puppy will tend to be assertive or timid by nature. If the puppy fights this action tooth and nail, you probably have a more aggressive puppy and one that is likely to be a bit on the feisty side. Although this is not necessarily a bad quality, it is something you should know prior to selecting the puppy as your ideal pet. This is a dog that will take a firmer hand in training and is likely to be a bit more stubborn growing up. It also is one that will defend you ferociously, however, if it feels you are being threatened.

Again, refer back to the type of dog you set out to find. If you are looking for a quiet dog that will curl up at your feet each night and that will socialize well with other dogs and people, you might want to look for a puppy that exhibits a more laid-back behavior, at least by JRT standards. If you are looking for a dog to go hunting with you or to wrestle with you and your buddies, the more assertive puppy would be the perfect match.

Remember that, when I refer to a quiet JRT, I am not referring to a Labrador or a Great Dane. Terriers are terriers, and there is no such thing as a truly docile JRT. The Jack Russell was bred to have boundless energy and remarkable stamina, and they live up to their heritage quite nicely. Although these qualities are great for people with an active lifestyle, they aren't so hot if you and your family would rather snuggle by the fire and read a book. Of course, Jack Russells *will* wind down after a long day, but they never will be described as mellow dogs.

Doggy Don'ts

Don't choose a puppy based strictly on emotion. Try to evaluate your desires and to include everyone in the family decision. If it doesn't feel just right, pass on the puppy until you find one that does. This is a big commitment!

Aim for the Center

In general, it is good to pick a puppy that is active and friendly but that is not the leader of the pack. If you choose a puppy that falls on either end of the scale—one that is very timid or very aggressive— you need to accept that this puppy will take special handling and training to fit into your lifestyle. Be forewarned that an overly timid puppy might become a dog that is so intimidated it lashes out by biting. This is especially important if you have young children because they often will unintentionally overwhelm a more timid dog. Likewise, an aggressive puppy could grow into a dog that inadvertently knocks down a child or that "plays" with children by grabbing their pant legs and shaking its head. This could cause your child to take an unnecessary tumble.

Don't assume you will be able to change the puppy as it grows. Rarely is an owner able to effectively change the basic personality of a dog. An active or assertive puppy is likely to stay that way as it matures, and a puppy that is fearful might well be a danger as an adult—withdrawing one minute and snapping the next. Instead of trying to buy a puppy and mold it into your perfect terrier, it is to your benefit to choose a dog with a personality you like. You still need to train your dog, but the training will be more successful.

None of us can change the world, and trying to change a terrier's personality can be frustrating at best, futile at worst. Know what you want and pick the puppy that best fits that description.

The Family Poll

Remember to ask the opinion of all family members before deciding on one particular puppy. What might be perfect to you might rub your partner the wrong way. And what might be great for the two of you might be totally wrong for your child. All these factors are important and should be weighed equally before a decision is made.

If Looks Matter

If you intend to show or breed your dog, you must be very selective about the puppy's adherence to the breed standard. If this is important to you, it must be high on your list of requirements, and you might have to pass on a particularly charming dog that just isn't show quality. See why making a list ahead of time is so important?

One last thing to remember is that both the JRTCA and the AKC lean toward the medium- to longer-legged dogs for their registered stock.

Although the short-legged dogs certainly are charming, they are frowned upon when it comes to the majority of the registries. If you want to register your dog, choose a pup from taller parents whose offspring fit the guidelines for the breed and steer clear from the short-legged dogs. If registration isn't important, enjoy the variety available to you in picking out your perfect pooch!

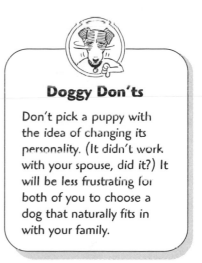

Doggy Don'ts

Don't pick a puppy with the idea of changing its personality. (It didn't work with your spouse, did it?) It will be less frustrating for both of you to choose a dog that naturally fits in with your family.

The Least You Need to Know

➤ Write out a list of the important traits and characteristics you want to find in your puppy before beginning your puppy search.

➤ Finding a reputable breeder is an important first step in finding a healthy puppy.

➤ View several litters before making your decision.

➤ Ask lots of questions while visiting the breeder to determine whether the litter and the breeder are right for you.

➤ Beware of breeders who don't ask you any questions or who think that Jack Russells are great for everyone.

➤ Spend plenty of time with the puppy you think might be "the one" to see whether it's true or just wishful thinking.

➤ Choose the puppy in the litter that most closely fits your predetermined description of your perfect pet.

Chapter 7

Club Jack Russell: Resort or Condo?

In This Chapter

➤ The wild, wild West

➤ The few, the proud, the JRT owners

➤ Kids and Russells—a good match?

So far, this book has covered environment, your special family circumstances and whether you have what it takes to be owned by a Jack Russell Terrier. Now it's time to take a good hard look at these factors and decide whether you are ready to take on the responsibility of a rotten Russell or if you should rethink your purchasing decision. Remember, Jack Russell Terriers are *not* for everyone. Deciding that you can't meet the demanding needs of this feisty little terrier does not mean you have failed as a pet owner. It simply means that this particular breed of dog isn't right for you. You should look for a lower-maintenance breed that will better suit your lifestyle.

The Wild, Wild West

If it seems like I'm suggesting that JRTs need acres and acres to roam just to be happy, rest assured that I'm not. Granted, the more space you can offer your Jack Russell, the easier it will be to control its energy level and, as a result, its zippy nature and potentially destructive behavior. Many JRTs, however, have been raised quite successfully in the city, provided their owners have the time and inclination to properly maintain an exercise schedule for their busy little friends. That, more than anything, is the key to success in managing these little terrorists.

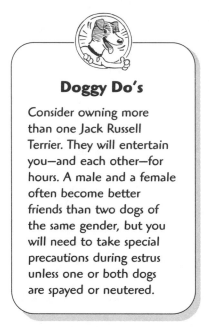

Doggy Do's

Consider owning more than one Jack Russell Terrier. They will entertain you—and each other—for hours. A male and a female often become better friends than two dogs of the same gender, but you will need to take special precautions during estrus unless one or both dogs are spayed or neutered.

You also need to consider the climate in your area. People who live in temperate climates such as southern California will have an easier time accommodating their JRTs with outside exercise than people living through tough New York winters. That's not to say it can't be done, however. Remember that JRTs came from England, and the winters there aren't exactly balmy. It just means you have to do some adapting. You need to provide your JRT with a sweater and possibly paw protectors for cold, winter walks, and you need to find a suitable indoor energy outlet for your terrier when the weather prohibits an outdoor excursion.

JRTs can romp in the snow, provided they have enough protection to keep their body heat up. You have to keep an eye on them, however, to make sure they do not become overly chilled. One puppy from our very first litter was flown to a family in Alaska and has adapted quite well to her new arctic home. The vet gave the family a few tips to prevent her from getting too cold and some warning signs to watch for in case she does. She's been happy and healthy ever since.

The Joy of the Fenced Yard

The best scenario is if you can provide a house with some type of enclosed yard for your puppy or dog. This gives it some room to run, jump and play in a controlled environment without harming itself or threatening your sanity. If at all possible, install a doggy door linking the inside of your house to your fenced yard. This arrangement gives your dog access to both your company and the great outdoors. It can decide whether to head outside to play or sun itself or to stay indoors to be with you. You will find that, if you provide an outdoor access and a few toys, your JRT often can amuse itself, taking some of the burden off your shoulders.

Bet You Didn't Know

Most pet stores and many home-improvement centers offer a wide assortment of doggy doors for your convenience. These doors come in various sizes and configurations to match your terrier's height and weight and to fit into virtually any door, including sliding glass doors. Check out all your options before deciding that adding a doggy door is impossible.

Potty training also is made easier by this arrangement. By teaching your terrier to go outside on its own when it has to eliminate, you won't constantly have to be on the lookout for "tinkle signs." It also provides your JRT with instant relief when it decides it has to go. Since it doesn't have to rely on you, it is more likely to head outside and prevent an accident, making your life and training easier.

If you have more than one puppy or dog, so much the better. Our terriers often wake up, bolt out the doggy door and spend the next thirty minutes in uninterrupted play with each other until they finally feel the urge to come back in and hang out. This takes the burden off you as an owner to amuse your furry little friends, and it gives them both the exercise they desperately need and the companionship they desire. It also allows them to check out perceived threats, such as an encroaching cat, without bothering you. Trust me, they will demand much of your attention through their regular activities. Any break you can give yourself by providing alternate forms of amusement will be greatly appreciated.

Play Dates

If the doggy door arrangement is not possible, regular play trips are imperative to keep your JRT's energy level under control. These can be simple jaunts around the block, trips to a nearby park, or escapades all the way to a beach or a field to really burn off energy.

A dog's home is its castle (but note the strong fencing around its domain).

All you need is your terrier, a little time and a Frisbee or a ball, and you have the makings for a very happy pooch! If you need more ideas about how to creatively exercise your JRT, check out Part 5 of this book. After reading that section, you should have no excuses!

Remember, most behavior problems stem from a lack of exercise and stimulation. If you have a quiet neighborhood with plenty of back streets, your dog will be happy just seeing the sights and enjoying your company while also burning off energy. Even if you only have a few minutes and can't take the time for a walk, go outside and play with your dog for even just ten or fifteen minutes. This goes a long way toward satisfying your dog's need for companionship. You also can choose a hallway in your home and your dog's favorite ball to get a few minutes of wonderful exercise. You can just play fetch for ten minutes without ever leaving the comfort of your own living room. As the saying goes, just do it.

Urban Life

Even if you live in an apartment or a condo, you still can make the arrangement work, provided you are committed to making an exercise program a regular routine for your dog and your family. Taking your JRT out for a five-minute walk once a week might seem like enough to you, but it won't be enough for your active little terrier. This type of exercise program only frustrates it, leaving its appetite for adventure whetted rather than sated. As soon as you bring your dog home from such a walk, it will be eager to go right back out. When that opportunity doesn't arise, it will seek its amusements elsewhere, often turning to destructive behavior to satisfy its energetic needs.

Because this type of arrangement isn't ideal for the JRT, you need to take some special steps to make the relationship work. If you truly are committed to your terrier and to your relationship together, you can make apartment dwelling tolerable, provided you are able and willing to take daily trips to the park to let your Jack Russell stretch its legs and satisfy its senses. These trips would probably include playing ball, chasing birds, meeting new people and just generally enjoying life. Keep in mind that you don't have to make a special trip. If you are headed out anyway, consider taking your JRT along to keep you company. It might do both of you some good.

Doggy Do's

Include your Jack Russell Terrier in as many activities as possible. It's a friendly little bugger that likes to explore new places and to meet new people.

The Few, the Proud, the JRT Owners

Does this mean your whole life must be committed to this cuddly little beast? Of course not. It simply means that, if space is limited, you must make up for it in other ways if your relationship is to be a happy one. Even when space is plentiful, however, your lifestyle might not allow you to give the time and attention necessary to satisfy your terrier.

If you work eighty-hour weeks and live alone, your dog will be left to its own devices for a significant part of the day. This could lead to problems. Even if your Jack Russell has its own room to run in, don't assume it will take advantage of it. JRTs need playmates, either human or canine. If you have two dogs that get along well and that don't squabble when left alone, they usually can amuse themselves without difficulty. No amount of canine fun, however, can be substituted for your love and attention at regular intervals. Because Jack Russells are people-loving dogs, they are not content to live solely with another dog as a companion. They need consistent, playful interaction with you as well.

Quality Time for You

To truly enjoy your JRT, you must spend time getting to know it and enjoying its unique personality quirks. All Jack Russell Terriers are distinctly unique, yet frighteningly similar. They all have odd behaviors that seem to permeate the breed, yet the way these behaviors manifest themselves and the way your terrier incorporates them into its own personality make it special indeed.

Bet You Didn't Know

The antics of your Jack Russell Terrier will keep you amused for hours. They can have as much fun chasing a ground squirrel in the field as chasing a rubber toy in your backyard.

No one can spend time around a Jack Russell without being thoroughly entertained by its antics and amazed by its intelligence and problem-solving capabilities. You must spend time with your dog, however, to see this very charming side of its personality. It takes commitment on your part to truly make your JRT part of the family rather than just another addition to your living room or yard. Given the chance, your Jack Russell Terrier gladly will assume the role of the family jester and will delight at doing funny things to make you laugh.

Spending time with your Jack Russell need not take an act of Congress or days of planning. Simply committing to fifteen or thirty minutes each day usually is enough to satisfy your furry friend, provided it has ample opportunity to play on its own to relieve any additional pent-up boredom or energy it builds up during the day. It enjoys the interaction the two of you have, regardless of the activity.

Remember that you likely will tire of your JRT's favorite game long before it does, so don't feel like you have to be creative or innovative to satisfy your dog. Grab its favorite ball and head outside for a quick game of fetch or reach for the nearest sock toy for a bout of tug-of-war. This goes miles toward keeping your dog sane and healthy. Afterwards, it is likely to curl up next to your feet for at least a few minutes before grabbing another toy and trying to entice you into another round of play.

Quality Time for Your JRT

Simple daily routines can provide an opportunity to spend time with your terrier. A hike to the mailbox accompanied by your Jack Russell or a walk to visit your neighbor might be the perfect solution for accomplishing two goals in one fell swoop. But be honest with yourself. If you know in your heart that finding even this much spare time in your busy life will be a chore, you should opt for another breed (or perhaps you should set up an aquarium instead).

You can't spend hours with your dog on the weekends and absolutely no time with it during the week and still expect your dog to be well mannered and adjusted. It simply has too much energy stored up to be satisfied with this arrangement. Smaller, more manageable time chunks work better for your Jack Russell, if not for you. Remember, time spent is not cumulative to a JRT. It needs some interaction time every day to be truly happy. Honestly evaluate your available time to see whether a JRT is right for you.

Kids and Russells— a Good Match?

In addition to honestly evaluating your lifestyle and available time to determine whether a Jack Russell Terrier will fit within your routine, you also must take a good long look at your family situation prior to making this decision. Although some JRT experts feel these terriers don't get along well with children, I wholeheartedly disagree. Great relationships can be formed, provided the child is old enough to handle the antics and energy of this breed. The child also must be well mannered and have enough respect for animals that your puppy or dog will not become a punching bag.

Doggy Don'ts

Don't leave your puppy alone for extended periods of time, especially in the house, unless you want to return to a demolition derby. Being alone is stressful to your dog.

A Little Maturity Helps

Everyone feels their own children are perfect little angels that would never do anything to hurt anyone or anything, but please be realistic. Some children are too aggressive with animals to accept the independent and strong personality of a JRT. Some children will spend hours roughhousing with or trying to one-up your dog. If this is the case, you need to choose a breed that is more tolerant of this behavior and that is less aggressive by nature. To throw two such assertive personalities together is a recipe for disaster and could possibly lead to your child being bitten by a dog fed up with being tormented.

A Jack Russell Terrier that feels cornered or threatened is likely to protect itself and act accordingly. You can't blame your dog for defending itself when it's put into a situation in which it feels its safety is at stake. Some children simply don't understand that dogs are not around solely for their amusement. They cannot treat a dog like one of their toys if the dog is to be happy. Evaluate your children's personalities honestly before deciding that a JRT will fit into your household.

Terriers and Young Kids

On the flip side, some children are either too young or too timid to handle the rambunctious JRT without becoming intimidated or frightened. Jack Russell Terriers are fast-moving targets, and they rarely slow down for corners, obstacles or even small children. Some children are overwhelmed by their activity and feel more like part of an obstacle course than part of the family. If you know your child can be easily startled or overwhelmed by lots of activity and commotion, either choose an older, more settled terrier or look for another breed. JRTs rarely have a slow mode. An older dog, of course, will be more controllable than a puppy, but it still will have plenty of get-up-and-go and isn't likely to spend life as a lap dog.

A very young child will likely be scared by the fast movements and boundless energy of a Jack Russell, and I don't recommend adding a new JRT puppy to a family with such a youngster. Just as the toddler is trying to walk on shaky legs, the Jack Russell no doubt will come flying through the room and inadvertently either trip the child or knock her over. As a protective parent, you undoubtedly will get angry with your dog, setting yourself up for resentment on both ends. Your JRT can't help feeling rambunctious any more than your child can help being wobbly on new legs. It just isn't a good combination.

When the Stork Arrives

Introducing a newborn to a family that already has a JRT can work, but only if the parents are committed to helping the Jack Russell understand that the rules of the road have to change. The parents must be willing to be patient with their terrier's curiosity about this new addition to the household. The dog and the baby will have enough time to grow together and to learn what is acceptable and what isn't, and your JRT will begin to understand that there are times when interaction is okay and times when it is not. Rest assured, however, that this will take patience and a firm commitment by the parents to understand the dog's mistakes and to teach the JRT what is acceptable behavior.

Doggy Don'ts

Don't become upset with your puppy or dog if it bites in self-defense when a child is abusing it. Your terrier doesn't understand teasing and is acting as any dog would in a threatening situation. Instead, teach the child compassion and kindness toward animals or keep the two separated for both of their sakes.

Be Honest with Yourself

If you have children and are considering adding a Jack Russell Terrier to the mix, honestly evaluate your children's responses to the puppies and to all the activity when you go looking for a puppy or a dog. You must be positive that your children will be comfortable with being jostled from time to time before selecting this particular breed (or any breed of terrier, for that matter). Focus primarily on the youngest member of the family because he or she is the individual most likely to be overwhelmed or startled by the dog. If possible, allow the children to interact with the parents of the litter to see if an adult JRT causes them concern or anxiety. If all goes well, let them interact with the puppies. Make an honest assessment of whether they are old enough to understand how to handle and take care of a puppy.

Remember, this new addition will be an integral part of your family, not an outside dog that will simply act as a burglar alarm. JRTs must interact with people to be happy. This means being a house dog at least part of the time. If you feel you will need to keep your JRT at an arm's length to make your child feel comfortable, pass on this particular breed. By forcing your terrier outside every time your child looks crosswise, you will be breeding resentment in your Jack Russell that will be aimed toward your child, and you could end up with an aggressive terrier. In addition, this situation sets up the JRT to feel unwanted and unloved.

You simply can't take the zip out of a terrier. They might mellow as they get older, but that's the best you can hope for. If you can't honestly say you are willing to accept this fuzzy little whirlwind into your family as an integral part of that unit, don't buy a Jack Russell. Your JRT will want to be a friend to all the family members. If you feel this dog will make one of your children uncomfortable, you need to accept that this might not be the right time for this addition or the right breed for you. Be honest with yourself and listen to your children's opinions before making this kind of commitment for your family.

The Least You Need to Know

➤ JRTs need room to romp, either in their own backyard or out playing with you.

➤ If you have the space, two JRTs often are a good choice. They can amuse themselves and can keep each other company when you are away.

➤ If you don't allow your JRT to burn off energy, it can become destructive and disobedient, making your life miserable.

➤ You must be sure you have the time, energy and lifestyle to include your JRT in your daily activities.

➤ JRTs need some of your time every day to stay happy and healthy.

➤ JRTs can get along famously with children, provided the children are old enough to handle the dog's energy level, are confident enough to play with it and are not so aggressive that they try to intimidate or harm your terrier.

➤ Adding a Jack Russell to a family with very small children is not recommended, although you often can successfully add a newborn to an existing JRT family.

➤ Consider your children's feelings and actions before you choose to add a JRT to the mix.

Chapter 8

Love at First Sight?

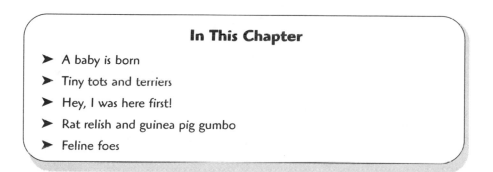

In This Chapter

➤ A baby is born

➤ Tiny tots and terriers

➤ Hey, I was here first!

➤ Rat relish and guinea pig gumbo

➤ Feline foes

Now that you have fully evaluated your home, schedule and commitments, have decided you are ready to be owned by a Jack Russell Terrier and have finally found that perfect pup, you are ready to introduce that puppy or dog to its new home. Although we all have visions of the perfect homecoming and a family that lives happily ever after, this isn't always the case. Careful consideration of your puppy and its new environment, however, can help make the transition go as smoothly as possible. The advice in this chapter should help you head off any potential disasters before they happen.

A Baby Is Born

Introducing your puppy or dog to a newborn usually can be accomplished smoothly and easily, especially if the newborn already is in the house and the puppy or dog is the newcomer. In this case, the dog has few expectations of who or what is higher in the hierarchy than it is and will accept all house dwellers simply as part of its new home. It will be looking for ways to fit in and will be most open to training and imprinting in its first few days in the house.

Preparing Your Dog

If you are bringing a newborn home to a puppy or dog already in the household, you need to take a few extra steps to let your terrier know that it is not being replaced and that it is still very much loved and wanted. The easiest way to do this is to prepare your dog in advance for the baby's homecoming.

Doggy Don'ts

Hard as it might be, don't be overly protective of your newborn. Chasing your dog away whenever it gets close to the baby only breeds resentment in your dog and could lead to aggressive behavior toward you or your baby.

All dogs have an acute sense of smell, and they learn much about their surroundings by using their noses. Your first step, before baby gets close to coming home, should be to bring home a blanket or a piece of clothing the baby has worn. Let the dog smell the clothing and grow accustomed to this new scent over a day or two. If possible, bring home one of the baby's swaddling blankets and place it in your Jack Russell's bed for it to sleep with a few days prior to your homecoming. This makes your terrier comfortable with the scent of your new little one, and it is a nonthreatening way to begin the introduction.

During this time, you also should play a recording of the newborn's cry as your spouse or another family member pets and reassures your terrier. This will prevent your Jack Russell from going nuts every time your baby wakes up and cries, and it will help your JRT grow accustomed to this new loud noise in its home. Watching programs on TV or videotapes that show babies crying also will help disarm your dog. Soon it will take a baby's cry in stride and will not become anxious at the noise.

Home from the Hospital

When you finally bring your newborn home, let the father hold the baby while the mother welcomes the dog. She should scratch and pet the dog, letting it know that Mom is very happy to be home and is equally happy to see her beloved Jack Russell. After a few minutes, Dad can hand the baby back to Mom; he, too, should make a bit of a fuss about seeing the family JRT again. Resist the temptation to rush this step. It could easily be the key to either your success or your failure. The main thing is to make your Jack Russell feel that, in spite of the new bundle, it still has a place of importance in the family.

Once situated, place the baby in your arms and let your dog look at the baby and smell his blankets and clothing. Because you already have introduced your baby's scent to your Jack Russell, the dog won't be totally taken off guard by this new intrusion. Let your dog be curious, look, and gently touch, but don't allow it to jump on the chair or couch with you. Remember your awe and curiosity at seeing this new little being for the first time? Your Jack Russell feels the same way. It simply wants to see what this new little bundle is and to know that its place is not being threatened by your new addition.

Doggy Do's

Let your Jack Russell sniff, touch and even nuzzle your newborn while you stay alert so it doesn't try to jump or get too rough. A terrier that is familiar with a baby is more likely to accept and even protect it.

Pet and talk to your Jack Russell—or even feed it small cookies or treats—while holding the baby. This shows the dog that it is still a cherished part of your home and that it should not be threatened by the baby. Allow your terrier into the baby's room with you, but only when you are in the room. By making it pleasant for your JRT to be around the baby, the dog will come to associate the baby with good things and will look forward to being with him. Spend some extra time reassuring your dog during this period of transition, and it will be more willing to welcome your new baby as a positive addition to the family.

When I brought my newborn home to our two terriers, I followed all the preceding steps. I was shocked to find that, not only did my two terriers adore our new baby, they were bound and determined to protect her at all costs—even from each other! The dog that followed me into the baby's room first wouldn't let the other one in, and whenever she would cry, both would come running to make sure no one was threatening their "baby sister." If you've ever doubted the intelligence of these dogs, watch them in action and your doubts will be put to rest forever. They are truly amazing little animals!

Tiny Tots and Terriers

Introducing a young child to a new dog is easier than bringing a new baby home for the first time. Because the dog is in a new environment, it will be curious about its new surroundings. It won't be threatened by your children's attentions, provided they do not overwhelm it or try to intimidate it by poking or teasing. The success of this introduction rests solely on your children. If the puppy feels welcome and comfortable, all will go well. If your new addition to the family feels threatened and frightened, it will react either by tucking its tail and hiding in its crate or by turning to aggression to protect itself.

Doggy Do's

Discuss the "rules of the road" with your children and set up guidelines before you bring the puppy home. Jack Russells make nice pets for children, provided the children are not allowed to abuse or tease the terrier.

Keep the Moment Mellow

Children often are so excited about having a new puppy that they scream or shriek at the puppy's every move. This is likely to frighten a new puppy in totally foreign surroundings, and the dog will probably head for the nearest corner or dark spot. Talk to your children and let them know they should make the puppy feel welcome by gently petting it and by not making noises that could frighten it. If your children are old enough to understand logic, they usually will be quite willing to tone down their excitement if they realize the puppy is scared. Ask your children to talk to the puppy in a quiet voice and to keep their movements slow and purposeful. Show them how to gently pet the puppy and how the puppy likes to play with balls and chew toys on the ground.

Pickin' Up the Pup

Remember that young children are notoriously clumsy with items they hold, and they often drop whatever is in their clutches. For this reason, don't let a young child pick the puppy off the ground. If the child accidentally drops it, the puppy could be injured or, at the very least, frightened. How would you like to be dropped on your head on a first date? You would never go out with that person again and would likely avoid any further encounters at all costs. The same is true of your puppy. If you drop it even once, it is unlikely to be as forthcoming with its affections in the future.

If your young child wants to hold the puppy, have him sit on the floor and hold the puppy on his lap. An adult or older child always should be present when your child holds your puppy to make sure he is holding it gently and is not unduly restraining it. The child also should be taught to keep his hands and face away from the puppy's mouth to avoid injury. Puppies have sharp little teeth and are not always choosy about what they bite down on. An excited puppy is likely to playfully snap or nip. If your youngster's face is in the dog's line of site, it could receive a nasty bite.

Supervise!

Keep a close eye on both the puppy and your children for the first several days or even weeks after your terrier comes home. You need to make sure your children don't forget that the puppy is a living, breathing creature that has to be handled gently. It is easy for them to slip back into thinking a puppy is a stuffed animal that can be dropped or hurled across the room like their stuffed toys. Obviously, this could result in serious injury to your new puppy or could lead to aggressive behavior to protect itself. Remind your children to treat the puppy as a new playmate that has feelings of its own and to be very gentle when playing with their new dog. Encourage them to think of your new puppy as a member of the family and enforce the same "no biting, no hitting" rules as if it were another child.

Doggy Do's

It is more difficult for an older JRT to adjust to another adult dog than to a younger dog. Keep this in mind when selecting a dog for your family. If an older dog or cat already is present, opt for a puppy or a young dog as your new pet.

It's a Crate Life!

A crate can be very helpful during this time of transition. As you will see in later chapters, it also is helpful during training in general. The crate gives your puppy a safe place to be when it begins to feel overwhelmed, and it enables you to put the puppy someplace that is labeled off-limits to the children. This will keep both your sanity and that of your terrier intact. Make the crate a homey place for your pup by placing a soft, fuzzy blanket at the bottom and by providing fresh water and food plus a chew toy or two for the puppy to amuse itself if it so desires. The crate should be roomy, but it should not be so large that the puppy has room to run around. See Chapter 9 for more information about finding and purchasing a crate that's right for your dog.

When your puppy is playing with your children, give it free access to its crate by leaving the door open. This way, if your terrier feels threatened, it easily can retreat to its comfortable cubbyhole. By letting the children know that the crate is off-limits, your puppy can feel safe and can choose when it wants to come out to play. This keeps the puppy from feeling cornered with no place to go, and it teaches your children how to read your JRT's actions.

Bet You Didn't Know

Every year, hundreds of puppies are injured by swinging or slamming doors. Educate your children about the importance of watching for the puppy whenever entering or leaving the house. Even better, install a doggy door that leads to an enclosed area. Teach the puppy how to use it so that it can enter and exit by its own route.

When introducing a new dog to your home, be patient. After a time, there's a good chance the two canines will become good pals.

Hey, I Was Here First!

The success of introducing a puppy or dog into a household that already has a dog or cat depends greatly on the attitude of the other pet. Some pets get very possessive of their family and would rather not share that attention with an intruder. Some even resort to violent behavior to try to chase off the new pet. This especially is common with older dogs or cats that have had the run of the house and family for many years. They have grown accustomed to their lifestyle and are unlikely to welcome a dramatic change.

Try to see the situation from your other pet's point of view. For months or even years, the pet has had your family's attention all to itself and is secure in knowing its needs will be met. It can sleep when it wants, can play when it wants and never has to share its food, water or toys with anyone else. Suddenly, this interloper shows up and starts sniffing around its food dish and getting loads of attention from members of the family. The older pet feels insecure, not knowing whether its place within the family is still intact. Like any threatened animal, it will respond by protecting its territory and by trying to run off the offending addition. Some dogs even resort to violence to protect what they feels are their rights. It is up to you to play referee and to ease your pet's anxieties during this difficult time.

For the Intro—Easy Does It!

You can lessen these anxious feelings by slowly introducing your puppy to your other pets. You don't like to be forced into actions against your will and neither does your pet. Likewise, your pet will resent lengthy introductions and forced periods of play. Allow the relationship to develop slowly, and you will have much better success in the long run.

To start out, let your pet have the run of its usual area (whether a yard, a room, or the whole house) and restrict the puppy to one area of the home that is all its own. Keep their feeding areas well separated and spend time alone with each so they both feel wanted and secure. When things have settled down a bit, you can bring the puppy and the other pet into the living room or into the yard for supervised time together, allowing each one to explore the other. Allow both pets to approach each other in their own time and in their own way. They will be curious about one another, and the older pet likely will show signs of dominance toward the puppy.

Watch, but Don't Get in the Way

Don't try to play referee unless the situation really gets out of hand. It's best to let the animals work it out between themselves, provided no one is in serious danger. Letting your puppy get smacked in the nose a time or two by the cat will teach the puppy that the cat has claws and should be respected. Likewise, letting your excited pup get pinned down or snapped at by an older dog will teach it to back off when the dog growls. The puppy then will be more likely to give your older dog a wide berth in the future. If things do start to get out of hand, startle both pets by making a loud noise and then separate them until another day. If you gradually increase the time they spend together, they will become friends (or at least tolerable cohabitants) in no time.

Avoid the temptation to put your pets together before spending some quality, supervised time with them to judge their reactions. Although a cat is likely to hit the high road and escape to places your puppy can't reach, another dog is likely to turn on your new puppy and act aggressively, sometimes causing injury. Even after a day or two of playing nicely together, the relationship can go downhill. Don't assume that, because they've been tolerant of each other for a while, everything is fine. Spending a few days supervising your pets will prevent possible injuries and vet bills. Don't rush the process. The pets will make progress in their own time and in their own way.

Even after they've adjusted to each other, keep their feeding areas separate to prevent fights over food and treats. If you give treats by hand, make sure each dog gets an equal amount and don't play favorites.

Doggy Don'ts

Don't force your older dog to approach your new puppy by placing it on a leash and dragging it over or by locking the two in an enclosed space together. Not only will the older pet resent the introduction, it will resent you as well. Instead, let them approach each other whenever they are ready and be close by to intervene if things get nasty.

Playing favorites builds resentment and erodes any trust your pets may be building together. Give them treats in their respective dishes and avoid hand-feeding for a while. Be sure to spend plenty of time with each pet, and remember that abundant exercise will help keep tempers in check.

Rat Relish and Guinea Pig Gumbo

If you look back at the breeding and evolution of the Jack Russell Terrier, it is clear that they were, first and foremost, hunting dogs entrusted with tracking foxes and with keeping stables clear of rats and other rodents. With this in mind, it is easy to see why a guinea pig or a domestic rat is a lousy match with a new Jack Russell Terrier. Try as you might to make these two become friends, your JRT is more likely to view your small, furry friend as its next meal.

Hatred of rodents has been inbred into these terriers for hundreds of years. No amount of training will ever truly rid the JRT of its desire to hunt and to destroy anything that smells even remotely like a rodent. Instead of setting yourself up for heartache, it is best to avoid mixing these two very different beasts. Guinea pigs, rats, mice, rabbits, ferrets and even snakes all should be avoided if you plan to have a JRT in your household. Otherwise, you could come home to a dead rat and a smiling terrier when you least expect it.

Doggy Don'ts

Don't ever leave your Jack Russell Terrier alone with a cat, a guinea pig, a rabbit, a rat or a mouse. Your dog sees these animals as prey and is likely to hunt and kill them.

Even if you keep the rodent in another room or high out of reach, your terrier could find a way to penetrate the barriers you set up. Remember that Jack Russells are crafty little dogs and have remarkable jumping abilities. They also are great demolition dogs and can claw and bite their way through even the toughest cage. Add to this a persistence bordering on obsession that is unmatched by any other breed, and you will see that having one of these pets in the house or a surrounding area is a bad idea. It might not happen right away, but sooner or later, your Jack Russell will find a way to make relish out of your rat or make gumbo out of your guinea pig.

Feline Foes

Cats can pose a problem if your JRT is more than 2 years old when you bring it home. I know of many JRT puppies that were successfully raised in a kitty household; they were able to adjust and learn respect for the cats. Most adult Jack Russells that have not previously been exposed to cats, however, will view cats as prey and will try to hunt and kill them.

Male JRTs seem to be especially aggressive when it comes to cats, but I have known several females that were just as intent on murder and mayhem. Again, the JRT was meant to hunt. No amount of punishment will change the basic temperament of the breed. If you have a cat you want to stick around, avoid bringing an older JRT into the home. It would be a tragedy to lose a pet over a preventable mistake.

If you are introducing your new puppy to an older cat, make sure that the cat has plenty of room to retreat away from the puppy and that the cat is allowed to approach at its own rate. Don't punish the cat for slapping your puppy in the nose. The puppy must learn that the cat has claws and is not another play toy. If the puppy seems to get overly excited, separate the two for a while and then try the introduction again. By letting the two approach each other at will, both will feel they are in control of the situation. They will be less likely to turn aggressive, at least beyond a hiss or a bark.

Doggy Don'ts

Don't assume your JRT cannot live peacefully with your cat. Just know that you need to make introductions when the Jack Russell is still a puppy, and you need to take some special steps to ensure a happy relationship.

The Least You Need to Know

➤ If you are planning to introduce a new baby to your JRT, first bring home an article of clothing or a blanket that smells like your baby as well as a recording of his cries.

➤ Don't be too protective of your newborn. Let your Jack Russell sniff and explore your new baby—within reason—and pay lots of attention to your terrier when holding your new baby.

➤ Set guidelines with your older children regarding behaviors that are acceptable and unacceptable with your new puppy. It can be easily injured and intimidated.

➤ Let your puppy have free access to its crate and deem the crate off-limits to your children. This way, your puppy has a place to go when it is overwhelmed.

➤ Be compassionate of other pets when introducing a new puppy to the household. The new puppy will disrupt their lives for a while until everyone adjusts.

➤ Don't leave two unacquainted pets alone together until they have had plenty of time to get to know one another.

➤ Rodents, rabbits, snakes and JRTs don't mix and should never be left alone together.

➤ Cats and JRTs can safely live together if the dog is introduced as a puppy and if each is allowed to approach the other at its own pace.

Chapter 9

The Frustrations of Housetraining

Perhaps the most frustrating training task you will embark upon with your Jack Russell is housetraining. Why, you might ask? The answer is simple. Although JRTs are extremely intelligent and learn very quickly, they also can be bull-headed and defiant. Because your dog has an agenda of its own, it might not readily accept your version of how life should be. What this means to a fledgling trainer is that your Jack Russell will easily learn that it isn't supposed to do its business on your bed, but it might decide it still *wants* to do its business on your bed. Prepare yourself for a battle of wills.

To keep this problem from arising, it is best to start training your JRT the moment you get it home. This helps set the ground rules right from the beginning and starts you on your way to housetraining success. Keep in mind, however, that you might do all the right things but still have a hard time with this seemingly simple task. Don't despair. Many Jack Russell owners have walked down this frustrating path before you. Rest assured that almost all eventually ended up with a properly housetrained dog. It can take up to six or even eight months, however, so be patient.

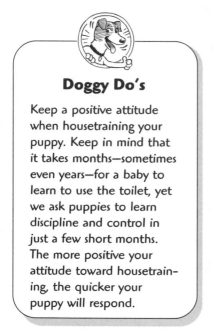

Doggy Do's

Keep a positive attitude when housetraining your puppy. Keep in mind that it takes months—sometimes even years—for a baby to learn to use the toilet, yet we ask puppies to learn discipline and control in just a few short months. The more positive your attitude toward housetraining, the quicker your puppy will respond.

Don't They Make Doggy Diapers?

Depending on how old your puppy is when you get it, it might not be physically ready to be completely housetrained. Most puppies come home to their new families when they are 8 to 10 weeks of age. At this stage, they are unable to control their bladder for an entire night and must relieve themselves every few hours. If your puppy is under 6 months old when you bring it home, be empathetic to the fact that you might be asking it to do something it is physically incapable of doing. Does this mean you should wait until your puppy is 6 months old to begin housetraining? Absolutely not! But it does mean that, mentally, you need to be prepared for less-than-perfect compliance for a while until your puppy understands what you are asking of it and until it can physically control its functions to comply with your wishes.

Select an Indoor Confinement Area

Before you bring your puppy home, you should select a place where it will be kept at night. It should be a place that can be readily closed off, that is small enough to be manageable and that has an easy-to-clean floor. This will be your puppy's bedroom, at least until housetraining is well on its way to being a habit. You need to purchase a crate for your puppy, and you should plan ahead to have lots of newspaper or housetraining pads on hand. You can purchase housetraining pads from most pet stores in your area. They have a water-resistant backing and are scented to tempt your puppy to eliminate on the pads instead of on the floor or the rug. Either newspapers or pads will work, but puppy pads are easier to clean up. On the other hand, they also are more expensive.

A *Lot* of **Potty Trips**

Someone needs to stay with the puppy for the first few days it resides with you. Taking a week off from work really is the best idea. If someone is available to watch your puppy for signs that it needs to go out and can immediately take it outside to eliminate, the chances for more immediate success increase. If, however, it is left to its own devices as to when and where to eliminate,

Doggy Don'ts

Don't leave your very young puppy in a crate all night with no place to relieve itself. This forces your puppy to soil its bed, making both of you unhappy. It also can cause problems in the future with housetraining. Dogs naturally eliminate away from their beds. If your puppy has no choice but to soil its bed, however, this instinct is diminished.

it will take longer to train your puppy to eliminate outside. It will incorrectly assume that other places in the house are acceptable alternatives to its outside toilet.

The more often you can catch your puppy *before* it eliminates in the house and can take it outside to do its business, the more quickly it will associate outside and grass with going potty. This is a situation in which success invariably breeds success. The dog also will be more willing to go when it is convenient for you. The addition of a doggy door can be very helpful with this step because it enables the puppy to head outside the moment it "feels the need." This takes some of the burden off your shoulders, and it allows the puppy the luxury of instant gratification.

The Crate—Your Best Friend

The crate truly is one of the best inventions on the market for dog training and is an invaluable tool for housetraining. Although you might be inclined to look at a crate and think "I can't possibly lock up my poor puppy in that thing!", keep in mind that your puppy

Not only is a crate a great housetraining tool, it serves as a private place for your terrier when it needs some time out.

will view its crate as a comforting refuge rather than as a jail. This only is true, however, if you use the crate as a training tool and not as a method of punishment. A puppy likes to curl up in cozy corners. It feels safe in its little refuge and views it as a place all its own. As long as your puppy sees its crate as a positive place to be, it will look forward to curling up within its comforting confines.

Once a puppy learns that its crate is its personal cubbyhole, it will respect that space as its bed. This means the puppy's natural instinct will be to keep that bed clean. As long as your puppy isn't forced to wait longer than its immature bladder can endure, it will be willing and grateful to have an alternate and more appropriate place to relieve itself (such as outside or on a newspaper). By providing an "escape" from its den, you will keep intact your puppy's natural instinct not to soil its bed—this ultimately will help you in your housetraining goals.

If possible, prepare an enclosed area with flooring such as linoleum or cement where you can place the puppy's crate and training pads. Be sure to place the pads or newspaper near the crate's open door so that, when your puppy wakes up in the middle of the night, it will naturally leave its sleeping place and look for a suitable place to relieve itself. With a little luck, this should be the paper. This routine should be maintained for several days or even for a few weeks until your puppy is predictably paper-trained.

When your puppy consistently relieves itself on the paper, you can move to the next step—slowly moving the paper closer to a door leading to the outside. This teaches your puppy that, ultimately, outside is where you want it to relieve itself. Each day, move the paper a bit closer to the door until the newspaper is just inside the opening. Watch for signs that your puppy is about to relieve itself and then pick it up and take it outside.

Doggy Don'ts

When shopping for your puppy's crate, make sure you don't buy one that is too large. If your puppy has loads of room to move around, it will use a corner of the crate to relieve itself, thinking that the corner is far enough away from its bed.

Both after it eats or when it first wakes up are good times to catch your puppy in the act and advance your housetraining goals. Be sure to pay close attention to its actions after a good round of play or if you know it has been a while since it last took a potty break. When, through either luck on its part or vigilance on yours, it goes outside as requested, give it lots of hugs and treats to signal that you are very pleased with its progress.

As your puppy comes to understand that relieving itself outside pleases you and that it is where you want it to go, it will accept housetraining and will begin to signal you that it needs to go outside by going to the door or by acting anxious. This is a big step for a puppy, and you must be sure to praise and reward this effort with lots of love. As soon as you notice one of these signs (circling and

When to Call the Vet

If you notice blood in either your puppy's urine or its stool, call the vet immediately. These are signs of internal problems.

sniffing are typical), take your puppy outside immediately and attempt to get it to relieve itself. When it does, reward it as before with lots of praise. As the behavior is reinforced, so is your puppy's desire to please you, cementing your housetraining efforts.

Great Expectations

Even after your pup has learned to signal when it wants to go out, it still will have accidents. No one is perfect, and this applies to your puppy as well. Many factors can contribute to your puppy's lapse in control. A visitor to your house, for example, could over-stimulate it. It might become so excited at the sight of a new person that it loses its ability to control its bladder. A long or rambunctious bout of playing or roughhousing also could distract your puppy long enough that it forgets it has to control itself and go outside. Your puppy plays and plays and, before it realizes it's past time to go, it is caught with a full bladder and does not have enough time or self-control to hold it in. The result is a wet spot on the carpet. All these scenarios can be prevented with a bit of planning and attention on your part.

Spot the Patterns

To avoid accidents, remember that puppies have patterns they tend to follow. These patterns can help you predict the most likely times to further your housetraining. Your puppy will need to urinate as soon as it wakes up from a nap or in the morning and immediately following intense play. Drinking a lot of water all at once is a sign that a potty break is soon to follow. A recent meal or bout of excitement also can signal the need for relief.

Don't always wait for your puppy to show signs that it is about to have an accident. If you take your puppy out immediately after these events occur, your puppy likely will be quite ready to do its business wherever it happens to be. This is the time to carry your puppy outside or to the newspaper to encourage it to relieve itself in the desired spot. By preempting your puppy's needs, it will think that going outside is its idea. It will be more likely to continue to do so whenever the opportunity presents itself.

Being aware of your puppy's schedule enables you to create circumstances conducive to successful housetraining. If you are alert to your puppy's signals that it needs to "go," you soon will learn that it has a predictable pattern. By using this pattern, you can predict when your puppy most likely is ready to go outside. Don't wait for an accident to occur or almost occur. Take the initiative by predicting when your puppy needs to go and take it outside before it even is aware of the need.

Bathroom Body Language

To determine your puppy's pattern, you need to pay attention to its body language. Usually, a puppy circles an area several times, sniffing or whining, before settling on a spot to relieve itself. If you notice this behavior in time, you can take your puppy either outside or to the paper and let it know that this is where you want it to do its business. If the puppy complies, abundant praise and treats must quickly follow.

When to Call the Vet

If your dog begins eating its stools or those of another dog (coprophagia), call the vet. This could be a sign of improper digestion or a chemical imbalance that causes undigested food to be left in the stool. Although not life threatening, this unpleasant habit is best caught early.

Caught in the Act

Even if your puppy starts to relieve itself in the house, you still can save the situation if you act quickly. Calmly pick up your puppy saying "No!" and take it outside. Your puppy will be startled enough to stop in midstream (usually) and will let you take it outside without a problem. Most of the time, your puppy still will have to relieve itself and will comply by doing so outside. Again, heap on the praise and let it know it has done well. Adding a treat or two never hurts.

Avoid Common Housetraining Mistakes

Contrary to numerous books available on the subject (many of which are outdated), rubbing a dog's nose in its urine or feces does not promote housetraining. Neither does hitting a dog or puppy with a rolled newspaper if it has an accident. These reactions only breed fear and resentment in your terrier, and ultimately to a wet spot on your bed when you least expect it! These behaviors on your part also could lead to aggression from your puppy. If it feels threatened enough, it might try to fight back to protect itself, and you inadvertently could create a biter. This can be dangerous and obviously should be avoided. In addition, hitting with a newspaper can create a fear for the very object you want to promote—going to the bathroom on the newspaper!

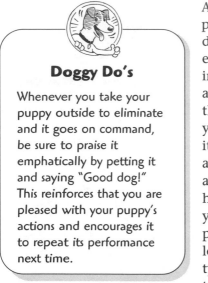

Another possible effect of overzealous punishment is that it teaches your dog not to relieve itself in your presence. Some dogs "learn" that to eliminate at all is wrong—now you have a *real* problem. This creates a puppy that either soils in the house when you are away or is afraid to relieve itself in front of you, whether you are inside or outside. Both scenarios are counter-productive to your housetraining goals. To be successful, you must be able to observe your puppy doing it right to quickly follow up with praise. If this opportunity is taken away, your training will take significantly longer. Keep this in mind when you are tempted to lose your cool and resort to punishment.

Clean Up Quickly

If your puppy has an accident, it is important to immediately clean the spot and thoroughly deodorize the area. Puppies tend to relieve themselves in areas that smell like previous "potty spots." By eliminating the odor, you reduce the possibility of your puppy visiting the same location. Vinegar and water works well, as do many nonammonia cleansers. The quicker you get to the scene of the accident, the smaller the chance a permanent odor will set—so act quickly. Better yet, keep your eyes open for signs of an impending accident and avoid it in the first place.

Battle of the Sexes

For many reasons, male dogs seem to be more difficult to housetrain than their female counterparts. The primary reason for this behavior is found in the male dog's natural instinct to mark its territory as a warning to other male dogs as well as to attract potential mates. To alleviate this problem, you might want to consider neutering your male puppy as soon as the veterinarian gives you the okay. This will catch your puppy early enough in its development to prevent this habit from becoming established or at least before it is firmly ingrained in its behavior.

If you wait too long to have your puppy neutered, it might urinate on your furniture, plastic bags, clothing, bedding or any number of leg-height objects in an attempt to warn other male dogs that these places are within its denning area. Although this is great for warding off other male dogs, it doesn't usually sit well with you, the home-owner, who has to clean up all the puddles. The benefits and draw-backs of spaying and neutering are discussed later in this book, but trust me on this one—a neutered male is much more pleasant to be around than an intact one.

Practice, Practice, Practice

I can't stress enough the importance of consistent training with your puppy or dog. If your puppy gets away with a bad behavior even once, it will continue to try for the exception rather than the rule. It is your job as trainer to set the bound-aries, to make sure your puppy understands the rules and to make sure these rules are followed. This means monitoring your dog each and every day. If you allow the rules to be broken just once, they will continue to be broken.

Doggy Don'ts

Don't assume that, just because your puppy has had a particularly successful week, it is fully house-trained. Even the best learners have setbacks. Expect mistakes to happen and deal with them calmly and without anger.

If you forget to praise your puppy for its conscious attempts to please you, it will see little value in complying with your wishes in the future. Likewise, if you allow your puppy to engage in unacceptable behavior even once, you are encouraging it to continue that behav-ior. If you are unable to consistently watch your puppy through certain times of the housetraining phase, place it outside or in a confined area and be patient if it doesn't do everything exactly right. Housetraining takes time even in the best of situations. If your time to devote to training is limited, understand that it will take your puppy longer to really understand what is expected of it. It is, after all, just a baby.

Your purpose as a Jack Russell Terrier owner is to make your puppy feels wanted and loved, not rejected or shunned. You wouldn't hit a baby for going to the bathroom in her diaper, and the same rules should apply to your baby dog. Like babies, puppies and adult dogs want your approval and will work hard to please you. Consistent, positive reinforcement goes a long way toward housetraining your dog and, in the long run, is much more rewarding and effective.

When all else fails and you are at the end of your rope, remember this: No matter how smart the trainer, how precocious the puppy or how vigilant you might be, most Jack Russells aren't fully house-trained until they are at least 6 months old, and some take even longer. Just keep your chin up, your temper in check and treats on hand, and you eventually will succeed. I promise!

The Least You Need to Know

➤ Jack Russell Terriers are notoriously difficult to housetrain, and they can take six months or longer to truly get it right.

➤ The age of your puppy plays a significant role in the success of your housetraining efforts.

➤ A properly prepared housetraining area is invaluable to your success.

➤ Every time you catch your puppy *before* a mistake occurs gets you closer to a housetrained pup.

➤ A properly sized crate can be your most important tool in housetraining.

➤ Consistency is the most important rule to housetraining.

➤ Punishing your dog if it makes a mistake does *not* further your housetraining goals.

Part 3

The Doggy Social Scene

Terriers, by nature, are rather difficult little beasts. If you know how to terrier-proof your house and some simple training techniques, you can make living with your Jack Russell Terrier a little more predictable. Although you never totally control your JRT's antics, this section gives you some valuable tools for tempering your terrier's irascible nature.

This part discusses how to set a command hierarchy for your terrier, some basic training guidelines that every JRT and terrier owner should know, the use of positive reinforcement and corrections in your training and how to make your family a cohesive unit. It also identifies specific danger zones in and around your house and provides directions to make these places a little safer. Finally, it gives you invaluable advice about how to deal with the dogs that have specific problems such as barking, digging, aggression, separation anxiety, chewing and chasing.

Who Owns Who?

> ## In This Chapter
>
> ➤ Setting the record straight
> ➤ Creating standards without causing problems
> ➤ Dealing with defiance
> ➤ Time–outs
> ➤ Crating success

As you've seen in previous chapters, the Jack Russell Terrier has a very distinct personality with strong opinions about who it is and how things should be run. There are times when you and your JRT will have differences of opinion about how a situation should be handled, and your terrier will use its not-insignificant mental capacities to slyly avoid your rules or to conveniently forget that there are any rules to follow in the first place. As a trainer, it then becomes your job to see that the rules are once again firmly established without losing your temper or your sanity.

You also must remember that training your Jack Russell Terrier will be far from easy. With a breed as smart as the JRT, you'd think training would be a breeze, but this simply is not the case. Because they are so smart, they also have strong opinions as to the behaviors they prefer. This often can lead to a battle of wills. You should know, however, that your JRT will be a much happier dog once it understands the rules. These rules provide structure in your terrier's life and create a feeling of stability that results from knowing what is expected of it from day to day. You cannot lose your patience, however, or your training sessions will be dismal failures.

Doggy Do's

Be realistic when setting rules for your terrier. A young puppy has physical limitations on its bodily functions, and asking too much of it too soon will cause frustration for both you and your pet. Remember, too, that JRTs are not mellow dogs. Asking your terrier to lie at your feet for hours on end simply isn't reasonable.

Setting the Record Straight

From the day your puppy comes home, it is important that you set some boundaries and rules for your terrier to follow. Dogs, and especially Jack Russells, do well with guidelines that keep their lives neat and orderly. Without these guidelines, havoc and chaos would eventually rule, making everyone in the household—including your terrier—absolutely crazy. Of course, a young puppy will have fewer "rules" than an older puppy, and an older puppy will not be held to the same standards as an adult dog. It also is important to remember that these are only guidelines. No dog is perfect; they all will have lapses in memory and judgment somewhere along the way. Getting angry will only frustrate both you and your terrier and will lead to unrealistic expectations and goals for both of you.

From day one, your Jack Russell Terrier must understand that you are "top dog" in the household and it is not. If you start this command hierarchy when the puppy is young, it is much easier to continue it throughout older life and training. If you are lulled into the fantasy that the puppy is so cute and that its little habits like gnawing on your slippers or ignoring your commands are so endearing, you are setting yourself up for some serious problems when you begin obedience training with your dog.

The best time to set the record straight is the moment your puppy comes home. Any form of aggression or defiance should be corrected immediately. Notice that I said corrected and not punished. JRTs don't do well with punishment and often retaliate with very deliberate and well-thought-out acts of defiance such as wetting on your pillow or bed in the middle of the night or chewing up your favorite slippers the day after your disagreement. Punishment often can lead to a more aggressive dog or, conversely, to a dog that cowers whenever you lift a hand and that is more likely to run when called than to come to you.

You Are the Leader of the Pack

Remember that dogs naturally work in packs. This translates to teamwork. The strength of a hunting pack of coyotes is that they can rely on one another to surround their prey, making it easier to bring home dinner. Your domesticated puppy has the same frame of mind. It needs to know who is the leader of the pack (you), who are the higher-ranked dogs (your family) and what its role is within your pack (your household). By providing a structured environment in which your puppy understands its role and the rules of the "pack," it will gladly work with the "team" to make a successful relationship.

Doggy Don'ts

Don't use spanking over vocal reprimands. Hitting your terrier will only create a timid or hostile dog, depending on its basic nature. A sharp "No!" or "Bad dog!" will go much further to train your dog what is right and wrong than a rolled up newspaper on its behind.

When training your Jack Russell Terrier, you must remember that it is a very smart breed of dog. Although you need to set the ranking of the hierarchy, it is important that you go into this ranking with the understanding that you must train your terrier and not dominate it. This distinction is a fine line. Your JRT must respect you and must understand that you are the head of the household, but it should not fear you or be intimidated.

You should take care to increase your terrier's experiences by exposing it to the correct stimuli and by teaching it what you want. It is easy to get frustrated with training your Jack Russell, and you might

All dogs, especially willful JRTs, need a leader—never forget that you are the top dog.
(photo by Stephanie Mohler)

be tempted to use force, but this will only be counterproductive. A dog that is fearful is unlikely to want to learn and will be reluctant to even participate in training sessions. A terrier that truly loves and respects its owner will bend over backwards—sometimes literally—to learn a skill and will put its mental energies into learning rather than evading.

Jack Russells have strong drives and desires that you can use when training. Some are drawn to balls and toys. Others will perform almost any feat for a treat. Still others are more concerned with pleasing you than with any morsel of food. Don't be afraid to use your Jack Russell's drive of choice to aid in your training. Food is often a good way to reinforce a desired behavior, as is rewarding you JRT with quick rounds of play whenever it has done a particularly good job of behaving itself.

You will explore the details of how to accomplish this in Chapter 11, but it is a good idea for you to start thinking about it now and to start getting the concept ingrained in your brain so it will be familiar to you when you begin working on training. Have you ever heard the expression that you catch more flies with honey than you do with vinegar? This holds true tenfold for your JRT. Eager to please and learn, these dogs will go to the ends of the earth for you if they understand what is expected of them. Once that trust and drive is broken, however, it is virtually impossible to regain.

Bet You Didn't Know

Your Jack Russell Terrier often will outsmart you. You might not like it, but you might as well get used to it. If you don't take it too personally, you might even find it amusing at times.

Consistency Is the Key

How do you set the rules without breaking your dog's spirit? Consistency. By consistently using the same commands, by consistently insisting that the commands be obeyed and by consistently rewarding your terrier when it performs correctly, you will create consistency in your dog's responses. If the dog is never sure whether "No!" really means no, why should it respond every time? If your terrier learns that at times there are no consequences for ignoring a command, it will quickly think of ways to test you to see when you mean it and when you don't.

You cannot be passive in your terrier's training and hope the dog will intuit right from wrong. There are times when, much to your dismay, you will physically have to get out off the couch to accomplish your desired objective. Sometimes this means you have to physically go over to your terrier, pick it up and bring it to you when you ask it to come. Sometimes you have to physically move your dog into its bed for a timeout after it's been bad. Understand that this is all part of the training process. If you take the time to do it right when your dog is a puppy, your training will be much less tiresome and time consuming than when your puppy is a grown dog.

Dealing with Defiance

Male dogs seem to exhibit defiance and rebelliousness more than females, though I have seen these traits in both genders. What do you do if your dog simply refuses to obey your command or, worse, if it retaliates when forced to comply? There are several ways to manage defiance, and it is best to try different methods to find out which works best for your terrier.

Dogs in general have their own natural hierarchy within different packs and among different individual dogs. The hierarchy is determined by each dog's confidence, ability to fight and ability to bluff. The dog that "rolls over" first usually is ranked lower than the confronting dog. Rarely will a submissive dog confront or attack a more aggressive dog (one that is higher up in the "pecking order"). This occurs in wild dogs and coyotes as well as in domestic dogs, and it is useful to understand when training your puppy or dog.

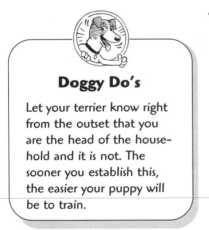

Doggy Do's

Let your terrier know right from the outset that you are the head of the household and it is not. The sooner you establish this, the easier your puppy will be to train.

The Gentle Roll-Over

Sometimes, especially with a male dog, it becomes necessary to force your dog to roll over. By this I don't mean to beat your dog until it falls down, although some terribly misguided owners have tried this method. Not only is it cruel, it also does not further your training one iota. Instead, physically roll your dog onto its back and hold it there. This method is used when a terrier is being particularly defiant or borderline aggressive. By rolling your puppy onto its back, you are exerting your dominance without hurting the dog. By holding it there for a few moments, you are showing your terrier that you are in control and that you are the "boss dog" of your family pack.

Now a word of caution. Be careful that you don't use this method on a dog known to be overly aggressive, or you could get bitten in the process. This is best used on young dogs, especially males, that are pushing their boundaries and testing the rules. An older, more aggressive dog should be dealt with in a far different manner, and confrontation with these dogs should be avoided rather than initiated. Chapter 13 will show you how to safely deal with an overly aggressive older dog.

Time-Outs

Like overactive children, Jack Russell Terriers often can become over-stimulated, creating a hyper, difficult dog that literally ignores you even if you are right in front of it. The most common time for this behavior is when someone comes over to visit. Your JRT undoubtedly will be excited to see this new intruder, will all but maul your visitor to get attention and will be jumping and barking in its excitement. Although this certainly is understandable in puppies, it is far less appealing in an older dog. At these times, you might need to employ the "time-out" method to get your terrier to settle down and come back to reality.

Time-outs can take several forms, depending on the terrier and its personality. Some dogs will settle down simply by putting on their harness. Others need to be sent to a "bad dog" corner to sit for a few minutes and think about their actions. Still others need to be sent to bed for a few minutes to settle down. Let's look at each method and discover which one might work best for your individual terrier.

Doggy Do's

Ask people who are unfamiliar with your puppy or dog to ignore it until it has had time to settle down. You then can control the meeting if they are unacquainted, or you can allow your puppy to greet the visitor after it has calmed down enough to be manageable.

Humbly Harnessed

Many JRTs love to put on their harnesses because it means they get to go somewhere; others see their harnesses as a means of confinement and become slightly intimidated. If your Jack Russell Terrier becomes even more wound up when you head for its harness, this is not the right time-out method for your puppy. If, however, your puppy becomes a bit subdued at the thought of being harnessed, this might be a good choice for your training.

If possible, you should put the harness on your puppy just *before* your company arrives to set the scene for the next half-hour or so. This helps your terrier to get into the right mind-set for the upcoming visit, and it allows you to judge whether just wearing the harness will be enough to temper your puppy's exuberance or whether you will need to put it on a leash for a few minutes to tone down its energy level. When your company arrives, hold the puppy until your friends are safely inside. This prevents your puppy from getting so excited that it runs outside, creating yet another problem. Your visitors can pet the puppy for a few moments while it is in your arms and then can ignore it once you set it down.

After you set your puppy down, watch carefully to see that it doesn't jump on your guests. If it does, gently push it down and tell it "No!" If the behavior persists after one or two commands, attach the leash to your puppy's harness and use it to help control your puppy. When your puppy goes to jump on a guest, apply one sharp tug on the leash accompanied by the command "No!" Bring your puppy off to your side and keep it there for a few seconds before letting it approach again. By doing this several times, each and every time you expect company, your puppy will soon learn that it has to control its enthusiasm to enjoy the company of friends and family.

Bet You Didn't Know

Jack Russell Terriers have been raised for so long as companion dogs that they often prefer the company of their owners to the companionship of other dogs. If your JRT is a real "people-dog," take advantage of its desire to please for training purposes.

The "Bad Dog" Corner

The "bad dog" corner is a corner of a room, usually the living room, where your dog gets to spend a few moments after it has ignored you or has done something wrong. Which corner you use really doesn't matter because the purpose is to get your puppy to sit still for several minutes to decrease its energy and anxiety level and to think about its behavior. Sometimes just getting the puppy to stop moving and to concentrate on sitting still will be enough to get it to click back into reality.

For this method to be effective, it must be started when the puppy is old enough to understand right from wrong but young enough to make an impression. This type of training usually can occur when the puppy is 5 to 6 months old. If you catch your puppy doing something wrong, such as tearing up a sock, grab your puppy by the scruff of the neck, the same way its mother did, and remove the object from its mouth. Say "No!" and then physically take your puppy over to the corner and sit it down. You will have to stay within an arm's reach for a while because your puppy is likely to get up and try to move away as soon as you let go of it.

If your puppy starts to move away, pick it back up, set it down in the corner again and say "No, go to your corner." Each time the puppy moves, you should repeat the command and physically put the puppy back into the corner. Younger puppies should only be kept in the corner for a few minutes; older puppies should have longer time-outs to instill the impression that their actions were not appreciated.

Each and every time your puppy must be reprimanded, send it to its corner. At the beginning, you will need to pick the puppy up and physically take it to the corner, making sure it doesn't cheat by moving away from the corner before being "released." Remember, though, to simply place your puppy in the corner without anger or aggression. It is a correction, not a physical punishment. Anger has no place in dog training, and your puppy will not understand if you are rough or angry. You will simply scare your puppy.

If your puppy stays in the corner without moving for a reasonable amount of time, say three minutes to

Doggy Don'ts

Don't yell "No!" at your puppy every time it does something wrong. Not only are you correcting your puppy at the wrong time—after it has misbehaved—you are assuming your terrier is deaf. The command has no added benefit when screamed at your dog, and it will quickly become annoying to the rest of your family if yelled fifty times a day.

start, you can then call your puppy onto your lap and pet it. As your puppy gets older, this time in the corner should increase to around ten minutes to be sure you have made an impression. If your puppy moves during this time, send it back to the corner. After your puppy has been in the corner for the allotted time without coming away on its own, call your puppy over to your side or to your feet and have it lay down there for a few moments. This effectively releases the puppy from its reprimand and lets it go about life as it will.

As your puppy gets older, it will know from the tone of your voice and your actions when it is in trouble. Soon, your puppy will anticipate your actions by going to its corner whenever it senses that it has goofed. All it will take is a stern look from you, and your puppy will head for the corner in embarrassment. While emphasizing that the puppy has done something to displease you, this does not create resentment or hostility from your terrier. It simply is a way to portray your displeasure and to let your puppy know it has misbehaved.

Doggy Don'ts

Don't tempt your puppy with dangling cords and slippers left close to its play area. Puppies encounter enough temptations every day and have to work hard at being good. Remove obvious temptations (and those that are not obvious) from your puppy's reach to encourage success.

Go to Bed!

Another effective place to send a puppy for a time-out is to its bed, provided the bed is in a location where it is easily accessible and where you can keep an eye on your puppy when it is in the bed. Again, consistency will be the key.

When your puppy misbehaves, send it to bed in much the same way you would send it to a corner by saying "Go to bed!" As with the corner, you need to physically pick up the puppy and place it in its bed the first few times. Remain next to the puppy's bed to make sure that it doesn't prematurely escape from its time-out and that it stays lying down and immobile. Your puppy will soon get the hint that this is the place to go when it is in trouble.

If you use the puppy's bed as its time-out place, remember that this is the puppy's own space. You never should physically intimidate a puppy or reprimand it in its own space. In other words, after you set the puppy in its bed, don't proceed to shake a finger and yell at it and do *not* spank its bottom. First, these actions do nothing to emphasize your point; second, this is the place the puppy can go to be "safe." You do not want the puppy to feel insecure in its "secure" place. Although you want the puppy to know it has done something wrong, you don't want it to be afraid of you and go running to the safest dark corner whenever you raise your voice.

Timing Is Crucial

For a correction to be meaningful, it must occur at the time of the misbehavior. It is futile to correct your puppy after the fact. It will never make the connection between the reprimand and the act. Its memory just isn't that long. If you don't catch your puppy literally in the act, don't bother with the correction. Wait until you do catch it in the middle of misbehaving and then act accordingly.

As important as it is to catch your puppy in the act, it is equally important to reward correct behavior when it responds to a command. If you see your puppy starting to wet on the carpet or chewing on something off-limits, give the command "No!" If your puppy stops, reward it! It has torn its attention away from either mother nature or a very tempting tidbit, and this is quite a commendable task for a puppy. It is showing to you that you deserve to be listened to and that it respects your voice. This is a big step, and rewards now will go a long way toward building respect and the desire to please in the future.

Doggy Don'ts

Do not ever strike your Jack Russell in anger. Physical violence has no legitimate place in training. The goal is to deepen the bond with your dog—hitting it sure won't help.

Doggy Do's

Try to catch your puppy doing something right or responding correctly to a command and reward it when it behaves. This can be a simple "Good dog!" with lots of pats and scratches, or it can be a small cookie or dog bone to emphasize the point.

Crating Success

Sometimes sending your puppy to a corner or to bed simply doesn't get the job done. These are the times when your terrier has gone past being able to listen to you and truly is on sensory overload. This can occur when the dog is in a new location for the first time in which there is an abundance of outside stimuli, or it can occur inside the home when several new things are going on at once. In this situation, crating your puppy becomes the best and safest way to handle the behavior.

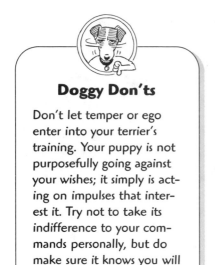

Doggy Don'ts

Don't let temper or ego enter into your terrier's training. Your puppy is not purposefully going against your wishes; it simply is acting on impulses that interest it. Try not to take its indifference to your commands personally, but do make sure it knows you will get its attention, one way or another. Always do so, however, without resorting to violence.

As with sending your puppy to bed, it is important not to view the crate as a place where you can exert your dominance over your puppy. Instead, it should be used as a safe haven for your puppy to calm down, to collect its thoughts, and to return its heartbeat to a normal level. Your puppy might not like being crated during these times. Most terriers will take offense at having their freedom taken away. It is important, however, to curb your puppy's natural excitement for its own good. When it is overly excited, your puppy might lose control over its physical functions or even work itself into a frenzy. Neither is good for your puppy. By allowing it to calm down for a brief period, your puppy will learn to regulate its excitement and will better be able to cope to new environments and stimuli.

If you see that your puppy is overstimulated, make sure there is a soft blanket in the crate and place your puppy inside. If possible, put the crate in a quiet corner where activity is at a minimum. You should only have to leave your puppy there for a short time (around fifteen minutes) to get it to settle down. You will know when the time is right because it will stop pacing and being anxious and will settle down in a corner or curl up and go to sleep. When this occurs, you can open the door and let your puppy out. Be sure to spend a few minutes talking and scratching your puppy when you let it out, but be careful not to rev it up again with too much enthusiastic praise.

Always remember to treat your Jack Russell with respect and kindness. This is your pet, and it relies on you for love and attention as well as for guidance. Although it is important that your terrier knows you are the top dog, it is just as important to show your puppy that you are fair and loving. You want to create a relationship with your dog that is free of intimidation and anxiety. Only by having a terrier that is comfortable in your presence will you fully gain your dog's cooperation.

The Least You Need to Know

➤ It is important for you to let your puppy know right from the beginning that there are guidelines it must follow.

➤ Violence has no place in training or working with your terrier.

➤ The use of your voice will often go a long way toward getting your puppy to listen.

➤ Catching your puppy doing something right is just as important, or even more important, than catching it doing something wrong.

➤ Treats and praise are good reinforcements for positive behavior.

➤ Sending your puppy to a corner or to bed for a few minutes of inactivity often is an effective time-out.

➤ Crating your puppy when it is overstimulated will help it calm itself down and learn to cope with outside stimuli.

Chapter 11

Time to Lay Down the Law!

In This Chapter

➤ Why obedience training is so important

➤ Baby basics every puppy should learn

➤ The power of praise

➤ Nixing negative behaviors

➤ United we stand—making the family a cohesive unit

You've learned about the importance of setting a command hierarchy as soon as your puppy gets home and about some training techniques that could be helpful with your new little bundle. Now the time has come to broach the subject of obedience training with your new terrier.

Why Obedience Training Is So Important

If you know anything at all about Jack Russell Terriers, you know that obedience and JRTs don't exactly go hand in hand. These willful little terrors often are the bane of a formerly sane owner's existence, sometimes to the point of surrender. But it really doesn't have to be this way.

Contrary to popular belief, Jack Russell Terriers can be trained quite effectively. It takes patience, understanding and discipline, however,

125

and the sooner you start training your terrier, the easier time you will have. I recommend that *all* new terrier owners enroll in a basic obedience course with their puppies as soon as the puppy is old enough to walk on a leash and to stay focused for a decent amount of time. This usually occurs when the puppy is around 4 to 5 months old.

Bet You Didn't Know

Obedience classes are divided into sub-novice, novice, open, utility, brace and junior handler divisions, depending on the skill and the training of the dog and the skill and the age of the handler.

Setting Goals

Obedience training classes are important for many reasons. First, they give you and your puppy a goal to work toward together, and they provide a strong support group if you start to get frustrated with your puppy's progress. The class instructor can be a valuable resource, not only for training tips and ideas but for suggestions of how to have fun with your dog.

Staying Focused

By enrolling in a structured class setting, you are making a commitment to your new puppy to get out with it regularly and to devote time to its training. You are less likely to quit midstream if you have spent a few dollars to sign up for the class, and you also will be more apt to practice at home if you have someone giving you homework assignments and checking your progress on a regular basis.

Emotional Support

As an added benefit, you have a place to ask questions and to vent frustrations should the lessons prove to be more challenging than you anticipated. This one-on-one personal touch is much easier than looking information up in a book every time you get frustrated with a specific behavior your puppy has invented, seemingly just to thwart you.

Charting Progress

Finally, you will receive guidance regarding which lessons and tasks are appropriate for your puppy's age and development, and you will not be as tempted to ask something of your puppy that it is not developmentally prepared to do. Your instructor will be able to shed some light on your puppy's physical and mental limitations at each stage of the game and will guide you through the increasingly difficult stages of training as your puppy is ready and able to accept them. This helps to teach your puppy social skills because she will be repeatedly asked to interact with the other puppies in the group and will be less likely to be an overaggressive terrier.

Pretraining Tips

Before discussing the basic commands every puppy should learn early on, let's look at some hints to help you down the road to training success. By understanding how your puppy thinks and learns, you can make your short training sessions effective and fun for your puppy.

Doggy Do's

Jack Russell Terriers require a long and loyal commitment to obedience, discipline, exercise and companionship. Be prepared to commit to time with your dog to keep it happy, healthy and well exercised.

Train Before Meals

Plan to hold your training sessions before the puppy eats a big meal. This encourages your puppy to be active, and you will more effectively be able to use treats in your training session. After a puppy eats, its system slows down. This leads to a more lethargic dog that will not be as motivated by food.

Gather up the Goods

Always make sure you have the proper equipment on hand to have a productive training session. This should include a harness or a humane choke collar, a strong 6-foot leash, a 20-foot lightweight lead and plenty of cookies or treats. I prefer a harness on smaller puppies because they will be less likely to choke themselves and to create inadvertent corrections. An older dog does well with a lightweight

127

chain or a leather choke collar, although keep in mind that, despite its name, the intention of this collar is to correct, *not* to choke. Let the puppy wear its harness or collar around the house for a week or two (always while supervised) so it gets accustomed to the feel of having something on its neck or body. Never leave a choke collar on an unattended dog.

Less Is More

Keep your training sessions short and productive. Always end on a good note. Your puppy gets bored easily, and several very short sessions will be much more productive in the long run than a few long sessions. Also make sure your sessions are fun and entertaining for your puppy. You want it to look forward to training, not head for the hills the moment it sees you coming.

Keep It Simple

Give your puppy simple commands that are not more than one or two words long. Use your puppy's name before giving a command to get its attention and then give the command in a strong, clear voice. The command should be given before you move your puppy into action so the puppy learns the sequence of command-response. Always use exactly the same word for a requested action. Puppies get confused easily, so keep your puppy's new vocabulary short and concise. And always remember to reward or treat for each and every positive response. The reward doesn't always have to be food, though in the beginning this system is highly effective. As your puppy ages, pats on the head and scratches should replace some of the treats.

Accentuate the Positive

Remember that you are engaged in a training session, not an intimidation session. All your commands and responses should be positive. If you ask your puppy to sit and it ignores you, guide your puppy into a sit position and reward your puppy as if it did it on its own. You should view your training as requests, corrections and rewards—punishment never should enter the picture. Make sure you get the desired response, either voluntarily or by correction, each and every time you give the command and be patient with your puppy's learning process.

Bet You Didn't Know

Puppies and dogs learn best through repetition. Every time a command and response is repeated, the puppy learns to connect one with the other. Remember, however, that this can be a bad thing as well as a good thing. If you inadvertently reward your puppy's bad behavior with attention, even negative attention, you will be teaching your puppy that bad behavior gets it noticed.

Consistency Is the Key

Say what you mean and mean what you say. Don't allow yourself to be diverted from the command at hand just because your terrier has devised a particularly fetching avoidance technique. Likewise, don't train only when it is convenient for you. If you don't want your dog to jump on you, you must correct it every time it jumps on you, even if your hands are full or the phone is ringing. Consistency is the golden rule in dog training.

Be Patient

Remember that your puppy will not always be in the mood for training. There will be times when, try as you might, you simply cannot get anything worthwhile accomplished. Sometimes your puppy needs to mull things over a little, and what seemed like an unproductive training session will magically resolve itself the next time around. Always end on a positive note and always keep your training times fun.

Come Hither Yon Terrier

Teaching your puppy to come is one of the easiest fundamentals of training. It is easy for you and is easy for your puppy. Why? Because you practice daily without even realizing it. When you feed your puppy or when you come home from work and meet it at the door, you are calling your puppy by name and are rewarding it when it comes to you, either through praise or through food. Your puppy learns that, whenever it responds to its name, it will get either petted, fed or taken outside, all of which are viewed as positive events by your puppy.

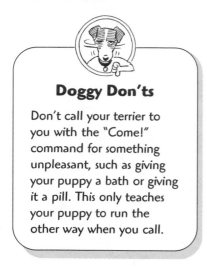

Doggy Don'ts

Don't call your terrier to you with the "Come!" command for something unpleasant, such as giving your puppy a bath or giving it a pill. This only teaches your puppy to run the other way when you call.

Getting your puppy to come when it is outdoors and surrounded by many other distractions is a bit more difficult than getting its attention around the home, but it is a very important response. It could even save your puppy's life. Be sure to reward each and every effort your puppy makes to respond correctly to "Come!" and try to make your dog's reward far more pleasurable than what it is missing out on by not coming. This is a situation in which it is virtually impossible to make too much of a fuss over your puppy's response.

You can begin training "Come!" outside with just a short distance separating you from your dog. As you say "Come!", run backwards a few steps and encourage your puppy to follow. If it does, even for a few steps, generously reward your puppy for its efforts. As your terrier masters this important first step, increase the amount of steps you take back before rewarding your puppy. This teaches it that it might have to come from a longer distance before receiving a reward.

If you have trouble with this and if, despite all your coaxing, your puppy still has a hard time putting two and two together, use the longer lead to help encourage your puppy. Put your puppy at the end of the lead and call your puppy to you. If it responds, reward it generously. If it ignores you, give a slight tug on the line and call your puppy again. Only tug the lead if your puppy ignores you and gently reel it in if necessary to get the ball rolling. As your puppy makes the connection, use the lead less and less until your puppy is coming regularly without the leash reminders. Then remove the leash from the puppy and continue to work on "Come!" without the leash.

Bet You Didn't Know

Puppies and dogs work best if you have their full attention. You always should say your puppy's name first to get its attention and to get it to look at you before saying the command. Many beginning trainers forget this step and wind up giving a command to a puppy whose attention is focused elsewhere. Then they wonder why the puppy never responds correctly!

Sitting Pretty

"Sit" is another fundamental command. It is fairly easy to teach and is one of the most useful commands in your puppy's repertoire. Because it is easy to teach and is easy for your terrier to understand, it is a good command to use in early obedience training.

Place your puppy on your left side next to your leg and hold its leash snugly to encourage it to look up at you. Say your puppy's name to get its attention and, in a firm, clear voice, give the command "Sit!" Immediately after saying the command, apply a firm downward pressure on your puppy's hind quarters until it is in a sitting position. As soon as your puppy sits, praise it and give it a treat.

Sometimes it is helpful to hold a treat just above your puppy's eye level to get it to look up, thus lowering its rump. This naturally and easily puts the puppy's body into an almost-sitting position. All you have to do then is help the process along with the vocal command and a slight push downward on the puppy's rear end. As your puppy begins to get the idea, require a more complete sit on its own before handing over the treat. Soon your puppy will be sitting like a pro (and possibly even sitting up like a gopher) to get its favorite treat.

Stay

"Stay" is another useful command that not only will come in handy throughout the day, it also could help protect your terrier from danger. Jack Russells have a tendency to bolt out doors or across streets whenever something of interest catches their eye. Rarely do they pay attention to cars coming their way.

"Stay" is most easily taught with both vocal and hand commands. With your puppy sitting in front of you, place your open, flat hand in front of the puppy's nose and tell it to "Stay!" Take a few steps away (always beginning with your right foot) and then turn to face your dog. If your puppy stays put, tell it "Okay" and call it to you. Be sure to give it lots of praise for making such a good effort. If your puppy moves, move back into position and repeat the command. Keep practicing until you can take ten or fifteen steps away while your dog stays put.

It is important to always step away from your puppy with your right foot when you want your dog to stay immobile. When you teach your puppy to heel later in the chapter, you will step off with your left foot. This will indicate to your puppy that you want it to go forward. Don't confuse the two or you will invariably confuse your puppy as well.

Doggy Don'ts

Don't look your puppy directly in the eye when teaching it to stay. Some dogs take this as an aggressive stance on your part and might squirm, wiggle or lie down to avert your stare. Instead, look over your puppy's head when giving the command.

When your puppy has mastered the art of staying from quite a distance, you can make things a little more difficult. Try jumping up and down or waving your arms to try to lure your puppy out of the "Stay!" command. If your terrier comes and tries to play with you, put it back on "Sit-stay" and try again. Your puppy needs to learn that it cannot move off the "Stay!" command without being called with "Okay." When your puppy won't respond to movement, try adding noise distractions. Yell, scream, talk, sing, do anything but say the command "Okay." Gradually increase the distractions until you're sure your dog can sit and stay through almost anything.

Down and Out

Like sitting, lying down is a natural act for your puppy. It's often easiest to catch your puppy in the act to begin this training. If you see your puppy position itself to lie down, give the command "Down!" and let it finish its action. If it continues as planned and lies down, praise it for being so perceptive.

You can further this training by putting your puppy on a leash and placing it in a sitting position in front of you. Say the puppy's name to get its attention and then tell it "Down!" Reach down and gently pull the puppy's front legs in front of it until it reaches a prone position and then give it lots of hugs and treats. When your puppy gets the general idea, you can switch to using a slight downward pressure between the puppy's shoulder blades to remind your puppy what is expected of it.

Bet You Didn't Know

Lying down is a position of submission for your dog, as well as a sign of respect. It is important that your puppy trusts you for your "Down!" training to be successful. Be patient when working on this command.

Some dogs will stiffen their bodies as you try to push them down. This can lead to a battle of wills and an unproductive training session. To address this problem, use an alternate method of asking your puppy to lie down. While kneeling at your puppy's side, give the "Down!" command, reach across your puppy's shoulder with the hand nearest to the puppy and take a paw in each hand. Using your elbow, gently press down on the puppy's back while using your hands to place the puppy's paws out in front of it. This combines both the placement of the paws and the downward pressure to encourage your puppy to lie down. If it even begins to relax downward, praise your puppy and show your pleasure. As your puppy starts to relax, it will accept this correction with greater ease and will soon lie down willingly.

If you've maintained your position as the dog's leader, you should not have too much trouble teaching your JRT the "Down!" command.

When giving a treat after the "Down!" command, it is helpful to place the treat on the floor to encourage your puppy to stay in the down position when getting its treat. You also can scratch your puppy on top of its head or at the base of its tail, both of which can be accomplished while the dog is still down. The more comfortable your puppy is with the down position, the easier it will accept this training.

Heads and Heels

Although stationary commands are great for calming your puppy down when it gets hyper and for keeping it from bouncing off the walls, there comes a time when you want to take your terrier with you and you need its cooperation. This is when the "Heel!" command comes in handy.

Remember that your puppy never has had to control its energies while on the move, and it is used to romping here and there as it moves about the house or yard. To teach your puppy to heel, you must first teach it that it has to pay attention to your movements and that it can move about on a leash without feeling unduly confined.

Many puppies freeze when they realize there is something on them that will restrict their movement. They might lie down and refuse to move or might sit back against the leash, causing an unproductive tug-of-war. Other, more aggressive or curious puppies will run ahead of you and try to take you for a walk instead of the other way around. Either way, your puppy must learn that its job is to stay next to your leg, neither falling behind nor rushing ahead.

If your puppy is the reluctant type, use tidbits of food or small pieces of a doggy cracker to entice your puppy forward. Don't drag your puppy along in a misguided attempt to get it to follow you. You will only further ingrain in your puppy's brain that heeling is not a fun thing to do. Instead, use your puppy's desire for treats and its curiosity for what's in your hand to entice it forward. Praise it whenever it steps with you.

At this stage, even a few steps forward should be praised because your puppy is working hard to overcome

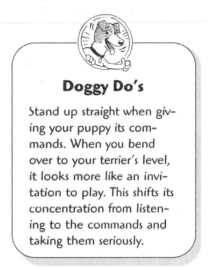

Doggy Do's

Stand up straight when giving your puppy its commands. When you bend over to your terrier's level, it looks more like an invitation to play. This shifts its concentration from listening to the commands and taking them seriously.

its fears and to trust your judgment. Be sure that the leash is somewhat slack and that your puppy truly is moving forward on its own accord. Remember to use the command "Heel!" each time you strike off (and remember to lead with your left foot). Continue walking and praising until your puppy gains some confidence and is willing to walk forward without being timid.

The Terrier That Tugs

If your JRT has a bold streak, you might have a harder time holding it back than getting it to go forward. This is a puppy that needs to learn, first and foremost, that it has to pay attention to you regardless of the other interesting things going on around it. The easiest way to remedy this situation is to allow the puppy to train itself.

Begin by holding your puppy on a fairly short leash so there is not much extra slack between your hand and the puppy. You should be holding the majority of the leash in your right hand, with your left hand picking up the slack between your right hand and your dog. Say "Heel!" and begin to walk forward, encouraging your puppy to walk with you. If you puppy runs forward, simply stop. Don't jerk the lead. This unnecessarily punishes your puppy. This is where the self-training comes in.

The mere act of stopping will effectively control the amount of leash your puppy has to work with, limiting its range of motion. When your puppy reaches the end of its short leash, it will find that it can't go forward any further and will turn back to look at you. Just stand there and look back for several moments and then walk forward again. Remember, lead with your left foot when you step forward. If your puppy runs ahead again, stop and stare at your puppy. Repeat the process until your puppy figures out that running ahead will get it nowhere. It might want to pay a little more attention to you to see what you have in mind.

At this stage, some puppies will decide that this is no fun and will jump and fight to try to gain their freedom. It is important that you not respond to these terrier temper tantrums. Instead, stand quietly, keeping the leash firmly in your hand, and wait for your puppy to stop fighting. When your puppy stops venting, bend down, pet it to reassure it and then continue with your lesson.

The proper position for heeling is with the puppy's neck even with your left leg. Its front feet should stay even with yours, and it should look up at you every few strides to make sure it is in the proper position. This shows that your puppy is looking to you for direction and is trying hard to anticipate your next move. An occasional "Good dog!" will encourage your JRT to continue its actions.

Doggy Do's

Keep your walking pace brisk. If you walk too slowly, your puppy will have too many opportunities to be distracted by the things around it. If you walk too fast, your terrier will have a hard time keeping up and will get frustrated.

When your puppy is heeling consistently, add a "Sit!" command each time you stop. This makes it easier to control your puppy or dog at intersections or when you see another dog approaching. Each and every time you stop, use the command "Sit!" Your terrier should remain at your left side and should sit even with your leg and with its front toes in line with your toes. If your puppy has a temporary lapse in memory, bring its head up to look at you and then press it down on its haunches to remind it how to sit. Encourage your puppy to look at you while sitting so it knows when you are ready to move into "Heel!" again. You can do this by offering treats when your puppy performs correctly and by using your puppy's name before striking off.

When your puppy has mastered the straight-away "Heel!" and the "Sit!" when stopping, practice making turns so your puppy learns to follow you regardless of which way you are moving. Keep the turns simple at first and then progress to quicker turns that occur more often to keep your puppy's attention. You also can vary your pace to make things more interesting. All these techniques will improve your terrier's responses and will focus its attention on your next move. Soon it will be heeling on the leash like a pro.

After your puppy has mastered the basic heel on the leash, you can work toward heeling off the leash. Make sure you always have your leash close by in case your terrier has a lapse in concentration and starts to wander off. Also, when you are sure your puppy firmly grasps the concept of "Heel!", you can use the collar to reprimand it should your puppy forget that it is supposed to stay at your side. If the puppy lunges forward after something due to lack of concentration, snap the leash back once and repeat the command "Heel!" Do not use this as a punishment, just as a reminder that it is not okay for your puppy to decide that something else is more interesting on the other side of the road and that heeling no longer is important.

The Power of Praise

With all this schooling, teaching and training going on, it is easy to forget to praise your puppy with each and every correct response. Sometimes we get so focused on *expecting* our terriers to do it right that we forget this kind of training is hard for the puppy. Not only are you asking it to use a lot of concentration to focus on you, you are asking it to control its own natural energy to do what you want it to do. You also are asking it to repeat it several times. This is hard for a baby!

Doggy Don'ts

Don't get so wrapped up in your lessons that you forget to praise and treat your puppy for good behavior. This is supposed to be fun for both of you, not a challenge to see how much you can teach your puppy in one day.

Consistency in each and every step of training is the key to success—consistency in your commands, consistency in your praises and consistency in your corrections. It is unfair to correct your puppy once for making a mistake and then let it go the next time it happens. This simply confuses the puppy and makes it wonder which way is really right. The same holds true for praise when the puppy responds correctly. If you praise it one time but not the next, and the response was the same both times, how does your puppy know whether it is responding correctly?

Nixing Negative Behavior

There will come a time during training that your JRT will decide there are far more interesting things to do than listen to you. You will need to regain your puppy's attention and will want a way to prevent its attention from wandering in the first place. By making yourself an important factor in your puppy's environment, it will learn to respect your wishes and will look to you for direction for its behavior. There are several ways to accomplish this.

No—More Than Just a Two-Letter Word

"No!" is one of the most overused and misunderstood commands in dog training. More often than not, the puppy begins to think of "No!" as part of its name rather than as a separate command. Many of these problems exist because either the word is screamed as the owner chases the dog through the house or it is said so many times that it fails to sound like the original command. To your dog's ears, "No, no, no!" sounds totally different than a firm "No!" To further add to your puppy's confusion, "No!" usually is used after the fact rather than before it. This leaves the puppy guessing as to what action caused your displeasure. Is it any wonder that terriers often ignore their owners?

Let's look at how to make "No!" a bit more effective so it will actually have some meaning to your dog. "No!" should be used to stop an action from occurring. When you notice your puppy starting to look at a passing bicycle instead of concentrating on "Heel!", snap the lead once and tell it "No!" If your puppy focuses its attention back on you, ask it to "Heel!" If it responds correctly, give it a treat. If you walk by a ball and your puppy starts to head towards it, snap the lead and tell it "No!" If it ignores you, snap the lead again and repeat the command. Give your puppy a treat and some praise if it responds by bringing its attention back to you.

Other Diversion Tactics

There are times when you need to divert your puppy's attention, and you don't have the leash attached to use. What do you do? As with children, you can use toys or noise to divert your puppy's attention away from the negative behavior and back to more positive things.

This technique can apply to anything from housetraining to chewing on cords. A terrier is, by nature, a rather obsessive little beast. When it sets its mind on an action, it will continue to focus on that one thing until something else grabs its attention. This is where diversionary tactics come in very handy.

Try to keep a can with a few coins in it or a squirt bottle within reach when relaxing in your home. If you see your puppy start to have an accident on the carpet, either rattle the can or squirt the puppy with a stream of water as you tell the puppy "No!" Your puppy will be startled by either the noise or the water, and it will literally stop midstream. You then can pick the puppy up and take it outside, where hopefully mother nature will once again take over and your puppy will finish its business. Now you have created an opportunity to praise the puppy for doing such a good job of relieving itself in the appropriate place.

Bet You Didn't Know

Several major bookstores, including Barnes & Noble, have sites on the Internet that list books devoted to JRT care and training.

This same technique can be used with any number of bad behaviors. The idea is to divert your terrier's attention from the negative behavior so that it forgets what it was going to do. You then can praise your dog for its good judgment and for being so well behaved. These techniques enable you to catch your puppy doing something right, instead of having to correct it for doing something wrong. It keeps things positive, and it saves you from always feeling like the bad guy.

United We Stand

Perhaps the most challenging hurdles to overcome during puppy training are presented by children in the family. Children love to play and often will encourage your puppy into destructive behavior because they think it is funny or cute. It is frustrating to spend hours teaching your puppy not to jump on people only to have your child encourage the puppy to jump on the couch! Not only is it frustrating to you, it also is frustrating to your puppy. Sometimes it is rewarded for jumping, and sometimes it is rewarded for *not* jumping—so which behavior is correct? It's easy to see the dilemma.

It is important for you to talk to your children *before* you begin your training. Explain to them the importance of keeping things consistent for your puppy. Involving them in your training lessons and obedience classes is a good way to help them understand the importance of consistency with your puppy's handling. Unless all involved parties are working together, training your puppy will take far more time and will be much more difficult that it would be otherwise. Trust me, training your JRT will be hard enough as it is. You don't need any outside factors making it even more difficult.

The Least You Need to Know

➤ Jack Russell Terriers can be trained and often can learn quite quickly, but you must be committed to your puppy's training for it to succeed.

➤ Your JRT needs guidance and discipline in its life. Enroll in an obedience class as soon as your puppy is old enough.

➤ By following some helpful hints, your training times will be fun and productive for both you and your puppy.

➤ "Come!", Sit!", "Stay!", "Down!" and "Heel!" all are basic commands you should teach your puppy—not only for your convenience but for your terrier's safety as well.

➤ Consistent praise and corrections are the keys to success in dog training.

➤ "No!" must be said in a firm, commanding voice and should be said only once to be effective. It must be used *before* the negative behavior occurs.

➤ There are times when diversion is a good training tool.

➤ Involve children when training your puppy so they will understand the importance of keeping expectations consistent.

Chapter 12

The Danger Zone

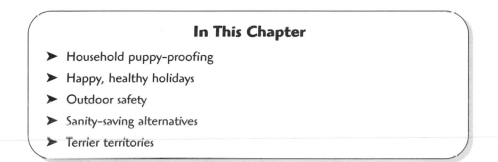

In This Chapter

➤ Household puppy-proofing

➤ Happy, healthy holidays

➤ Outdoor safety

➤ Sanity-saving alternatives

➤ Terrier territories

Your home and your yard can be full of hazards for a young, exuberant puppy. Prevention often is the best strategy for a Jack Russell Terrier. A few steps now can save you headaches and heartaches in the future.

Household Puppy-Proofing

By providing a suitable environment for your puppy and by taking some measures to "puppy-proof" your home prior to bringing your terrier home, you can prevent many accidents that could frustrate you and be dangerous for your pet. Many times, these accidents come about because new owners simply don't look at their homes from a puppy's point of view, and they overlook obvious temptations that could prove hazardous or just too tempting for the little explorer to resist.

141

Like small children who learn by exploring, your JRT puppy will find every cord, string and sock to be an amusing toy or a convenient teething target. It sees things much differently than an adult dog would and uses all its senses to explore and understand its surroundings. And like a small child, almost everything a puppy finds will soon make its way into its mouth.

When to Call the Vet

Chocolate, especially baker's chocolate, can be deadly to your JRT. It takes very little to act as a potent poison to your puppy's system. You should call your vet immediately if you suspect your puppy has ingested chocolate.

As a new puppy owner, you need to understand that your JRT is not trying to be purposefully destructive; it simply is using its mouth as an instrument to learn about its new surroundings. Although a sock or favorite slipper finding its way into your puppy's mouth will do more to frustrate you than to harm your puppy, other tempting toys could injure or kill your JRT if they end up within its reach. This is where you need to think like a JRT and locate obvious tempting trouble areas *before* your puppy does.

Zap Attack

Puppies love to chew on electrical cords and often are equally fascinated by their outlet cousins. Although it can be frustrating for you to come home to no lights on in the house, these lights can be dangerous or even deadly to your Jack Russell Terrier. If the cord is plugged into the socket and your dog happens upon the live portion of the cord, your puppy could receive a serious shock resulting in burns, cauterized tissue or even death. The same can occur if your puppy licks a wall socket and the saliva comes in contact with a live connection.

To prevent this from happening, make a conscious effort to keep all loose cords from dangling within your puppy's reach and use plastic socket covers to eliminate exposed socket connections. If the cord has to run along the baseboard or along the base of a lamp or appliance, anchor the cord securely along its path to prevent it from moving about as the puppy brushes against it, a sure lure for your puppy's attention. If your puppy does sustain a shock, wrap it in a towel and call your veterinarian immediately for further instructions.

Tower Terrors

Puppies love to look at new and enticing things, and they aren't often picky about where those things are located. Because puppies are small, more often than not the interesting item is above its head, and it will go to great lengths to get a closer look. Many puppies and dogs are injured every year by jumping up onto or against unstable pieces of furniture such as an end table or a bookcase. If the puppy hits something with enough force, it could fall on top of it, crushing it beneath its bulk. Make sure that all furniture within the puppy's realm is base-stable and that no balls or other interesting toys are placed on objects with the potential to tip over and crush the puppy, just in case it tries to reach the item on its own.

Friends in High Places

Like many young children, puppies like to climb on things so they can feel on top of the world and everything in it. Depending on your individual house, this can mean climbing everything from staircases to balconies. The only problem with this particular fascination is that puppies also have short attention spans and can become fixated on an object. When this happens, the puppy easily can forget that it is several feet off the ground and will literally walk off an edge to explore something several feet away.

Bet You Didn't Know

Jack Russell Terriers are born jumpers and often can jump several feet in the air to get their favorite sock or ball. They can also misjudge a drop-off, however, and can break or sprain a leg if they jump too far.

To prevent your puppy from inadvertently taking a header over a dangerous edge, place temporary fencing around all high, enticing places. Better yet, place a removable gate at the base of the stairs leading to these places to prevent your puppy from getting itself too high off the ground. If the balcony is outside, a temporary barrier of chicken wire or fine mesh fencing can be used to keep your puppy safe and sound. It won't exactly make an exterior design fashion statement, but it's easy to put up, is easy to remove and is worth the peace of mind you will gain with regard to your puppy's safety.

Dealing with Doors

Doors are an unavoidable feature in every house, but they also can be a hidden danger for your dog or puppy. Because of a Jack Russell Terrier's size and its penchant for always following you around the house, it's easy to forget that your puppy might be at your heels. You might slam a door without even thinking about it, catching your puppy between the door and the jam. Every year, hundreds of dogs are treated for broken legs and tails caused by just this scenario, and some suffer even worse injuries as a result of their owners' unintended actions.

To prevent this from happening, use doorstops on the back of your doors to prevent a person or the wind from slamming the door shut on your puppy. This will at least minimize any damage that might occur by providing a cushion of space for the leg or the tail should the door suddenly swing shut, trapping the limb.

Keep an especially close eye on swinging doors. Not only can they pick up speed and force by swinging to and fro, the puppy also could try to ease itself through and then get its head caught as the door closes, leading to possible strangulation. Whenever a puppy is around these doors, they should be either blocked open or blocked closed to prevent an inquiring mind from getting itself in trouble.

Glass doors also pose a threat to your high-energy JRT puppy. Remember that your terrier is likely to go flying through your house at breakneck speeds, and a clear-glass door easily could look like no door at all. It is not hard to envision the damage that could ensue should your puppy decide to go flying through what it thinks is an open space. An accompanying sliding screen door or a few decals placed at doggy level can help your puppy realize that a door is coming up and should help prevent an injury of this type.

Realize, too, that any door leading outside should be carefully watched unless it leads to a secure, fenced yard. Open doors are irresistible to most JRTs, and they often are out like a flash before you even realize they were nearby. Screen doors are invaluable if you own a terrier because even the most conscientious owners have been caught unaware by their Jack Russells streaking through their legs when they least expected it. At least a screen door gives them something to bounce off of if they hit it.

If you have children or visitors in the house, make sure they are aware of the importance of keeping all exterior doors closed. Instill in your terrier a sense of respect for the words "No!" and "Stay!" so you can prevent it from dashing outside and getting into trouble.

Garage Door Warning

Garage doors, especially electric ones, also can pose a threat to your terrier. The best solution is to keep your JRT out of the garage when opening or closing the door. If this isn't possible, however, you should catch and hold your terrier whenever closing the door. Even doors with sensors can exert enough pressure to crush your dog, so these "safety features" should not be relied on to protect your puppy. A manual door that is allowed to swing closed on its own also can crush your puppy, so it's best to be positive about your terrier's whereabouts before closing any garage doors.

Doggy Do's

Immobilize your dog's leg if it is injured in an accident or if the dog is reluctant to put weight on it and then take it to the vet. It could have a broken leg and moving it could further injure the limb and cause your dog considerable pain.

Perilous Poisons

Curious by nature, JRTs seem to have a way of finding the most dangerous substances in the most unlikely places. By being aware of common household cleaners and plants that could be toxic to your puppy, you can minimize, if not eliminate, the threat of accidental poisoning.

Plants that are no-no's in the JRT abode include azaleas, castor bean, corn cockle, English holly berries, foxglove, jimson weed, milkweed, mistletoe, oleander, philodendron and their rhododendron cousins, rattlebox and water hemlock. Check with local nurseries to find out about other plants indigenous to your area that could pose a threat to your puppy.

When to Call the Vet

Call your vet if your dog has convulsions, is vomiting, is staggering or has collapsed. All can be signs of poisoning and should be attended to immediately.

Cleaners and common household utensils also can be life-threatening to your dog, and you might not even realize they pose a threat until it's too late. Keep obvious poisons such as insect and rodent baits and all household cleaners away from your puppy, but don't forget also to keep such items as paint thinner, gasoline, antifreeze, prescription and over-the-counter drugs, toilet and air fresheners, and laundry and dish detergents away from your curious terrier. Many of these substances have a sweet smell or taste that can be enticing to dogs.

Even such common items as nuts, bolts, loose change and beads can pose a choking hazard to your puppy, and sharp objects such as pins and needles can wreck havoc on your dog's internal organs. If you don't want your children getting into something, it's probably equally unsafe for your puppy. Keep all such items out of the sight and reach of your terrier.

Happy, Healthy Holidays

The holidays can present their own temptations and troubles for your Jack Russell Terrier. Even older dogs can get lured into trouble by the brightly colored baubles and enticingly wrapped packages. As with the furniture, a Christmas tree easily can crush a puppy if it falls. If at all possible, the two should never be in the same room together. Likewise, a puppy might mistake the scent of the tree for the scent of the great outdoors, and your packages could end up with a decidedly doggy touch. Try explaining that to friends and family! But always remember that your puppy is not intentionally misbehaving. It simply is getting confused by the decorations and temptations and is acting as any youngster would do—with curiosity.

Packages and their wrappings can be too tempting for your puppy to ignore and could result in a toxic reaction or strangulation if you're not careful. A balled up piece of wrapping paper might look like trash to you, but it looks like a fun toy to your puppy. Some of today's wrapping papers contain dyes and foils that could wreak havoc on your puppy's digestive tract. If it swallows a piece, it could lead to a toxic reaction.

Likewise, long ribbons are fun to roll around with, but they easily can get wrapped around your puppy's neck and can cause strangulation. Both scenarios would put a serious damper on your holiday festivities. When opening presents, your puppy should be left in another room or in an area where it can't get to the presents and wrappings.

Holiday foods and trimmings also can pose a threat to your puppy or dog. Foods such as chocolate, turkey, and chicken bones (or any bones small enough to be swallowed) and holiday decorations such as mistletoe and poinsettias can be deadly if ingested by your

> **When to Call the Vet**
>
> If you notice that your terrier's breathing has become labored, extremely rapid, shallow, loud or irregular, or if it gasps for breath, displays a blue tongue or loses consciousness, call the vet immediately. Any of these symptoms can indicate that your dog is choking.

Jack Russell Terrier. Make sure that neither you nor your guests, even with the best of intentions, share the holiday meal with your dog. You also need to keep all dangerous plants and decorations out of your terrier's reach. If you want to be generous, buy your puppy a present of its own such as a new chew toy.

Outdoor Safety Tips

In addition to removing any toxic plants from your yard that could be dangerous to your puppy, you also must consider your puppy's fencing to make sure it is truly terrier-proof. Sometimes small holes or weaknesses in the fence go unnoticed by you but act like magnets to your roaming JRT. If it finds one of these weaknesses, it will be sure to capitalize on its good fortune.

Terriers of all types are known to be diggers, and a yard that seems dig-proofed to you might be easily circumvented by your crafty canine. All fences surrounding your puppy's play area should extend below the ground's surface and should be at least 5 feet tall. If the fence already is in place and cannot be changed, add a sturdy mesh barrier below the fence that extends at least 8 to 12 inches underground to keep your digging demon safely at home. Eyeball the span of the fence to make sure there are no obvious holes or weak spots that your terrier could take advantage of.

If you must leave your puppy or dog alone in the backyard, check that all gates are securely closed and locked both to keep your terrier inside and to keep any intruders or doggy-nappers out. Make sure all plants and trees are free from any sharp or jagged edges that could impale a jumping or running puppy, and remove any fruits or pine cones in danger of falling or too close to the ground. If you own a pool, the surrounding fence and gate should be in good shape without any penetrable holes, and the gate must be securely shut and fastened.

Terrier Territories

When you leave your terrier alone, your natural tendency will be to give the puppy as much room to burn off energy as possible in the hopes of dampening any destructive tendencies your puppy might have. This might work outside in a protected area, but it rarely works within the confines of the home. There are just too many temptations!

Bet You Didn't Know

Chewing for a puppy is more than just an urge. Puppies, like children, go through phases of teething. Chewing helps the teeth break through the gums and helps ease the pain caused by the emerging teeth. Punishing your dog for chewing is like punishing it for eating. Instead, be sensitive to your puppy's plight and provide lots of safe, acceptable alternatives to help your teething pet along.

Remember that your puppy views the world through totally different eyes than you do. Although your leather couch or loveseat might be a sign of prestige and success to your friends and family, your puppy sees it as a giant chew bone. Likewise, any upholstery with loose edges and anything with wood or wicker legs are sure targets for your

It's so easy—give your JRT plenty of chewies and it won't feel the need to munch on your furniture.
(photo by Brandon Lucas)

puppy's sharp little teeth. After all, it feels so good on its uncomfortable teething gums to have something chewy or crunchy between its small jaws. This might be amusing to your terrorist, but it can prove to be frustrating—not to mention expensive—for you.

Most Jack Russell Terriers eventually can be left alone without significant problems, provided they have plenty of chew toys and are not left alone for too long. Another terrier or another buddy dog often can help this process along, especially if the other dog already is solidly housetrained and is trustworthy in your absence. Many terriers sleep with their owners and only have to be confined when traveling or when exposed to a new environment.

By providing your puppy with plenty of energy outlets, such as playing ball or going for walks, you help to ensure that its exercise needs are being met. This decreases both your puppy's energy level and its anxiety level. If you give your pup plenty of exercise, it will be ready for a nap during the day (providing you with a moment of down time). Remember that your puppy also needs to spend time with you in your house, free but supervised, to help it understand what is acceptable and what is not. Only by experiencing some freedom will it learn proper behavior.

Sanity Savers

What about before you reach this milestone in your puppy's training? Or what if, no matter how much you play with your dog, it insists on redecorating your home each and every time you are away, regardless of the length of time it is left alone? This is when a gate, a solid exercise pen or a dog crate can be invaluable to you as a terrier owner. Keep in mind that not all puppies outgrow this stage. Some fully-grown dogs cannot be left alone without turning into a terrier demolition derby. These dogs have to be crated or confined during your absence, to keep them from ruining your home. This is known as separation anxiety and is discussed in Chapter 13.

Baby Gates

If you choose to use a gate to cordon off your puppy's area, be sure to select one that is high enough to prevent your puppy from jumping or climbing over the top and that easily and firmly spans the width of the door opening. You need to provide a soft place for your puppy to lie down, such as a blanket or a doggy bed. To prevent boredom, give your puppy toys and chewies to amuse itself while you are gone.

Doggy Don'ts

JRT puppies can be frustrating little creatures, but don't leave your terrier in its crate or separated from you and your family when you're home as well as when you're away. Jack Russells want to be involved. As frustrating as they can be, they learn from interaction with you and your family and from periods of freedom away from their safe enclosures.

Doggy Crates

If you choose the crate approach, remember to choose one that is the correct size, and never leave your dog or puppy crated for a long period of time. This creates a frustrated dog that learns to sleep while you are away and that drives you crazy for attention while you're home. If you must leave your dog for an extended period of time, leave it either outside in a backyard or in a large dog exercise area so its abundant energy has an outlet. Better yet, provide a companion dog to keep your terrier company.

For the short haul, a crate can be a sanity saver and actually can be comforting for your dog. Whether you choose the plastic travel crate or the wire mesh variety, your dog actually can learn to love its makeshift den. The crate is best used when housebreaking a puppy, during the night for destructive or mischievous dogs or for short periods while you are away from home if your dog has a hard time controlling its destructive tendencies. It can also be used as a way to separate dogs as necessary or, as previously mentioned, as a place for a time-out when your dog becomes overstimulated.

The X-Pen

A nice way to confine your dog is to use an exercise pen that provides a small or large enclosure, depending on your needs. These pens are portable, so you can use them when traveling with your dog or when attending terrier trials and play-days. Because they're flexible, you only need to take as many panels as you need, and they even can be made into two pens if you have more than one pet.

Alternative uses for X pens are discussed in later chapters, but for a daytime kennel, these exercise pens

Doggy Do's

Make your puppy's crate or confined area a pleasant place to be by paying attention to its surroundings. It should be a quiet place that is neither too hot nor too cold, and it should have good ventilation. Of course, always provide fresh water while you're away.

can be great for curtailing destructive behavior and for limiting housetraining problems. These pens can be placed inside or outside, and they don't rely on a suitable doorway or opening as a gate does. They stand alone and allow you to place them almost anywhere. You also can use puppy pads or newspaper in one corner to minimize the mess when housetraining.

As with all enclosures and crates, make sure to provide plenty of water during your absence, a soft place to take a nap and plenty of toys and chewies for amusement. Try to make the area as quiet and soothing as possible so your puppy will learn to relax when placed in this area. Soon your puppy will learn to enjoy its own little domain!

The Least You Need to Know

➤ Puppy-proofing your house *before* your puppy arrives helps keep frustrations and injuries to a minimum.

➤ Doors can pose a very real threat to your puppy. All doors should be equipped with door stops, and you should have screen doors on all doors leading outside.

➤ Never close a garage door until you are sure of your dog's whereabouts.

➤ Check your house and your yard for plants that could be toxic to your terrier and remove any that are.

➤ Many common household items can be dangerous to your puppy. If you wouldn't let your kids have access to it (from cleaners to needles), keep it away from your puppy too.

➤ Holidays are wonderful occasions, but they can be dangerous for your puppy. Let your dog enjoy the festivities from afar.

➤ Check your yard before leaving your dog alone. Make sure there are no weak spots in or under your fence and no sharp branches or corners that could be dangerous to your dog.

➤ The more positive energy outlets you can offer your puppy, the less it will be tempted to resort to destructive behaviors.

➤ Gates, crates and exercise pens all are safe, humane ways to limit your dog's roaming space and to keep destructive tendencies to a minimum.

➤ Give your puppy periods of supervised play throughout the house so it can learn how to behave without always being confined.

Chapter 13

The Problem Child

In This Chapter

➤ Separation anxiety

➤ Digging demons

➤ Chewing

➤ Baffled by barking

➤ The chase is on!

This book already has touched on some of the possible problems you might encounter with your new Jack Russell Terrier, and all the previously mentioned behaviors are pretty typical of a "normal" JRT. What if your terrier is truly a terrorist, however, and has a taste for even more destruction than normal, even for this breed? Don't worry too much yet. There are steps you can take to understand and minimize your terrier's destructive tendencies, and most JRTs can be made to understand that some conduct just is not acceptable. But you have to be understanding as well. Some behaviors are just typically terrier, and no amount of training, punishment or bribery will eliminate these habits.

Separation Anxiety

All dogs are social by nature, as proven by the formation of packs. When you separate your puppy from its littermates, you and your family effectively become its pack. When you have to be gone, whether for work or play, your puppy is left without its playmates. You can make this time easier for your puppy by doing the following:

➤ Exercising the dog right before you leave the house

➤ Leaving special chew toys for your puppy to use during your absence

➤ Providing a quiet, peaceful area with food, water and a soft bed for your puppy to enjoy while you are away

Bet You Didn't Know

Separation anxiety is very real for your dog and is actually akin to a human anxiety attack or claustrophobia. Your dog is not being destructive out of spite. It simply becomes so agitated that it can't control its anxiety.

Sometimes, regardless of your best efforts to provide a peaceful oasis for your puppy, it will still view your absence with some trepidation. You might find that your puppy barks for a few moments when left to its own devices but then settles into a quiet nap until you return. Or your puppy might get excited in the hopes of going with you but then, when it's convinced you are going out alone, resolve itself to playing solo until your return. In extreme examples, your dog might succumb to separation anxiety.

Dogs that truly suffer from separation anxiety exhibit classic signs of claustrophobia when left alone. Basically, they panic. In their efforts to calm their fears, these dogs might tear up carpet, try to claw their way through doors, or bark until they can't bark any more. Although puppies are natural demolition derbies and usually will outgrow this destructive phase, an adult dog that suffers from separation anxiety is a different kettle of fish altogether.

You first need to understand why this behavior occurs. Because you have become your terrier's pack, it feels very vulnerable when you are away. Essentially, its backup buddies have left it all alone. Instead of taking a deep breath and waiting it out as humans might do, your dog begins to fret about the fact that you might not return. The more it frets, the more anxious it gets. The more anxious it gets, the more it tries to escape the confines of the house to reunite itself with its pack. As its concern builds into panic, its actions escalate. It begins to claw at the carpet surrounding the doors or the screens covering the windows. It might lose control of its bodily functions and soil the carpet, or it might dig frantically at the door jam to try to open the door. All these things can lead to significant destruction of property in a very short time.

Managing the Anxious Dog

It's easy to become frustrated with an overly anxious dog, and your first instinct will be to punish the dog for its destructiveness. This probably is the worst course of action you can take. If you look at what caused the situation and at what effect your punishment will have on your dog, you will understand why.

Imagine that your child gets separated from you in a grocery store. He calls out for you, but you are out of earshot. At first, your child isn't too concerned because you usually respond promptly to his calls for help. But as time passes and you don't reappear, your child gets more anxious. Pretty soon he is crying and then screaming, trying to find you. When at last you discover that he isn't where you thought he was, you go searching and finally find him a few aisles away. Instead of consoling his frantic wails, you yell at your child and swat him on the behind for not staying close to you.

Doggy Do's

When faced with particularly troublesome behavior from your terrier, try to think like your dog thinks. Sometimes this can significantly change your perspective and can help you come up with more effective, nonpunitive ways of solving the problem.

What have you really taught your child? You've taught him that, not only is getting separated scary, it's even scarier when mom shows up because then you're really in trouble. Now you've created a catch-22. The child is anxious about getting separated and is equally anxious about the reunion.

By punishing your dog for its destructive behavior, you are teaching it to dread your departure and also to dread your arrival home, doubling your dog's anxiety level. The more anxious the dog is, the more destructive its behavior is. By punishing your dog after the fact, you are, in essence, creating a vicious cycle of escalating destructive behavior.

The best way to diminish this problem is through constructive training. Remember the golden rule—never correct your dog after the fact. It simply has no meaning for your terrier and adds to its already-established anxiety level. Keeping that in mind, let's look at some steps you can take to try to help your terrier through this troubling behavior.

Bet You Didn't Know

Separation anxiety occurs in both passive and aggressive dogs. The passive dog feels you will leave and never return, causing it to be anxious about its future safety. The aggressive dog always needs to know where the members of the pack are and suffers from a loss of control when it can't keep tabs on you.

Tips to Remember

Create the best environment possible for your dog while you are away. Leave a radio on so your terrier hears voices and does not feel quite so alone. Provide several toys and chewies that your dog can use to safely release its anxiety and rub your hands on them before you leave so they smell like you. Make sure the area is at a comfortable temperature and dim any glaring lights. By the same token, make sure your dog isn't left in total darkness either.

Decrease the attention you give to your dog before you leave the house. If you always play and amuse it just before you go away, it makes separation that much harder. You will inadvertently show your dog why it should miss you even more! Instead, quietly go about your business and, when it is time to leave, simply gather up your things and go. Don't say good-bye or tell it how much you'll miss it. Again, this might make you feel better, but it actually increases your dog's nervousness and anxiety.

Leave of Absence

Start by acclimating your terrier to your necessary periods of absence by taking short walks away from home. Make sure your dog has a doggy bed nearby and leave the house for ten or fifteen minutes. Avoid any drawn-out good-byes or threats about what you'd better find or not find when you get home. When you return, ignore your dog for the first several minutes, regardless of the condition of the house.

If some destruction has occurred, resist the temptation to begin yelling about how a dog can do so much damage in such a short amount of time. It won't make you feel any better, and it will nullify any benefit of this training session. If the dog has managed to resist its destructive impulses, you have good cause to praise it quietly. Once you have set the stage for a calm reunion, either praise your terrier for its good behavior or ask it to perform a simple obedience task such as sit or down and then praise its cooperation.

Gradually increase the amount of time you are away until your dog gets the idea that you eventually will return and that your departure does not herald the end of the world. With a lot of practice and patience, you should be able to leave for a few hours without causing your dog to regress. Some dogs will permanently respond to this training; others will only stay calm for a few hours before giving in to their anxieties. If your dog falls into the latter category, it is best to simply confine it while you are away. This is less stressful for your dog, and it ensures that your house will remain intact.

Digging Demons

Terriers dig. Period. They were bred to dig down to their quarry, and no amount of training will completely eliminate their natural instinct to explore the nether regions for rodents and prey. If you

157

have a perfectly manicured lawn or garden and expect your terrier to never disturb a blade of grass or leaf of lettuce, you will be sorely disappointed.

Doggy Don'ts

Don't try to stop your Jack Russell Terrier from digging. It is an inbred trait and trying to curb it will only make you both frustrated and angry.

Instead of trying to train, beat or coerce your dog into not digging, try to think of ways to allow your terrier to satisfy these natural urges without wreaking havoc to your landscaping. Usually, this means providing a time and a place where your terrier can dig to its heart's content without being scolded. This might be a corner of your yard or an area of an abandoned dirt parking lot. It doesn't matter where it is, it just matters that it's okay for your dog to dig there. You even can make it more fun for your JRT by hiding doggy treats and biscuits under a few inches of dirt and then allowing your rotten Russeller to dig them up. By providing a place for your dog to "legally" dig and by visiting these digs several times a week, you can divert your dog's natural digging tendencies into a fun behavior.

If your safe digging spot is close by, take the time to train your dog to use it. If you see your dog digging in an area that is unacceptable, direct its attention to the acceptable area or simply pick it up and take it there. Tell it "Okay, dig." This will effectively turn digging into a command performance in which you control what is unearthed and where.

Who's the Boss?

Some forms of aggression can be prevented; others seem to be inbred in the dog and controlling them could prove difficult. The best and easiest solution is to buy your Jack Russell Terrier from a reputable breeder who is known for having dogs with mild temperaments. Choose a puppy that had parents with a friendly nature and that does not consider itself the leader of the pack.

Aside from this obvious preventative first step, what can you do if your puppy seems to be getting rougher and rougher in its play or if

Jack Russells were bred to dig after their quarry, so it's in your best interest to find an acceptable space for your dog to dig.
(photo by Laurie Mercer)

you see signs of escalating aggressive behavior? The answer is to correct this behavior quickly and effectively before it gets out of control, and never lose your temper when you are dealing with a puppy with aggressive tendencies.

Puppy Aggression

Tiny terrier teeth can do considerable damage to the flesh of your arms and hands. If you've ever had those little teeth sink into your finger instead of the sock you were holding, you don't need any convincing. Puppies naturally snarl, bite and snap as they play with their littermates. Playing with you seems no different to them, and it is up to you to make your puppy see the distinction.

Doggy Don'ts

Don't allow your terrier to win an aggression game. It sends the wrong message and could create a more difficult problem.

Although a rousing game is good for everyone, it is important that you make sure your puppy knows roughhousing hurts. If your puppy

159

puts your hand into its mouth, hold the puppy with your other hand, extricate your finger and tell the puppy "No!" Stop playing with your puppy for several minutes to reinforce the point that nipping or mouthing human hands is unacceptable. After your puppy has calmed down for a few minutes, try playing with it again. Remember to correct your puppy each and every time it grabs too hard, and don't lose your temper no matter how much those little teeth hurt. Remember that the best way to prevent aggressiveness is by showing your puppy kindness. If it doesn't feel threatened by you, it won't be aggressive toward you.

Doggy Do's

Correct your puppy by using understandable commands and by praising it for correct behavior. If you use physical punishment to correct a bad habit, you could be setting yourself up for another bad habit—aggression.

Dog to Human Aggression

Aggressive behavior in an older dog is a bit more difficult to deal with. It can manifest itself in several ways, including mounting, growling and barking directly at a human. This is often caused by spoiling a dog, by reprimanding a dog too harshly or by showing submission, thus encouraging more aggression. Keep in mind, however, that some JRTs growl just to growl. These dogs use growling more as a grumble than as a threat. As an owner, you will know the difference. Dogs that grumble at you seldom raise their hackles, bare their teeth or show any other outward signs of aggression.

If you find your dog doing things such as barking at you for attention, grabbing a toy and running away before turning back and trying to entice you to play or rubbing against you for attention, you have a dog that is displaying signs of dominance. Although this in itself might not turn into signs of aggression, it might very well eventually do just that. Then it will be up to you to solve the problem and to reassert your position as leader of the pack.

One of the best ways to assert yourself without confrontation is to teach your terrier the basics listed in Chapter 11. This sets the ground rules in your dog's mind that there are commands it must obey. By gaining its cooperation in learning commands, you are teaching it that you, not it, are head of the household.

These commands also prove useful in other areas and should be started immediately. While your dog is showing some aggressive traits, it should be schooled every day for at least a few minutes a day. In addition, keep your dog off your bed if it is showing aggressive behavior. By allowing your dog on the bed, you are signaling to it a need for protection, thus granting your terrier a dominant position over you. If the dog views you as submissive, it could lead to escalating aggressive responses.

Seriously dominant dogs will exhibit behaviors such as raising their hackles and growling if you walk by. You should not try to confront your dog when it is doing this. If you find yourself getting into a battle of wills or if your dog growls at you when you try to move or position it, you should seek professional help. A truly aggressive dog can be dangerous to you and your family. Prompt attention to the problem from a professional who does not condone physical punishment will be your best answer.

Some dogs only show aggression at feeding time or over a special toy or area. These terriers actually are protecting something they feel is theirs, and they feel must defend their prize from outside theft. Again, confrontation is not the way to handle this type of aggression. Instead, you need to let your terrier know that you are not there to steal its food or toy but that it must tolerate your presence to get a reward. You can do this by using training biscuits or distracting it with the can of pennies.

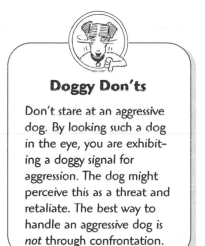

Doggy Don'ts

Don't stare at an aggressive dog. By looking such a dog in the eye, you are exhibiting a doggy signal for aggression. The dog might perceive this as a threat and retaliate. The best way to handle an aggressive dog is *not* through confrontation.

If you approach your dog's food bowl and it growls at you, call the dog over and show it a biscuit or rattle the can to get its attention. If it comes willingly, reward your terrier with one of the biscuits. You also can use cheese, pieces of hot dog, or any treat your dog has a taste for. The important thing is to be able to approach the toy or food without your dog feeling threatened. By making your presence even more rewarding, your dog will soon look forward to having you around and will not be so inclined to chase you off.

Dog-to-Dog Aggression

Some terriers are not aggressive with their owners but are extremely aggressive with other dogs. I'm not talking about a dog that runs up to anything and everything wagging its tail or wanting to play. I'm talking about a Jack Russell Terrier that wants to eat every other living, breathing dog, regardless of size. Not only can this be frustrating when trying to socialize your terrier, it also can be downright dangerous if the dog it chooses to attack is ten times its size.

Early socialization through park play and obedience classes is the best solution for this type of aggressiveness. If your puppy is introduced to other dogs and learns the social ins and outs of doggy behavior, it is less likely to turn aggressive. Because some of the puppies it meets will be more aggressive and some will be more timid, your puppy will learn to judge the other dogs' reactions and to act accordingly. Sometimes it will win and sometimes it will back down. This interaction will usually lead to acceptable behavior.

Doggy Don'ts

If faced with a dog fight, don't scream or yell to cause a distraction and don't try to get between the dogs. This will only escalate the tension that already exists between the two dogs. Instead, use water, a rattle can or a bag to break up the fight before extricating your terrier from the situation.

If, despite your efforts at socialization, you find your terrier in the middle of a dog fight, *do not* reach down in the middle of it to try to stop your dog. This is a good way to get bitten! Instead, you need to create a diversion either by spraying the dogs with water or by causing another distraction. Remember that the fighting dogs are focusing 100 percent on their disagreement and are not likely to notice you are nearby. A dog in this situation has little respect for human hands or feet and is likely to mistake your limbs for that of its opponent.

The best course of action is to control your terrier in the first place by keeping it firmly on a leash until you are sure of its reaction to the other doggy players. Only after you have assured yourself that everyone will get along should turn your terrier loose. Keep a close eye on it to satisfy yourself that your judgment was correct. By keeping your dog on a leash at the beginning, you can easily pull your dog out of harm's way should another dog begin to look aggressive.

Chewing

All dogs chew, though their reasons for chewing change as they move from puppyhood to adulthood. They do not chew to frustrate you or to cause you grief. Instead, they chew to help their puppy teeth cut through their gums, to strengthen permanent teeth and to clean their teeth and massage their gums. All dogs, and terriers in particular, use chewing as a type of pacifier to calm their nerves and to rid their systems of anxious energy.

The negative side of chewing is that, without proper guidance and direction, your terrier literally can chew you out of house and home. The positive side of chewing is that you can provide acceptable chew toys for your terrier and can rid your dog of excess energy and damaging dental tartar all at once!

Notice that I said *acceptable* chew toys. Not all of the toys, bones and chewies you see at the local pet store are acceptable for your dog to gnaw on. Some are made of soft rubber and are for structured play, not continuous chewing. Others have pieces that could pose a choking hazard to your dog should it chew through the supporting structure. Because Jack Russell Terriers have notoriously strong jaws, you must choose your chew toys with caution and a great deal of care.

Never give your terrier a bone that could break into small pieces or anything that is indigestible if swallowed. If the bone happens to break off with a sharp edge and your terrier ingests it, it could tear a hole in your dog's stomach or intestine and cause serious internal damage and even death. Likewise, indigestible material such as rubber or plastic could create an internal blockage leading to surgery or worse.

Perhaps the best chew toys available are the strong, nylon chew devices found on today's pet store shelves. These chew bones are made of strong, durable nylon and often come with a scent or a flavor added to make them more attractive to your terrier. Some are smooth and are shaped like knuckles or bones; others have raised bristles to help stimulate your dog's gums. These often are useful for dogs with a propensity for tartar build-up, though none is a good substitution for routine dental hygiene.

Doggy Do's

Provide a variety of chew devices for your dog and then stick with the ones it prefers the most. Although it is fine to leave the harder chew bones with your dog most of the time, rope chew toys can be easily shredded and strewn about the house, so let your dog use these only under close supervision.

These toys provide excellent resistance for your dog's jaws and are crucial for jaw strength and health. They have the added benefit of being soft enough to prevent the wearing down of dental surfaces, but they are hard enough to provide a satisfying chew toy for your terrier.

Rope and floss chew toys provide the added benefit of "doggy dental floss" and can be used in conjunction with the harder nylon bones to complete your dog's dental regimen. The rope chew toys can get between your dog's teeth and literally can act as dental floss to clean the space between the teeth that harder chew bones can't reach. Because the rope and floss toys work with a gentle tugging that your dog naturally performs by itself, all you have to do is sit back and watch it work!

Baffled by Barking

Barking is another aspect of canine behavior that is quite natural but can be quite annoying. Although you appreciate being notified of an intruder in your house, you don't appreciate being alerted to each and every passing car. Not only is excessive barking annoying to you, it will do nothing to endear you to your neighbors.

There is a big difference between a few warning barks to signal someone approaching the door and a half-hour barking jag that says your JRT is bored or irritated. Some JRTs also like to bark as a means of playing. Before you can be effective in changing your terrier's behavior, you need to determine the cause of your dog's barking. You then can choose the response most likely to succeed in that given situation.

Bet You Didn't Know

Digging, barking and chewing are normal doggy behaviors. Many dogs are abandoned every year because uneducated owners didn't take the time to learn how to manage these habits and were overwhelmed by them.

Like most tempting first responses, yelling at your dog when it barks will not stop it from barking. Instead, your terrier will think you are joining in the fun and will bark longer and louder. In fact, it will enjoy barking even more because it thinks it has your approval and input!

You need to teach your terrier that, although you appreciate the alarm for an approaching stranger, it must stop barking when commanded and must let you to deal with the person in peace. To begin the training, keep a leash handy so you can grab it as you head toward the door. As you approach the door, tell your dog "Enough!" in a firm, quiet voice and clip on the leash. If your dog barks after you have given the command, give the leash a sharp tug and repeat the command. Take special care not to raise your voice and not to escalate your response in any way. You need to stay calm if you expect your dog to calm down.

The tried-and-true can of coins also comes in handy for this training as will a spray bottle. If a leash is unavailable or if your dog is barking at an unknown sound or at you to get your attention, you can either ignore it or you can distract it. Don't pet or coddle a dog that is barking for attention. You will only create a spoiled dog that barks even more. If you can't ignore it, use the command "Enough!" again in a calm, commanding voice. If your dog continues, use the can or the spray bottle on your terrier to divert its attention.

Be sure not to telegraph your intentions with these devices. They work best when your dog thinks they occurred out of the blue and did not come from you. This way, your terrier will assume that the correction was caused directly by the barking, not by your actions.

You also can send your terrier to bed or to its time-out corner if it ignores your command to be quiet. Once your terrier is quiet, praise it for being so cooperative.

The Chase Is On!

Terriers, by nature, love a good chase. After all, they were bred to hunt foxes and to chase them out of their dens. Like digging and barking, chasing cats, cars, children and anything else that seems like a good sport are natural, inbred traits for your terrier and will prove to be particularly enticing.

Managing the chasing habit is especially important if your terrier likes to chase cars. For some unknown reason, Jack Russell Terriers have a particular penchant for anything with wheels and are almost obsessed with following these wheeled beasts. Unfortunately, the car can do a lot more damage to your terrier than your dog can inflict on the car.

The only way to correct this behavior is through leash training. Your dog must be made to respect your judgment. If your dog has been trained to respond to the command "No!" from Chapter 11, you will have a much easier time getting its attention away from the point of interest and firmly back on you. If not, now is a good time to teach this command. In every case, you must teach your terrier that "No!" means right now, not ten steps later. This takes consistent schooling and a lot of patience. When your dog can respond quickly and predictably on the leash, you need to continue to work without the leash so your dog's response will be both timely and consistent. This kind of schooling might get boring, but remember that it is very important. It could save your dog's life somewhere down the road.

To illustrate this point, one of our favorite terriers, Annie, was out with me at the ranch one day. I was giving a riding lesson to one of my students, and Annie was happily running here and there chasing squirrels and peering down holes. Suddenly, a coyote came out from the woods, walked across the arena and proceeded up the hill. Annie took one look at the coyote, decided it looked like a good prey and took off running after the coyote.

About 50 feet into the chase, the coyote decided to see what was pursuing it. Seeing the size of my little terrier and comparing it with its own mass, it decided that this tender little tidbit might make a great midday snack. I immediately yelled "Annie! No! Come!" and prayed that she would listen. Thanks to years of training and a strong respect for me, she stopped in her tracks and came running to me with the coyote not far behind. I was able to chase off the varmint and then thank my lucky stars that my training had paid off. I had my terrier in my arms to praise for her good behavior. Had I neglected this training, my dog might not be here today.

The Least You Need to Know

➤ Jack Russell Terriers can and do have destructive tendencies. If you understand why they occur, you can train your terrier more effectively.

➤ Separation anxiety is a very real fear for your dog. It can be rectified only through patient training and understanding.

➤ Digging is a natural behavior for Jack Russell Terriers, and no amount of training will stop them from digging.

➤ Aggression should be curbed early to prevent future problems.

➤ You might need professional help correcting an older dog that has an aggression problem.

➤ Dog-to-dog aggression could get you or your dog injured. Be sure to approach such meetings with care and control.

➤ By providing both hard-nylon bones and suitable rope or floss chews for your dog, you can satisfy its natural desire to chew while encouraging good dental hygiene.

➤ To solve a barking problem, you must first determine the cause of the barking and then train accordingly.

➤ The "No!" command is crucial when training your terrier not to chase. You must put enough time and effort into this training to be sure your dog understands and respects the command.

Part 4

Doctor Dog

Although playing, exercising and frolicking with your Jack Russell are by far the most fun parts of JRT ownership, with this fun comes responsibility. This includes caring for your terrier's health and well-being through proper diet, exercise and veterinary care throughout its various life stages.

This part guides you through the confusing and often daunting morass of health routines, problems and concerns most important to your JRT's well-being. It also explains some of the medical symptoms and disorders you might encounter. It gives you solid information about healthy diets for your Jack Russell and practical steps for routine health care. It also addresses the difficult dilemma of saying goodbye to an older friend. Taking care of your JRT doesn't have to be difficult. It can even be idiot-proof!

Chapter 14

Your Friendly Neighborhood Vet

In This Chapter

➤ Dr. Jekyll or Mr. Hyde?

➤ The lowdown on shots

➤ Watch out for the creepy crawlies

➤ Jack rabbits or Jack Russells?

➤ When to call 911

➤ Bumps and bruises

You should know that not all veterinarians are created equal. Depending on where you live, you might have many veterinarians available to you. You would be wise to check out several before deciding which vet is for you and your terrier. Some veterinarians have a very distinct opinion of JRTs, and this might not be in your best interest. This chapter will help guide you through the selection of a veterinarian for your Jack Russell, and it will give you some solid questions to ask your vet to make sure your terrier will remain happy and healthy.

Dr. Jekyll or Mr. Hyde?

You should exert the same care in selecting a veterinarian for your dog as you would in selecting a doctor for yourself and your family.

171

Ridiculous? Not in the least. After all, your dog *is* part of the family, isn't it? What do you look for in your personal physician? Experience, compassion, dependability, ability to communicate with you, closeness to home, and so on. All these factors are important, as is knowing that your doctor keeps up on new medical developments, medications and treatments.

In addition to the preceding, you will want to be sure that:

➤ The office has overnight facilities, in case your dog needs to stay there a day or two for observation or for treatment.

➤ The facilities are clean.

➤ Food and water are fresh and available.

➤ The doctor's fees are within your budget.

An older, more established veterinarian might charge more than a young vet just starting out. Some young vets are willing to charge less in order to establish a practice.

Bet You Didn't Know

A crate is a useful tool for transporting your dog to and from the vet's office. His favorite blanket and toy should be placed inside to minimize the trauma of a visit to the vet. Remember, however, that your dog also should be able to associate the crate with pleasurable and fun car rides such as trips to the beach.

Bedside Manners

Rapport with your vet is important. You need to be able to communicate well with him when explaining your terrier's symptoms and actions when it is ill, and you should feel comfortable that the veterinarian will explain your dog's condition without being condescending or impatient. Also, will the vet return your calls promptly? It sounds like an obvious question, but all too often the answer is no.

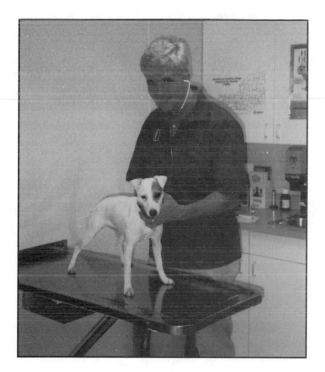

You should feel comfortable that your veterinarian has a good understanding of your dog's needs and that he is your friend in maintaining your dog's health. (photo by Catherine Romaine Brown)

When you are nursing a sick dog, a timely call-back from your vet is as appreciated as your pediatrician's response time when you are a first-time mother with a sick baby who can't tell you what hurts! Remember, your dog is part of the family, and it deserves your vet's best care and attention.

In truth, you and your vet should have as good a rapport as you and your personal physician have. Knowing what to expect from the beginning avoids unpleasantness and ill feelings in the long run. Your vet might assume you know all the ramifications of his diagnosis. If there is any question in your mind, you need to ask additional questions of your vet. Don't leave your vet's office until you are confident you understand everything that has been recommended and exactly what effort and costs those recommendations entail.

Fees

It is important that you understand the charges for specific procedures and treatments before you agree to the treatment so that, when the bill arrives, you are prepared and won't have to second-mortgage your home. This also enables you to make an educated decision whether to proceed with a given treatment. When taking your dog in for a yearly physical, for example, will you be charged just for a physical or, as in the case of an older dog, will special tests be required? If these tests determine that there is a problem, will you have the money to invest in additional treatment? How extensive will that treatment be? Will it be a one-time event? Or will it entail ongoing costs and treatment? As you can see, some early research will help you make a good decision at the start.

Doggy Do's

Ask whether your vet is accustomed to working specifically with Jack Russell Terriers. If so, he is more likely to understand and effectively treat inherent health problems specific to the breed. Moreover, a vet familiar with JRTs might have more patience with a rambunctious dog.

The Low-Down on Shots

Veterinary medicine has come a long way, and there are now vaccinations for almost every modern dog disease. It is incumbent upon you as a responsible JRT owner to make sure your terrier is immunized against diseases that often can be fatal. It would be a tragedy to lose your pet due to a lack of simple preventive medicine.

Some of the diseases currently preventable through vaccination include rabies, distemper, leptospirosis, canine hepatitis, kennel cough, Lyme disease and coronavirus. As your JRT gets older, other shots will be required. You should ask your vet whether he sends out shot reminders to keep you abreast of your JRT's vaccination schedule.

When you first get a puppy or dog, one of your first calls should be to your vet. You should tell him what shots your Jack Russell already has had and should ask him which shots are still needed and when. Vaccination recommendations vary from area to area and from vet to vet. The following paragraphs provide a brief summary of the most common vaccinations recommended and when they usually are administered.

At birth, puppies obtain a certain amount of immunity to disease through their dam if she herself has been immunized. This immunity, however, lasts only for a few weeks. At 6 to 8 weeks, your puppy will require vaccinations for canine distemper, infectious hepatitis, parainfluenza (CPI), canine adenovirus type 2, coronavirus and parvovirus.

Puppies should be revaccinated every two to three weeks until 16 weeks of age. At around 12 weeks of age, your puppy also should receive a leptospirosis shot and, if recommended by your vet, a Lyme disease vaccine. Many veterinarians wait until the puppy is 1 year old to administer the first rabies shot; others give the first shot at 14 to 16 weeks. Check with your vet for his recommendation because it might differ from those listed here. Boosters for all vaccinations are often given annually.

Watch Out for the Creepy Crawlies

Internal parasites include hookworms, whipcords, ascarids, threadworms, heart worms, lungworms and tapeworms. These and other unsavory creatures are a real threat to your dog's health. Most puppies are infected at birth, through their dam, with some type of worm. It is important to develop a vet-supervised worming schedule right from the start.

Doggy Don'ts

Resist the impulse to purchase over-the-counter worming medications for your puppy. These treatments are not as effective as those prescribed by your vet, and they often can even be dangerous to your puppy's health *if given* without prior parasite testing.

Worm Control

Worms can cause serious health problems, which is why a regular worming schedule is important. Like any other health maintenance program, however, it should not be administered willy-nilly. Your veterinarian is the best person to advise you if and when your terrier needs to be wormed. Usually he will ask you to bring in a stool sample for testing. From the results of that test, he will prescribe a wormer based on your JRT's individual needs.

You should contact your vet if you notice your dog scooting his rear end on the ground or if you see any other behavior that would seem odd or that would indicate that your dog has an itchy rear end. This might be a skin-related problem, impacted anal sacs, or it could indicate worms. In any event, have a medical professional examine your dog.

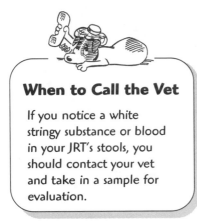

When to Call the Vet

If you notice a white stringy substance or blood in your JRT's stools, you should contact your vet and take in a sample for evaluation.

Jack Rabbits or Jack Russells?

Unless you plan to become a professional, responsible breeder, you should not decide at your dog's first heat that having a litter of puppies is a neat idea. Breeders choose their brood-stock with rigorous guidelines and an eagle eye. Unless you have chosen as your pet a superior JRT specimen and have bred dogs before, you are getting in way over your head. Doing so could produce litters of inferior-quality puppies, could create an influx of displaced dogs, and could put your family pet in jeopardy.

Doggy Don'ts

Don't breed your dog because you feel it would be a good experience for your children to see the wonders of nature. Rent a video!

Jack Russell Terriers are cute but, as stated elsewhere in this book, they aren't for everyone and aren't as portrayed on TV programs or movies. Witness the number of JRTs that end up in rescue organizations. Your female dog should not be looked at as a source of funding for your family's next trip, nor should well-meaning friends convince you that, because they would "love to have one of Spate's puppies," you should oblige by providing litters of them.

Breeding Is for Pros

Dog breeding is serious business. Unfortunately, the popularity of the breed has caused many people to purchase female Jack Russells for the sole purpose of breeding them and earning a few bucks on the side. This is *not* what a responsible breeding program should be about. Breeders rarely make a fortune on their litters because there are many costs that defray any profit that could be made. Puppies must have their tails docked, their dewclaws removed and their early shots provided. Breeding females must be routinely examined to ensure their health, and complications during the birthing process are not uncommon. Moreover, the original cost of breeding stock is significantly higher than that of a pet-quality animal, not to mention the cost of the stud fee to breed with a quality sire.

The Benefits of Spaying or Neutering

There are many advantages to spaying your female dog or neutering your male dog. In males, neutering reduces problem behaviors such as fighting, aggression, territorial marking and mounting. It also reduces the incidence of prostate problems and eliminates the possibility of testicular cancer. In females, spaying prevents diapering during heat cycles (the use of a plastic diaper and pad to collect the bleeding that occurs during estrus), unwanted litters and the considerable nuisance of having unwelcome males camp on your doorstep or against your fence like fawning Casanovas. It also can help prevent pyometra, which is a serious and potentially fatal uterus infection.

Bet You Didn't Know

Many sites, links and resources on the Internet are devoted to neutering, spaying, careless breeding and the pet overpopulation problem. These sites outline everything you need to know about these topics.

If you own male and female Jack Russell Terriers, spaying and neutering avoid the necessity of keeping your dogs separate every time the females are in heat (four to six weeks at a time, twice yearly). Many a backdoor screen has been shredded by the attentions of a male trying to get to his mate. Dogs also have been known to jump fences and to dig holes the size of the Grand Canyon to reach the object of their affections. An intact male Jack Russell kept away from a female in heat truly is a miserable animal, and he will do virtually anything to satisfy his natural urge to procreate.

Neutering, when performed by a competent vet, is relatively safe and painless. In some areas, license fees for neutered dogs are reduced, thus paying for the neutering procedure in the long run.

Neutered dogs are happier and are less apt to seek ways to roam the neighborhood. They are less aggressive and are less likely to be the object of aggression than their intact counterparts. They also are less likely to try to mate with the neighbor's Pit Bull or Rottweiler. As a result, risks of injuries are lessened, saving you expensive vet bills. Neutered males are more laid back, are better behaved and make for a more contented pet. Because their natural urges are diminished, their anxiety level is lessened, as is their propensity for destructive behavior.

When to Call 911

It is important to keep your veterinarian's phone number handy so you can quickly access it in case of an emergency. Emergencies come in many forms and, no matter how careful you are, they can and do occur. Jack Russell Terriers are such active little critters that a thorn deeply imbedded in a paw or a laceration from chasing a ground squirrel is not uncommon. Unless you are paying close attention to your JRT's actions, you might not notice these injuries until they become infected or until your terrier becomes noticeably lame. If you are familiar with the Jack Russell's busy nature, you know that this might be days after the fact.

Any signs of bleeding or infection should receive prompt attention, as should difficulty in breathing, limping, convulsions, excessive drooling, listlessness, inability to urinate, vomiting, swelling or fever. Symptoms can vary widely and can be signs of problems ranging from poisoning to a bee sting to hypothermia. If you aren't sure what's wrong with your terrier and it appears to be "not quite itself," a quick call or visit to the vet is warranted. He will be able to tell you whether further treatment will be necessary. Some external emergencies are obvious (open wounds, cuts, bruises, slivers in paws, or foreign objects in ears), but many are internal and only can be determined and treated by your veterinarian.

How to Check Your Dog's Vital Signs

So you can be prepared to answer your vet's questions, check to see that breathing passages are free of obstructions, write down any symptoms you have been noticing and take your dog's temperature. To do so, lubricate and insert a rectal thermometer (preferably digital) into your dog's anus about 1½ inches deep and leave it for one minute. Hold your terrier still and standing during this time. (You do *not* want it to sit on the thermometer!) A JRT's natural temperature ranges from 100° to 102° F.

When to Call the Vet

Call the vet and remove the collar on your JRT if you notice that your terrier's breathing is labored, very rapid, shallow, loud, irregular, or if it gasps for air, displays a blue tongue or loses consciousness. These symptoms suggest a respiratory problem that could be fatal.

If your vet asks you to check your dog's pulse, lay your dog down on its side. Place your hand on the femoral artery, which is located where the thigh meets the abdomen on the back leg. Count the pulse rate for one minute. A normal pulse is 80 to 100 beats per minute while resting.

Know Your Terrier's Typical Readings

During one of your routine visits to your vet, you should ask what temperature and pulse rate are normal for your individual JRT. It is a good idea to write this information down and to keep it in a safe place so you can compare it to the readings you get down the road should you suspect something is amiss with your terrier. Your vet will find this information useful when diagnosing whether the readings you are giving him are abnormal for your individual JRT.

Leave Some Things to the Pros

Don't try to remove a splinter or other object that appears to be deeply imbedded and *don't* try to straighten a limb that possibly has been broken. Similarly, you shouldn't try to induce vomiting if you suspect your dog has ingested a toxic or poisonous substance unless specifically directed to do so by your vet's office. These types of

treatment are best administered by a licensed vet, and you can cause more problems for your terrier by taking matters into your own hands. Many poisons are more dangerous if regurgitated and can cause additional danger to your JRT if vomiting is induced.

If your dog has been hit by a car or has suffered an extreme trauma, you should immobilize it and get it to the vet immediately. Wrap your dog in a blanket to keep it warm and place it in a small crate or on a board to keep it totally immobilized. Talk to your JRT and do all you can to comfort it on the way there to try to keep its shock and trauma to a minimum. Your presence and your voice can be very soothing to your Jack Russell in times of trauma; the more you do to keep it calm, the easier it will be for both of you to handle the situation. It is important for you to keep your own actions and demeanor calm so your JRT doesn't sense your emotional distress—this will only cause it additional anxiety.

Bumps and Bruises

With a dog as active as a JRT, injuries are difficult to avoid. A bit of knowledge as to what to do when one occurs can save your dog's life or, at the very least, can reduce its discomfort until you can get it to the vet. The following sections discuss some specific problems you might encounter and how to handle them if they do occur.

Bleeding

If your dog sustains an open wound that is bleeding profusely, control the bleeding immediately by covering the wound with a clean towel or cloth. Apply gentle pressure, adding additional coverings as necessary. Elevate the wound and use a cold pack, continuing to apply pressure to the wound. As soon as you notice such an injury, get your terrier to the vet as quickly as possible. In case of a chest wound, place a piece of plastic over the wound, securing it to make it as airtight as possible.

Eye Injuries

If your dog's eye comes into contact with an irritant, wash the affected eye with plenty of water. You can do this by using an ear bulb or a plastic syringe. Be careful that you keep the stream of water or saline gentle so as not to cause further damage. If your dog's eye has been punctured or lacerated, wrap the dog in a warm blanket and take it to the vet right away.

Injured Limbs

Digging is one of the Jack Russell's inbred traits. Sprains or even fractures can occur as a result of excessive, spirited digging. If your dog comes in limping and looks to be in pain, keep it warm and quiet, try to steady the injured limb with a support bandage without pulling or tugging on it and take your pet to the vet. A mild analgesic often will help. Active dogs that share their lives with horses also are apt to be kicked or stomped on occasionally. Again, avoid unnecessarily moving your dog and seek attention if the injury appears to be severe.

Bet You Didn't Know

Because of the Jack Russell Terrier's intense love of digging, one of their most common injuries is a torn or removed toenail. If you notice your JRT limping or laying down licking its paw, check to see whether it has damaged one of its toenails. If it is limping badly, call your vet.

Snake Bites

In the case of a snake bite, try to keep your dog as quiet as possible, keep it warm and, if you are unable to contact your vet immediately, apply pressure between the dog's heart and the bite. Symptoms of snake bite include nausea, listlessness and swelling at the site. Fang marks often are apparent. If you know the snake was venomous, you should get your JRT to the vet immediately.

Bet You Didn't Know

You can receive a shock yourself by touching a dog that has been electrocuted. Protect yourself by removing the cord from the socket or by pushing your JRT away from the electrical source before attempting to handle it.

Electric Shocks

JRT's love to chase and bite everything. If your dog gets hold of an electric cord or conduit and bites through it, use a plastic or wooden stick to move the cord away from your pet, look for burn signs inside its mouth, keep the dog warm, and rush it to the vet. Many times, the injuries caused by this electrocution are not readily apparent, so you should act quickly and get your Jack Russell immediate medical attention.

The Least You Need to Know

➤ Use the same care in choosing your vet as you use when choosing your physician.

➤ Keep your vet's number and your terrier's typical vital signs within easy reach in case of emergency.

➤ Keeping your JRT current on vaccinations is an easy way to prevent illness and even death.

➤ To treat worms, take your dog to the veterinarian and get professional advice.

➤ Have your terrier spayed or neutered as soon as the vet gives his okay.

➤ If your dog has been seriously traumatized, immobilize it, keep it warm, stay calm and get it to the vet immediately.

➤ Remember that not all injuries are immediately apparent. If you know your terrier isn't acting quite right, call your vet and let him make the decision whether additional treatment is necessary.

Taking Care of Business— Routine Health Care

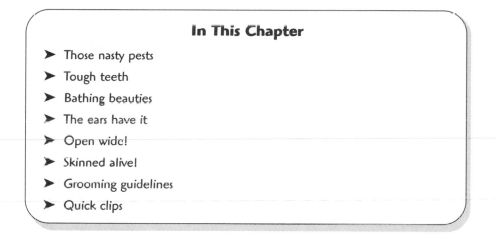

Because Jack Russells have reasonably short coats, caring for your terrier's coif, especially for a dog with a smooth coat, is fairly simple. But there is more to routine JRT health than an occasional bath, a good brushing and a daily walk. Preventive maintenance and upkeep can prevent many health problems that, if left unchecked, could pose a problem for your JRT. It's a bit like taking your car to the garage for a lube job to prevent engine problems. Like your car, a well-tuned and well-cared-for Jack Russell will be a happy pet that will give you many years of love and devoted companionship.

183

Those Nasty Pests

As if dealing with summer mosquitoes, ants and spiders around the house isn't enough, having a dog around creates a whole new environment for a different set of creepy crawlies. By paying attention to these little invaders *before* they become a problem, however, you can save your Jack Russell and yourself significant discomfort and frustration.

The JRT Flea Circus

Spring is the season when thoughts usually turn to planting a garden, spring cleaning, and summer vacation plans. It also harks the arrival of fleas and ticks, the teeny little pests that can make your dog's life miserable. Fleas are well adapted to survive, and an adult female flea can lay up to fifty eggs a day on your dog. Soon, these eggs fall off the dog's hair onto your beds, carpets and upholstery. After hatching, the eggs develop into tiny larvae and feed primarily on adult flea feces that accumulate in pet areas along with the eggs. This is not a very appetizing prospect, but it's one that reinforces the importance of ridding yourself not only of the fleas on your dog but also those both inside and outside of your home.

Doggy Do's

Kill fleas both indoors and outdoors and make sure you are using a flea treatment that is both safe and effective. Many flea treatments contain chemicals, which can be harmful to both you and your dog. Opt for natural remedies instead.

Does your dog scratch or chew its backside, chest or genital area? Does it sport bald and reddened spots? If so, there's a good chance those nasty little bugs are lurking among your terrier's hair. You shouldn't assume that because you can't see them, they aren't there. Only combing your dog's hair with a fine-toothed flea comb or giving it a bath with a good flea shampoo will verify whether they are present or not.

Remember, fighting fleas must be done on several fronts. First, determine how extensive a flea problem you have. Have dogs or cats lived in your home prior to you moving in with your terrier? Or is your pet the first one in the residence? In the former case, you might have an entrenched flea problem that requires treating not only your pet but also the rugs and upholstery. If the latter is true, it will be your job to keep these nasty little biters from ever taking up residence.

Only about 10 percent of fleas reside on your Jack Russell, so you need to pay special attention to the carpets inside and the yards around your house. You can treat carpets by sprinkling Borax—or any of the other products currently available on the market—on your carpet and then vacuuming thoroughly. Make sure you seal the collection bag and dispose of it outside your home. Because fleas require humidity to survive and Borax dehydrates them, it is a great flea treatment and it doesn't hurt your carpet. If the flea infestation is severe, you might consider a flea bomb or, in the worst scenarios, having a professional treat the house. If you choose all-out warfare, make sure all items on the floor are removed, put away or covered and be sure to thoroughly ventilate the area afterwards.

Bet You Didn't Know

Most flea sprays, shampoos and powders are not advisable for use on a pregnant or nursing dog or on very young puppies unless otherwise directed by your vet. Also, special preparations are available for homes with pregnant or lactating women, infants or young children.

Your veterinarian is an excellent source of information for products available that are both effective and safe for you and your dog. Keep in mind that professional rug cleaning does *not* rid your carpets of fleas unless a solution is included in the cleaning process that specifically kills fleas. Also remember that there are fleas outside your home as well, and the same care should be taken to rid your yard and the surrounding area of fleas and their friends. Although fleas do not carry diseases as severe as ticks, they do account for more than half of doggie dermatological problems and can cause similar problems in humans.

If you've ever been bitten by a flea, you know firsthand how irritating those itchy little bites can be. Take care to rid them from your home and from your Jack Russell.

Fleas that actually reside on your pet can be even more difficult to eliminate. Your veterinarian might suggest one of several products on the market that will safely kill fleas and will prevent them from propagating. Feed-through products work well, are easy to administer and pose fewer health risks than a topical treatment might. Natural remedies such as feeding your dog garlic and brewer's yeast also might work to rid you and your terrier of these pests. Many people swear by them, although there are no tests to prove the efficacy of these food supplements. If you want to try it, go ahead. It won't harm your JRT and it might work for your pet. Flea collars have produced mixed results, and some might even be harmful to your terrier. Check with your vet before strapping one on.

Tick, Tack, Oh No!

Fleas are not the only pests that threaten your Jack Russell. Ticks also can be a problem, though they are more common in wooded or rural areas than in the city. Ticks are somewhat easier to manage than fleas because they do not infest the inside of your house, but they do carry more serious diseases. It is important to check your JRT for ticks immediately after it has been out playing in the woods. Ticks can carry Lyme disease, Babesia, tick paralysis, tick fever or Rocky Mountain spotted fever, all of which are potentially fatal for your terrier and also can make humans quite sick.

Bet You Didn't Know

There are two basic kinds of ticks: soft ticks that blow up like a balloon when filled with blood and hard ticks that slice open the dog's skin with their mouth parts and attach to its skin. Ticks are thirsty little devils and can drink up to 100 percent of their body weight in blood.

Ticks are small and round and can be found on your dog's body around its ears, neck, head and feet. They cling to one spot, insert their heads into your dog, and feed on its blood. One easy way to remove them is by using your thumb and first finger or a pair of tweezers and pulling firmly but gently away from your dog's skin. Usually, the tick will detach in its entirety, although occasionally the head will stay in your Jack Russell. You should remove the head if you can to prevent infection of the site. If signs of an infection develop, take your JRT to the veterinarian immediately. If possible, drop the tick in alcohol to kill it. If alcohol is unavailable, find a rock and smash the tick to kill it.

Don't try to burn a tick with a match or use petroleum products such as gas or kerosene. These "remedies" could put both you and your Jack Russell in danger. Alcohol, on the other hand, is quite safe if you apply it only on the tick and not on the surrounding skin area. Be sure to wear gloves and to avoid contact with the ticks' body fluids to avoid infecting yourself. Make sure to thoroughly wash your hands with hot soapy water after removing it.

Ticks thrive in long grass near wooded locations. If you have a heavy tick infestation in your area and your dog spends a great deal of time outdoors, you should spray your backyard thoroughly to minimize the risk of tick bites. Keep the grass mowed and the weeds down to reduce areas where ticks can hide and make it a habit to check your terrier regularly for these little blood suckers. The sooner they are removed, the less discomfort they will cause your JRT.

Tough Teeth

Dogs, like humans, have two sets of teeth. Their baby teeth, all twenty-eight of them, come in when the puppy is between 3 and 6 weeks old and are replaced by forty-two permanent teeth when your dog is about 4 months old. Your dog uses its incisors to nibble meat from bones and to groom itself, the canine teeth for holding things in its mouth and for defending itself as needed and the premolars to rip meat off bones.

Just like humans, dogs are prone to tooth problems and require regular checkups and treatment. Don't allow dental care to slide because neglected plaque and tartar can cause infections along your dog's gumline. Your Jack Russell also can develop tooth decay, and puppies can have a condition called "retained baby teeth." This condition can cause a bad bite, or malocclusion, and misaligned adult teeth later on.

187

Bet You Didn't Know

With the invention of doggy bakeries and specialty stores, it's no wonder that doggy toothpaste can now be easily found by the conscientious canine owner. You can find it in any pet store and can even find a choice of flavors to satisfy your finicky pooch!

Keep 'em Clean

Ideally, you should brush your dog's teeth daily using a child's tooth-brush or one angled specifically for a dog's mouth and a toothpaste developed especially for dogs. If you don't have the time for such extensive dental care—and unfortunately most of us don't—at least brush its teeth once a week and make sure your terrier has plenty of hard biscuits, rawhide and other chewies to help remove plaque. If, despite your best efforts, plaque still accumulates, you need to take your Jack Russell to the vet yearly to have the plaque removed. As your dog ages, it might be necessary to have its teeth cleaned more often.

Doggy Don'ts

Don't forget to care for your dog's teeth. Neglect can cause more than bad breath. It can result in a bacterial infection that travels to your terrier's bloodstream and can even damage its heart's valves.

Dogs don't usually develop cavities, but if your dog eats too much soft food, debris can accumulate in pockets at the base of its teeth. This can cause infections that soften gums and cause them to recede. Ultimately, tooth loss might occur. In areas of hard water, tartar (the result of calcium salts' accumulation) also can be a problem. If severe, it might have to be removed by your vet. Mouth odor, a yellow-brownish crust of tartar around the gumline and pain or bleeding of the gums all are signs of trouble. If noticed, these symptoms should be attended to immediately.

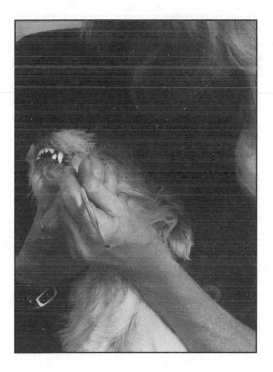

Have your JRT's teeth examined by a veterinarian on a regular basis. (photo by Laurie Mercer)

Removing the plaque, or treating other gum and dental problems, usually requires that your dog be sedated. Make sure to have your vet explain any ill effects that can be expected from these procedures.

Bathing Beauties

Depending on your Jack Russell's outside activities, you only should have to bathe it every month or so. Of course, if your terrier is out rolling in the dirt on a daily basis, you might have to bathe it a bit more frequently. Short, more frequent baths are better than long, infrequent ones. Get your dog used to baths when it's still a puppy. As with children, try to make bath time fun by combining it with a bit of playtime. Like all dog products on the market, you might find the selection of shampoos to be intimidating, but rest assured that most are fairly equal in effectiveness. A more costly shampoo is not necessarily better than an inexpensive one.

One particularly useful item you might want to check out is the dry shampoo that requires no water or rinsing. If you and your terrier are always on the go, you might want to invest in this handy cleaning solution. You'll be glad you have it on hand when you have a filthy Jack Russell and bathing your dog with regular shampoo and water isn't feasible.

Dry, Normal or Oily?

When using a shampoo with water, use one suited to your Jack Russell's coat or skin problems, if it has any. In other words, choose a moisturizing shampoo if its skin is dry and scaly or an oatmeal shampoo if your dog has a tendency to itch. Check to see that the water is warm but not hot. As you apply shampoo to its coat, work your way from the behind to the head, paying particular attention to the oily areas of its ears but avoiding the eyes. When rinsing, reverse the motion and rinse from head to rump, making sure no shampoo residue remains.

Post-Bath Prep

Keep a large towel nearby to prevent having a wet and exuberant JRT running through the house spraying water everywhere. Don't be surprised if your terrier is overcome by a bout of Jack Russell "turbo-itis" immediately after its bath. Just smile as it rockets through the house and know that this is the reason you bought a JRT in the first place.

The Ears Have It!

To avoid an unexpected ear infection or an infestation of ear mites, it's important to check your Jack Russell's ears frequently. Because JRTs frequently are out running around, they are prone to picking up infections caused by dirt and debris getting trapped in their ear canals after vigorous bouts of digging. They also can pick up ear mites, which can make your terrier miserable if left untreated. If at all possible, check your JRT's ears on a weekly basis. If you suspect that something is amiss, your vet can provide you with special ear drops to keep your dog's ears clean and wax-free. Place a few drops in each ear, massage gently and let them thoroughly penetrate if a wax buildup has already developed.

Bet You Didn't Know

Parasites in your dog's ears can be a source of infection. You often can remove ear ticks yourself, but ear mites and other types of mites usually are more insidious and require professional treatment.

If you notice your dog pawing or scratching at its ear or shaking its head, it might be a sign of an ear infection. Redness and a smelly discharge also are signs that something isn't right and that your dog needs immediate attention. These symptoms often can be caused by foreign bodies or dirt in your dog's ear, a severe case of wax buildup, ear mites, a yeast infection or otitis, which is an inflammation of the area outside the eardrum. Its symptoms are the same as those just described, and pus might be present in severe cases. In the case of ear mites, remember that they are very small and often are difficult to detect with the naked eye. In any case, you should contact your vet to diagnose the exact cause of the problem.

If you suspect your dog might have a foreign object lodged in its ear, you can place a few drops of baby or mineral oil in the ear. Massage gently to soften the object and to relieve the pain until you can have the problem addressed by a trained professional. If you hike in rugged terrain where your dog might be apt to get twigs, dirt or other foreign substances in its ears, wads of cotton are useful as a preventive measure. Whatever you do, don't stick anything down deep into your dog's ear. You could push any wax or debris farther into the ear canal, making it more difficult to get out.

Open Wide!

The time will come when you need to open your dog's mouth either to check its teeth or to administer medication. To open your dog's mouth, put your hand across its muzzle, grasp gently, say "Open!" as you push a thumb on its lip behind its canine tooth and lift its upper jaw.

Pill Poppin'

If you are administering a tablet or a capsule, gently push it all the way to the back of your terrier's throat and place it in the center of your JRT's tongue. If your Jack Russell is particularly skilled in evasion tactics, it often helps to wet the tablet or capsule or to wrap it in a soft food your dog enjoys (such as cream cheese or a piece of hot dog) to help it go down more smoothly. Otherwise, you could find the pill laying on the carpet in the next room and your crafty JRT applauding itself at its ingenuity. Remember to give your terrier a treat after each successful attempt and to use slow, gentle movements to avoid startling or frightening your terrier.

Doggy Don'ts

Don't banish your Jack Russell to the great outdoors when it smells a bit gamey. If a bath doesn't solve the problem and your terrier has had its regular dental cleanup, something else is wrong. A smelly dog often is a symptom of a more serious medical problem.

Liquid Medication

In the case of liquid medication, slowly tilt your dog's head back and hold its muzzle shut by putting your hand around it. Using a medication syringe, work the plastic tip into the back corner of the mouth. Give the medication slowly enough so that it won't choke the dog or leak out through the corners of its mouth. Never give your Jack Russell medication meant for humans or anything that hasn't been prescribed by the vet. These remedies can be unsuitable or even dangerous to your dog. If you must administer foul-tasting medication, you might be in for a bit of a struggle. Most dogs don't like to have their mouth handled and probably will try to spit the ugly stuff out. As I always say, though, better a petulant dog than a sick one!

Skinned Alive!

Many skin irritations are the result of insect or flea bites that cause your dog to scratch itself, thus aggravating the problem. Some are the result of allergies to food, pollen, dust mites or mold. Symptoms include scratching, biting, chewing and constant licking. Treatments vary widely from cool baths to allergy shots or steroids that reduce inflammation (if present), depending on the type of skin irritation and its cause. Corticosteroids are not recommended because they can have negative side effects and should be considered only as a last resort.

Flea allergies are caused by the saliva in the flea's bite and can cause your dog to be miserable for days, especially if it hasn't been exposed to fleas for some time. Don't automatically assume, however, that your JRT's itching fits are caused by fleas. Dry skin also can be a common but less-serious cause of skin irritation, and it is often easily treated using topical treatments or special conditioning shampoos.

Bet You Didn't Know

Some skin allergies are caused by foods the dog eats. This type of allergy usually manifests itself with itchy skin, anal itching, rubbing its muzzle or face on the carpet and the like.

Grooming Guidelines and Quick Clips

Grooming not only keeps your terrier looking good, it's a boon to your dog's health, too.

Coat Clippin'

All dogs shed and your smooth-coated Jack Russell is no exception, so don't expect it to be "shed free." A good outside brushing with a bristle brush or a special mitt should keep your floors and carpets as free of hair as possible. It is perfectly okay to trim errant hairs on your dog's feet, rump and abdomen area. Naturally, a rough or broken-coated Jack Russell requires a bit more care than one with a smooth coat. If you have a rough or broken-coated terrier, a stripping comb is a great help in plucking your dog's dead hair. If you really are big on coat care, you also might enjoy the convenience of a combing table if you have the room and can afford one. Just remember that grooming need not be a time-consuming experience. A thorough once-a-week brushing and a good vacuum job on the house should do just fine.

A weekly brushing should do the job for a smooth-coated JRT.

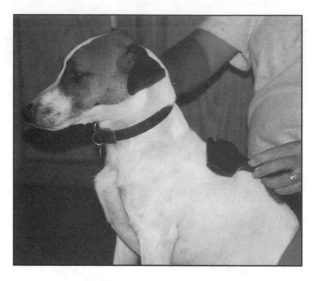

The Pedicure

Nail clipping doesn't have to be traumatic for either of you, but you should exercise a bit of caution when trimming your JRT's nails yourself. If you begin clipping your dog's nails when it is a puppy, it will become accustomed to the process and will be less likely to object. Nonetheless, don't expect your Jack Russell to be overjoyed when it sees you approaching with clippers in hand. A treat will go a long way toward softening your dog's disposition and making it a bit more accepting of its pedicure. The single-blade, guillotine-type nail clipper works best, but some people prefer the type that looks like diminutive pliers with a blade at the top and bottom.

Doggy Do's

Make sure the blades on your nail clippers are sharp. They will cut faster and with less effort and will be less apt to pinch or smash the dog's nail, which can be very painful.

To trim your terrier's nails, leave it on the ground rather than on a high table to make it feel more secure. It also makes things easier if someone can keep your terrier distracted by feeding it treats and by keeping it from moving around. Start with the rear feet, grasping its foot gently but firmly with pads facing up. Work your way forward until all twenty toenails are clipped and accounted for. Talk to your dog in a low voice to reassure it that there's nothing to worry about and give it a good hug and a treat when you are done to ease its traumatized mind.

Do not clip the nail too close to the quick. A dog's nails contain nerves and blood. Cutting them too short will hurt your terrier and will cause bleeding. You can easily distinguish the live part of the nail from the dead part (the part you want to cut) by holding your JRT's foot with the pad facing upward and observing which part is pink and which part is clear or white. The sensitive part is the red or pink part closest to the toe; the dead part is lower towards the tip.

For dogs with black toenails, you have to trim carefully to avoid accidentally nipping too close to the live part. When you're done, fuss over your dog and offer another treat. Soon your pet will become less resistant to nail cutting, making the entire experience more enjoyable for you both.

The Least You Need to Know

➤ Fleas and ticks can carry diseases and can make your JRT sick and miserable. Control them outside and inside your home as well as on your pet.

➤ Some flea and tick sprays and powders can be harmful to both you and your Jack Russell. Be sure to ask your vet what type to use.

➤ Make sure your JRT has regular dental care. It can develop not only bad breath but gumline infections that can travel into its blood stream.

➤ Give your Jack Russell short, more frequent baths rather than longer, infrequent ones.

➤ Clean and check your dog's ears often to avoid wax buildup. If your terrier paws at its ears or shakes its head, it might have an ear infection or an object lodged in its ear.

➤ Administer pills or liquid medication gently and give your JRT a treat afterward to ease its anxiety. Disguising pills in food also helps.

➤ Skin irritations usually are not serious, although they can cause your dog serious discomfort. Remember that they also can be a symptom of something more problematic.

➤ Groom your JRT once a week and trim its nails regularly. Use sharp clippers for better results and avoid the live area of the nail to prevent pain and bleeding.

Chapter 16

Chow Time!

In This Chapter

➤ Baby care basics

➤ Adult dinners

➤ Older options

It is your responsibility as a pet owner to supply your Jack Russell with the best nutrition possible, just as you do for your family. Don't base your choice of dog food on price alone. The fact that a particular brand is on sale should not be the determining factor. Carefully check the listed ingredients. After you find a brand that meets your terrier's nutritional requirements and that your JRT seems to like, stick with it.

Dogs are not like people; they do not require variety in their diet. In fact, frequent changes in food are likely to upset your dog's stomach and cause intestinal distress every time you switch brands. Some dogs might appear to like the new dog food at first but then become bored with it, so there is something to be said about buying new dog food in small quantities. This way, you won't waste your money and get stuck with a 50-pound bag of dog food that your finicky Jack won't touch.

You usually are safe buying a well-known, high-quality dog food that has undergone rigorous feeding trials and that meets the Association of American Feed Control Officials (AAFCO) recommendations. If you still are lost among the morass of available choices, check with your veterinarian for a recommended brand that will meet your JRT's needs. The lamb and rice varieties seem to prevent many skin irritations that the varieties containing corn can cause, so consider this option if your dog seems to get "hot spots" or has itchy skin.

Doggy Don'ts

Don't feed your JRT on an irregular schedule. This can affect its digestive system and can cause chronic digestive disorders. It also can make your dog frustrated and hungry at perhaps the wrong times.

Jack Russells are incredibly energetic machines. Studies have shown that their aerobic capacity exceeds that of humans by more than 200 percent, especially during exercise. Like humans, however, they need a proper balance of protein, carbohydrates and fat. The meat in dog foods provides the protein your high-octane Jack Russell needs. Many of the best dog foods on the market advertise their high-protein content as a selling point—and with good reason. Protein is the foundation upon which your dog's growth and well-being is built. Dogs are omnivores, but they primarily are carnivorous by nature. The protein derived from meat is more easily digested and is of higher quality than plant protein. Fat also is an important factor in your dog's diet, as are minerals and vitamins. Minerals and vitamins are easily overlooked, but they also should be part of the equation.

The selection of dog food on supermarket shelves is mind-boggling. There is "gourmet" food as well as food for dogs under stress, for puppies, for dogs that hunt, for fat dogs, for pregnant dogs, for skinny dogs, for middle-aged dogs and for elderly dogs. The list is endless. Then there is the choice between dry food, semimoist food and canned food. Naturally, each has pros and cons.

Dry, Canned or Semimoist

Dry food, while less appealing to your Jack Russell, is more convenient and is the preferred dog food choice. The hard nuggets give your JRT's teeth a subtle cleaning as it eats, and the texture forces your dog to work a little at its meal. This provides the "crunch resistance" your terrier needs for strong teeth and jaws.

Canned food is more expensive, has a higher moisture content, and contains color enhancers and sugar your JRT doesn't need. Because it offers no fiber substance, its prolonged use can cause plaque on your dog's teeth. It also lacks the hard texture your terrier needs to develop normal chewing action and good teeth. If your JRT is on a canned-food-only diet, you need to supplement it with plenty of chew sticks, rawhide bones, and dog biscuits so these needs can be met in other ways.

Semimoist food tastes good and is handy, especially when you travel with your dog. It is high in sugar content, however, and is the least favored as a nutritional choice. It offers so little resistance that it provides no strengthening value to your dog's jaws, and its clingy texture can play havoc on your terrier's pearly whites. Use this type of food only as a last resort or as a supplement to your JRT's hard food.

Scraps from the table, while okay as an occasional treat, should *not* become a regular part of your dog's diet. Your intentions might be good, but you actually could be giving your terrier a case of gas or diarrhea as soon as the foreign food works its way through your JRT's system. I know, I know! Who can resist those begging eyes as you wolf down your pizza or the last bite of a hot dog without sharing with your pet? Give in when you *must*, but try to keep these kinds of treats to a minimum.

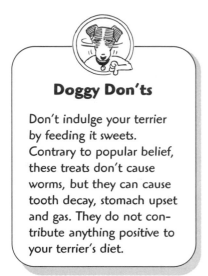

Doggy Don'ts

Don't indulge your terrier by feeding it sweets. Contrary to popular belief, these treats don't cause worms, but they can cause tooth decay, stomach upset and gas. They do not contribute anything positive to your terrier's diet.

Baby Care Basics

It's important to know that a puppy will multiply its birth body weight eight times before becoming a full-grown dog. It is easy to see how important it is to feed your puppy a formula specifically designed for its growing needs to ensure a healthy, happy puppy and, eventually, a healthy, well-formed dog.

Puppies get all their nourishment from their mother until they are about 4 weeks old. Around that time, the breeder will begin to introduce puppy foods. After you bring your puppy home, it's up to you to select a dog food geared to your growing little bundle's nutritional needs. Although protein is very important in your puppy's growth and development, there is evidence that too much protein can cause skeletal, joint and ligament problems. Your puppy's food should be balanced with vitamins, minerals, fats, carbohydrates and proteins. Again, when in doubt, choose a dog food your veterinarian recommends and stick with it.

Remember that puppies, like small children, have tiny stomachs. Feed your baby dog small quantities several times a day instead of expecting it to get its nutritional needs from one big meal. It's a good idea to mix dry and canned meat food to create a blend your puppy will enjoy. Be sure to remove the dish about thirty or forty-five minutes after your dog has eaten, discard the unused food and serve fresh food at the next feeding. Once the puppy is eating well, feed it dry food only and let it access its food whenever it likes. This way your puppy learns to eat when it's hungry, and it will not gorge itself whenever food is in sight. JRTs are active little dogs; rarely will you see an overweight JRT puppy unless it is being fed something other than dog food.

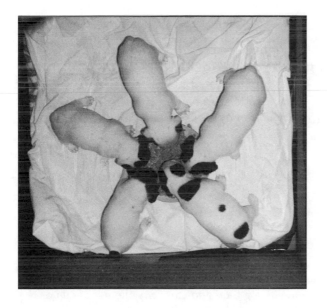

At the breeder's facility, puppies are fed a good-quality puppy chow. It's a good idea to start your pup on the same food it was used to eating. If you have questions about what type of food to buy, ask your vet.

The puppy will gradually reduce its food intake to twice a day. Again, keep in mind that table tidbits are not recommended, particularly for puppies. The calorie content is high and the nutrition is negligible. In no time, you will create a begging puppy that is sure to grow into a full-fledged begging hound. After one year, you can begin to introduce your puppy to adult dog food. Be sure to do so gradually, however, and make sure it has plenty of water to drink with its food. You also can feed your puppy in its crate. This helps create the feeling that the crate is a good place to be, and the dog gradually will look forward to meals in its own private dining room. As an added bonus, this acclimates your puppy to the crate for future fun trips with you.

If you have more than one puppy or dog, each one should have its own food and water bowls. This prevents fighting over food or one puppy getting more to eat than another. If you free-feed, such bickering will be minimized because both dogs can eat whenever they are hungry. Free-feeding, however, doesn't work for all breeds or all dogs. If one dog has a weight problem or is significantly bigger than the other, this arrangement won't work. But two Jack Russells of basically the same age (or same stage of life) should have no problem free-feeding and maintaining their fit figure.

Adult Dinners

Just like humans, it isn't healthy for a dog to be overweight. Like you, your dog is what it eats. Don't fall for the myth that, if you want a strong, healthy dog, you must feed it plenty of meat and feed it often. Your terrier's appearance is a pretty good indication of its health. If you are starting to see dramatic weight gain or scratchy spots on its coat, the dog food you have chosen could be the culprit.

Bet You Didn't Know

Dogs and humans metabolize protein in much the same way. Because eggs are too expensive to use in dog food and can carry the risk of salmonella, beef, lamb and chicken commonly are used to supply the protein needed by your dog.

Feed your adult dog kibble or dry food as its basic meal, and remember to buy the best you can afford. In the long run, this food will save you money in vet bills. Another benefit of premium food is that your dog needs less food to feel full than with a cheaper brand. Premium dog foods have all the nutrients your dog needs, other than the water you provide. Barring specific problems, your adult dog should not need additional vitamin or mineral supplements. An acceptable premium dog food should contain 22 to 26 percent protein and 12 to 15 percent fat for both puppies and adults and should provide all the vitamins and minerals the dog needs. The food also should be easily digested and should be tested as having a low probability for food allergies.

Naturally, your Jack Russell's food requirements will vary depending on its level of activity, its stress level and its health. A lactating dam feeding seven puppies needs to eat more often than an adult male, and outdoor pets require more fuel than indoor dogs. Jack Russells that are active in show and hunting competitions require the most calories, and the quality of dog food becomes even more important for these active athletes. If your terrier is involved in any of these activities, watch it closely to make sure it doesn't drop weight.

Watch for Weight Loss

Be aware that some terriers can lose weight rapidly. All of a sudden, you might wake up one morning to find that your JRT looks like a Greyhound. A dramatic weight loss usually is caused by an increase in exercise with no corresponding increase in food intake. If you know your dog will be changing its activity level, increase its food quality or amount just prior to undertaking the activity. If no such change has occurred, your terrier might have a digestive tract problem and should be taken to the vet for diagnosis. It is not normal for your JRT to experience significant weight fluctuations, and your dog should be evaluated by a professional if this occurs.

And for Weight Gain

If it looks like your dog is getting a bit pudgy and you can't afford a membership to the nearest canine gym, slowly decrease its food intake and increase its exercise. You can accomplish this by playing ball in your yard, taking trips to the nearest park, going on more frequent beach excursions or taking additional walks—anything that provides some added physical exertion in your terrier's day. Remember, your JRT is high energy by nature. If you make the commitment to own a Jack Russell, you make the commitment to provide a suitable, healthy environment. If the pudginess continues, consult your veterinarian.

Doggy Don'ts

Never feed your Jack Russell chicken, pork, lamb or fish bones, which can penetrate your dog's intestine or stomach and can be fatal. Also avoid chocolate, raw meat and alcohol. Dogs have died as the result of their owner's misguided sense of humor in giving them alcohol.

Because of their energy level, young and middle-aged Jack Russell Terriers rarely have a problem with obesity as long as they are on a healthy diet and have plenty of room to run and play. If your dog's coat seems lackluster and its energy level is low, don't take it upon yourself to add vitamins or minerals to its diet. Consult your vet for the appropriate course of action. These problems can be signs of something more serious.

Dinnertime Hi-Jinks

Now is a good time for a word of warning. Many Jack Russells are hit-and-run eaters. If you have hardwood floors, they can make you nuts with the pitter-patter of tiny toenails. Their favorite method of dining is to go to the dog-food bowl, take out four or five nuggets of food, walk to the nearest carpet, drop the nuggets and eat them one by one. They then walk back to the bowl and repeat the procedure. If your terrier is one of these sniper eaters, it doesn't matter how hungry it is or how hard you try to convince it otherwise—it will not stay at the bowl and chow down. This is why it is wise to place your terrier's food bowl on some type of carpet. Not all JRTs eat using this method, but it is prevalent enough to be worth mentioning.

Older Dog Options

Modern veterinary science has progressed by leaps and bounds to protect the health of older dogs and to increase their longevity. Now, more than ever, it is imperative that you shun cheaper dog food and stick to what your Jack Russell is used to. Keep in mind that, as your terrier gets older and less active, it should consume fewer calories to keep it from getting fat or even obese. Like all older dogs, even JRTs slow down a little as they mature. You should keep an eye on your older dog's weight.

Doggy Don'ts

Don't punish your older JRT if it relieves itself in the house. Older Jack Russells can lose control of their bladders as they age, and they are not soiling the house on purpose. They simply can't control their bladders long enough to head outside.

Older dogs often develop kidney problems, and it is important that your aging JRT be fed lower levels of protein. The protein does not cause kidney dysfunction, but high levels of protein can escalate an existing problem. Like a puppy, your older Jack Russell should be fed smaller meals more often. Dietary fat, especially human food scraps, should be kept to a minimum.

Don't forget to provide plenty of steady, low-impact exercise for your aging terrier. Just because it is slowing down a bit doesn't mean it wants to become a couch potato. Older terriers still love to go on walks and to play a toned-down game of fetch. They still can accompany you on trips to the park and will want to be included in your daily activities. Just use common sense to know when to quit and make sure your older JRT doesn't get overheated.

Internal body changes occur as your dog ages, resulting in decreased utilization and intestinal absorption of nutrients. This is when, under your veterinarian's supervision, vitamin and mineral supplements come into play. Keep in mind that, if a weight gain occurs due to fewer calories being burned, this places additional stress on your dog's heart and lungs. Conversely, if its digestive system becomes less efficient as it gets older, your dog might have difficulty maintaining its body weight.

The Least You Need to Know

➤ Buy the best, most well-balanced dog food you can afford. When in doubt, consult your vet.

➤ Protein is important in your terrier's diet, but so are carbohydrates, fats, minerals and vitamins.

➤ Because of the enormous selection of dog foods available, you need to learn to read the labels. Buy one that meets the AAFCO feeding trial standards.

➤ Feed your puppy several small meals a day, or let your puppy access its food at all times during the day.

➤ Feed your adult JRT good-quality, dry kibble. If you have more than one adult dog, feed them with separate bowls.

➤ As they age, Jack Russells require less food and lower protein in their diets.

➤ Don't forget to provide exercise for your older terrier. It actually needs exercise more than ever, just in more sedate doses.

Special Needs

In This Chapter

➤ General genetics

➤ Disabilities demystified

➤ Elegant elders

➤ When at last we say goodbye

In spite of the efforts of Jack Russell breeders to rid the breed of all genetic problems, some disorders still pop up from time to time. Under JRTCA rules, veterinary examinations and photographs are necessary to register a dog. These practices have helped shore up the breed's gene pool. Nonetheless, inherited health issues continue in JRTs.

General Genetics

This section discusses some of the more common problems found in the breed. It should be understood, however, that this is *not* an all-inclusive list, and it should not be used as a guide to diagnosis. Always seek your vet's advice for any symptom or problem you might encounter in your JRT.

Bet You Didn't Know

Jack Russell Terriers enjoy good health and, compared to most purebred breeds, are remarkably free of inherited diseases. Responsible and careful breeding can help ensure that this trend continues, as can continued loving care and attention on the part of the owner.

Lens Luxation

Lens luxation is a fairly common inherited disease of the eye in which one or both lenses become partially or completely dislocated from their normal location behind the cornea. In the case of complete dislocation, the lens will be painful and the eye will look red or opaque. Lens luxation, if left untreated, can develop into glaucoma. The condition usually manifests itself later in life and should be treated as soon as it is diagnosed to prevent blindness. This condition seems to be relatively common among terriers and, particularly, among Jack Russell Terriers.

Cerebellar Ataxia

Cerebellar ataxia is a neurological disorder resulting from degeneration of the cerebellum's cortex. The degeneration can progress steadily and cause a stagger in the dog's gait. If your terrier appears wobbly on its feet or disoriented from time to time, this disorder could be the cause.

Cardiomyopathy

Cardiomyopathy, an abnormality of the heart muscle, can result in lung edema (water in the lung), weakness during exercise and even sudden death. This defect is difficult for the average owner to detect, but if you notice your JRT having trouble after a walk or a run in the park or if you hear it wheezing when it breathes, you should explore this possibility.

208

Legg-Calve-Perthes Disease

Legg-Calve-Perthes (Legg-Calve) disease is a septic necrosis, or degeneration, of the head of the femur (the thigh bone). It usually does not manifest itself until a puppy is at least 6 months old, and it can result in progressive rear-leg lameness. It primarily affects small breeds. If you notice that one of your terrier's legs looks different than the other three or that one is particularly susceptible to becoming sore, this disease could be causing the problem.

High Toes

The term short, or "high," toes applies to a condition in which the toes are shorter than normal in a full-grown terrier, giving the appearance of toes that do not touch the ground. This occurs primarily on the front feet, but it has been seen on hind feet as well. Although not a debilitating defect, it is considered a breeding fault. JRTs with this disorder should not be bred.

Cryptorchidism

Cryptorchidism is the failure of one or both testicles to descend into the scrotum. The testicle is retained in the abdomen or inguinal area, and it may slide in and out of the scrotum. You can easily detect this problem because your male terrier will appear to have only one testicle in the scrotum or will alternately have two and then one, depending on the day. Although this is not a life-threatening problem, it is best to neuter a terrier born with chryptorchidism. Even if you choose not to neuter, a cryptorchid dog should never be bred.

When to Call the Vet

Symptoms of Cushing's Syndrome include increased drinking and urination, hair loss and a darkening of the skin. If you notice any of these symptoms in your Jack Russell, schedule an appointment with your veterinarian and have your dog examined.

Hernias

Hernias occur when a one of the dog's organs or tissues protrudes through a body wall. The most common of these are the inguinal hernia and the umbilical hernia. These occur when a portion of the intestine falls through the scrotal opening or through the umbilical opening. You will notice a bulge in the dog's stomach or scrotum that looks like a growth. Take your dog to a veterinarian immediately. A dog born with a hernia should not be bred.

Bet You Didn't Know

Oligodontia is not the name of a new fat substitute. It is the absence of most, if not all, teeth in JRTs.

Hydrocephaly

Hydrocephaly results from an accumulation of fluid in the brain, and it causes the brain to degenerate. The afflicted dog often becomes disoriented or runs into objects while walking. Sadly, dogs with this condition do not usually live long. For those that survive, treatment often is ineffective. Hydrocephalic dogs often are euthanized.

Progressive Neuronal Abiotrophy

Progressive neuronal abiotrophy (or ataxia) causes tremors and a lack of coordination in dogs and is caused by degeneration of the cerebellum's cortex responsible for coordinating movements. As a result, a dog develops a staggering gait and becomes unable to stand or even eat.

Patent Ductus Arteriosus

Patent Ductus Arteriosus is caused by the failure of the fetal vessel between the aorta and the pulmonary artery to close at birth, causing heart murmurs, weakness and even death. Special care must be taken of dogs with this condition because they are susceptible when exerted even with moderate exercise. Surgery for this disorder can be quite effective, especially if performed when the dog is young. Again, this is a problem that cannot be diagnosed unless the dog is examined by a veterinarian. Whenever you suspect your terrier might have a problem, even if you don't know what it might be, schedule an appointment with your vet.

Von Willebrand's Disease

Von Willebrand's disease, also referred to as vWD, is a common, inherited bleeding disorder that manifests itself through abnormal platelet function. Symptoms include ongoing bleeding of the gums and nose, bloody urine, prolonged bleeding during estrus or after the birth of a litter and excessive bleeding after surgery or even a slight nick while trimming your Jack Russell's nails. It is caused by an insufficient von Willebrand factor, a blood protein that binds platelets to blood vessels.

The disease usually attacks purebred dogs, although mixed breeds also can be affected. The good news is that it is not as common in JRTs as in other breeds. The bad news is that it can crop up from time to time, and it is serious enough to warrant testing if you suspect your terrier might be a victim. It is important to test for vWD early on, and many experienced and responsible breeders have their breeding stock tested prior to breeding. Breeders often advertise their litters as having been tested for von Willebrand's disease.

Continued bleeding in humans is nothing to laugh at, and it is no laughing matter in the case of your Jack Russell Terrier either. If you notice that your JRT has a tendency to bleed easily or that bleeding continues for a significant amount of time after a small nick or cut, notify your veterinarian and ask for his advice. Mention the fact that your terrier bleeds easily and that the bleeding is difficult to stop.

Disabilities Demystified

Some JRTs suffer from sensory disorders. With the right treatment and/or care, most disabled dogs can live a long and happy life.

Deafness

Deafness is not uncommon in Jack Russells, and it can occur in one (unilateral) or both (bilateral) ears. It often is possible to detect bilateral deafness in young dogs. A Brainstem Auditory Evoked Response (BAER) test can be performed on puppies as young as 5 weeks old;

the test monitors the puppy's brain's electrical impulses. Most responsible breeders advertise their stock as being BAER tested and clear.

Glaucoma

Untreated glaucoma is a serious problem that can lead to partial or total blindness if not quickly addressed. The pressure from fluid built up within the eye can crush the retina's cells and can cause damage to the iris and the cornea. Symptoms include a dilated pupil, cloudiness in the cornea, an increase in the size of the blood vessels in the eye's white portion and pain causing the dog to paw or rub at its eye. For more information about eye-related disorders, contact the Canine Eye Registration Foundation (CERF). This organization is an excellent resource that is dedicated to the public's education about canine eye disease. CERF can provide considerable information about eye disease and about breed-specific eye problems.

When to Call the Vet

If you notice blood in your Jack Russell's stool or urine, call the vet right away. It could be a symptom of bladder, urethra or prostate problems, or it could be a sign of kidney disease. An increase in water intake frequently is recommended for dogs with kidney problems.

Don't Panic

Although this list certainly is daunting, rest assured that there are far fewer occurrences of the preceding disorders and diseases in JRTs than in many other breeds. If all this medical mumbo-jumbo makes your head swim, just follow some simple advice. If you notice any of these symptoms in your dog or if you suspect something isn't right, you should notify your vet right away. Some disorders can be managed and treated; others are irreversible, and you will need to make an informed decision regarding your dog's future.

Elegant Elders

You and your dog are headed for your daily walk. As you bend down to hook up its leash, you suddenly notice that its muzzle looks grayer. As you trot down the street together, its gait is slower and it seems to tire more easily.

You might not have noticed the passage of time, and the realization that your beloved terrier is getting older can be difficult to accept. As your dog ages, there are some things that you, as a loving, caring owner, must watch for.

Fitness for Seniors

Jack Russell Terriers are known to retain their pep far longer than many breeds. As a general rule, they age very well. Even the feistiest terrier, however, is likely to become less active over time. Your dog might sleep more and might look a bit stiff after lying down for extended periods of time. It might exhibit signs of arthritis and often will prefer to sun itself in the backyard rather than chase a Frisbee.

You must exercise your older JRT using any physical activity it enjoys. If you don't, its internal workings will slow, and age will creep more

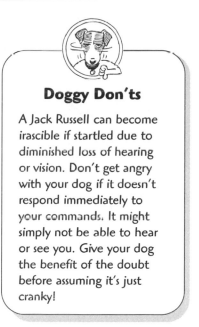

Doggy Don'ts

A Jack Russell can become irascible if startled due to diminished loss of hearing or vision. Don't get angry with your dog if it doesn't respond immediately to your commands. It might simply not be able to hear or see you. Give your dog the benefit of the doubt before assuming it's just cranky!

quickly into its joints. Its toenails will grow longer and will need to be trimmed more often. It also might gain weight and begin to appear more lethargic. Keep in mind, however, reasons other than age might keep your dog from being active. If your dog suddenly favors the rug near the fire rather than a walk down the street, and if it greets you with less than enthusiasm as you approach with leash in hand, your vet should check it for arthritis, heart problems, lameness or any number of problems that could account for its lack of energy.

I cannot overemphasize the importance of exercise to help your older dog keep its weight down, its joints more flexible, its heart strong and its *joie de vivre* intact. Part of a Jack Russell Terrier's charm is its bright, happy nature and its willingness to play. Just because it doesn't voluntarily leap and jump like it used to doesn't mean it won't enjoy a good game of fetch or a walk around the park. You should encourage as much activity as your terrier can comfortably handle. If you keep your older Jack Russell active, it will reward you with many good years of love and companionship.

Your senior JRT might be content to spend a lot of time just watching the world go by. But it still needs (and probably wants) to get consistent exercise.
(photo by Catherine Romaine Brown)

Weather Woes

Cold weather often will take its toll on your older JRT, and you often will find it buried under the comforter on your bed during the winter months. Extreme temperatures should be avoided because your older dog will find it more difficult to adjust to extreme cold or heat. If you must take it to Alaska or to some other chilly place, a heating pad and a warm sweater will help. You still should be very careful not to get it overly chilled. Conversely, if Death Valley is your destination, make sure your Jack Russell has plenty of fresh water to drink and keep the air conditioner on cool.

Never leave your dog unattended in a car during the summer, no matter what its age or how short a time you plan to stop. The temperature in a car can escalate in minutes to well over 100 degrees, and this can quickly cause a life-threatening situation for your dog. Surely you've encountered the two-minute pit stop that turned into a fifteen-minute expedition. Although this usually is just a cause of aggravation and frustration, with your beloved JRT waiting in the sweltering car, you could be signing its death warrant. Resist temptation and either have your passenger take your JRT for a walk while you're in the store or bypass the stop altogether.

The Elder Appetite

A diet change can be traumatic for an older dog, so forget about introducing it to Beluga caviar or Camembert. An older dog needs a balanced diet consistent with its current needs. Choose a good-quality dog food recommended by your veterinarian or one your dog enjoys and stick with it. Two or more feedings a day are better than one big meal. It is not unusual for an older dog to eat more slowly and sometimes pick at its food, but if you notice a marked change in its eating habits or a sudden gain or loss in weight, call the vet to make sure your dog is not ill. A sick dog often stops eating or drinking altogether, which can lead to rapid weight loss and dehydration.

Overweight Jack Russell Terriers are rare because they are so active, but this can become a problem for a senior dog that doesn't exercise as much as before. The added pounds are likely to tax its heart and joints. Just because your older JRT begins packing on the pounds, however, doesn't necessarily mean it's eating too much. Weight gain also can be the result of illness or disease rather than a slower metabolism. If arthritis develops, a heating pad, aspirin or a drug prescribed by your vet can help.

Bet You Didn't Know

It often is more difficult for an older Jack Russell Terrier to adjust to another adult dog or to the family children than to adjust to a puppy or a younger dog.

Other Aging Issues

Sight and hearing decrease as your dog ages. Your dog might experience a hardening of the lens, making its eyes look a blue-gray color that nature never intended. This does not significantly affect its vision, but cataracts resulting from diabetes can make your older Jack

Russell's vision blurry. These problems easily can be corrected with the help of surgery. Again, ask your vet if you see any of these signs or have any questions.

Older dogs often develop an unpleasant odor as the result of poor dental hygiene, impacted anal sacs, ear problems or kidney dysfunction. Any malodorous and unusual smells should be investigated. Breath mints won't help here, but a vet's thorough cleaning of accumulated tartar, usually done under anesthesia, will. Although this routine is easily performed on younger dogs, your older JRT might be at a greater risk from being put under. A general checkup is advisable prior to subjecting your dog to anesthesia. Your vet can inform you of the options available to solve the problem without taking too much risk with your old-timer.

When at Last We Say Goodbye

Parting is such sweet sorrow and, despite all your tender, loving care and your JRT's long lifespan, the time inevitably will come when your best efforts, your love and your vet's most devoted care no longer can prevent the advance of time or can remedy its ravages. You will have to say goodbye to your old loyal friend.

Bet You Didn't Know

Jack Russell Terriers have been known to live more than 15 years, and some live considerably longer. Better choose your dog wisely—it could be around for a while!

It is a cruel fact of life that dogs don't live as long as humans. Tough as they are, they eventually will succumb to either illness, injury or old age.

Don't be ashamed or embarrassed to cry at the loss of your Jack Russell. It's normal after the many years of love and companionship you and your JRT have shared, and you have earned the right to grieve for your terrier. Ignore the oafish, insensitive comments of people who say "It was just a dog." If they have never owned a pet, they don't know what they have missed and can't relate to what you are feeling. Instead, try to surround yourself with friends and family who also knew and loved your JRT. Know that, as much as it hurts, you will feel better with the passage of time.

Talk with your vet and decide on an appropriate time to say goodbye. If your dog is in pain and the vet feels further treatment would only prolong that pain, it would be kindest to ease any obvious suffering by having your dog humanely euthanized. You can and should enlist your vet's help when making this very personal and difficult decision. By preventing your Jack Russell from further suffering, you are giving it the gift of freedom from pain, and it will appreciate your sacrifice.

The time might come when you want to purchase another JRT. A new dog can never replace the one you lost, but it can give you a second opportunity to love a member of that very special breed. Take your time, however, before entering into another friendship. You need to grieve and to resolve your feelings before you can open your heart to another rotten Russell. Although it might never be the same, remember that each terrier is unique in its own wonderful way. The new JRT might bring you different joys than your lost friend did.

The Least You Need to Know

➤ Jack Russells are a relatively healthy breed, but an awareness of genetic disorders and their symptoms is important for any JRT owner.

➤ Deafness can occur in one or both ears, and it can be detected through a BAER test on puppies as young as 5 weeks old.

➤ Untreated glaucoma can lead to blindness in your dog.

➤ Your JRT probably will slow down as it ages, making frequent exercise and a balanced diet increasingly important.

➤ Older terriers have unique physical problems. By staying vigilant for changes in your JRT's ability and behavior, you can gauge when to ask for your vet's advice and when a problem might be lurking.

➤ Losing your Jack Russell or deciding on euthanasia is an extremely difficult time for you and your family. Don't be ashamed of your feelings and allow yourself time to grieve before purchasing another JRT.

Part 5

Free-for-All Fun!

Although training is undeniably important, it's even more important to have fun with your Jack Russell Terrier. After all, that's why you bought a dog in the first place, isn't it? If you are the unimaginative sort, however, or if you just need a nudge toward a place to start, this is the section for you!

Having fun with your terrier doesn't have to be limited to playing ball or going for a walk. When you think about it, the possibilities truly are endless. This part helps focus your efforts on activities that fit within your lifestyle. From having fun at the beach to Jack Russell Terrier trials to trips to faraway places, this section helps get you on your way and helps make your planned outing a successful one. It might even prompt you and your family to take up a new pastime. So get off the couch and have some fun!

Chapter 18

Let's Play Ball

In This Chapter

➤ Bouncing balls

➤ Frisbee fun

➤ Laser tag

➤ Jogging, jetsetting and other amusements

➤ Dog parks

➤ Nature at its best

➤ Winter wonderland

This book has discussed how to train your JRT puppy, how to make your home a safe haven for your terrier and some of the health problems your dog may encounter. But what are some of the ways to have loads of fun with both your terrier and your family and still keep everyone safe? The only limitation is your imagination.

Bouncing Balls

Talk to any Jack Russell Terrier owner and he will tell you that his JRT's favorite toy is a ball of some sort. The ball can be hard or soft, old or new, big or small; regardless of its size or texture, your Jack Russell Terrier will absolutely love it. Unlike your child's favorite toy that was outgrown within a few months, a JRT's ball is a toy for life. Terriers that are old and gray still respond to a ball with the same glee and excitement as a 6-month-old puppy. Don't you wish your children were so easy to please?

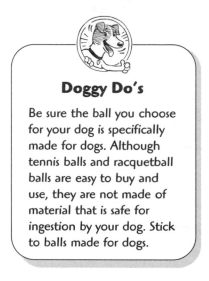

Doggy Do's

Be sure the ball you choose for your dog is specifically made for dogs. Although tennis balls and racquetball balls are easy to buy and use, they are not made of material that is safe for ingestion by your dog. Stick to balls made for dogs.

The type of ball you choose will depend on your needs and your plans for its use. If you will be leaving the ball on your living room floor or in your yard so your dog has easy access to a play toy, you need to choose a ball made of tough nylon. These balls are made with strong jaws in mind and can withstand the rigors of constant chewing. Keep in mind, though, that these tough balls always should be rolled and should never be thrown or used for catch. Because they are extremely hard, you could unintentionally injure your dog by accidentally hitting it, or it could break a tooth by trying to catch the ball in mid-air.

Other balls, such as the balls made with softer nylon or polyurethane, are great for throwing. They bounce and are soft on your terrier's mouth for catching, but they cannot take being constantly gnawed on. Plan to use these balls for games of fetch and toss (where you are in possession of the ball most of the time) and be sure to put the ball in a safe place that is out of reach from your terrier when you are through playing catch.

Balls made of other substances—such as string, cotton and plastic—also work well for structured play, provided they are put away afterward. Don't forget that your crafty Jack Russell will remember where you hide its favorite ball, and any hiding place should be secure enough that your terrier can't injure itself by trying to get to it.

Remember to use your imagination when playing ball with your Jack Russell Terrier. Try playing ball inside your house, where the ball can ricochet down hallways or into different rooms. Your JRT will be amused for hours chasing and trying to find the ball when it seemingly disappears behind an open door. You also can bounce the ball on the ground, encouraging your JRT to jump up after it. Because Jack Russells are natural jumpers, they love to watch the ball bounce and try to gauge when the perfect time is to jump up and meet it on the way down. I guess you could say this increases eye-mouth coordination!

When playing outside, the possibilities for fun are almost limitless. Throw the ball against a fence to really make your JRT jump, or teach it to wait away from you as you throw the ball high into the air for it to catch. Active JRTs love this game and will run at full speed. They carefully watch the air so they can time both their distance and their jump departure to perfectly match the course of the ball in the air.

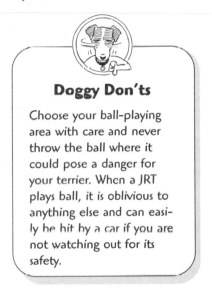

Doggy Don'ts

Choose your ball-playing area with care and never throw the ball where it could pose a danger for your terrier. When a JRT plays ball, it is oblivious to anything else and can easily be hit by a car if you are not watching out for its safety.

For added fun, get several dogs involved (after proper introduction, of course) and have a race to see who can get to the thrown ball the quickest. You can arrange an obstacle course in which the dogs have to go through, over or around one or more obstacles to fetch the ball. It's fun to see which dog figures it out first, though it is likely to be your own terrier. Enjoy your dog and enjoy being creative with it. It will make your play time more fun and enjoyable for both you and your pooch.

Frisbee Fun

Like balls, your Jack Russell loves a good game of Frisbee. Whether in the park or in your backyard, JRTs have a natural propensity to watch things and, coupled with their extraordinary jumping ability, are naturals for flying, spinning objects. Using a Frisbee made just for dogs adds an even more amusing element because these Frisbees have "mouth-holds" that make the Frisbee easier to catch and hold than Frisbees made only for human hands.

Although playing Frisbee inside might prove difficult without rearranging all the valuables in your living room, outside possibilities abound. You can use the Frisbee for long, bounding sprints or for sky-high catch targets. You even can roll it on edge on the ground; this makes

Let your dog work off some excess energy with a game of Frisbee. You'll both have a great time!

for a great spinning, rolling toy. We all know how much JRTs like objects that look like wheels! Regardless of how you use the Frisbee, encourage your terrier to leap, jump, run and catch. You will have a healthy, happy terrier when it returns to the confines of your home.

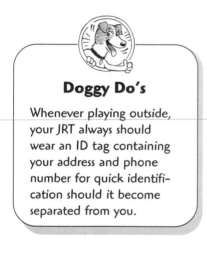

Doggy Do's

Whenever playing outside, your JRT always should wear an ID tag containing your address and phone number for quick identification should it become separated from you.

Laser Tag

What can you do in the winter months when neither of you are interested in braving the elements to fit in a little exercise? Does this mean you are doomed to months of dealing with a hyperactive terrier? Or are there toys made specifically for indoor play? Of course there are, and some might be as close as your nearest toy store.

Jack Russells are fascinating little creatures, and they are amused by a wide variety of play toys. From motorized stuffed animals to tiny laser beams of light, indoor playtime can be just as satisfying and as exhausting as an outdoor romp for your terrier. It just takes a little ingenuity on your part and a ready-to-play terrier.

One of the best toys on the market for your JRT's indoor amusement is the pet laser. This tiny toy will lead to hours of fun and hilarity in your household, and your JRT will never tire of chasing it around the floor and up the walls. The toy is actually a small, cylindrical tube that holds a tiny light source. When turned on, a pin-point colored beam of light glows on whatever surface the light is aimed at. To your JRT, it looks like a bug on the wall or the floor. Given that most terriers are fascinated with hunting bugs or other such prey, this toy has become a favorite of Jack Russell Terrier owners across the nation.

You can use the pet laser to draw intricate patterns on the ground, up the walls and even onto the ceiling, and your terrier terror will follow it every step of the way. Some JRTs get so intent on catching the elusive little light that they actually jump several feet off the ground trying to grab it from the wall or the ceiling. All this usually keeps family members in hysterics as they watch the dog perform amazing acts of contortion in an effort to catch the tiny light beam. It also is highly amusing to friends and neighbors who have never seen this side of your JRT.

Other toys originally meant for human use, such as light sabers, cones, plastic wands and the like, can keep your dog more than satisfied when the weather won't cooperate. Just go to the toy store with your dog in mind and make sure whatever you choose is durable enough to stand up to your dog's strong jaws. Remember never to leave such toys laying about for your dog to chew on. They weren't made for this type of abuse, and your dog could be injured if it ingests part or all of such a toy.

Toys for Tugging

Old socks and T-shirts also can make great chew and tug-of-war toys for your terrier, especially if you have two dogs that can play together. Tie knots in them to give your terrier something to hold on to and then hold the other end and let it pull to its heart's content. Be careful not to pull back too hard because you could loosen a tooth. You probably will be amazed at just how strong your Jack Russell really is.

Two dogs together really can get a workout with these tug-of-war toys. Put one dog on each end and watch the fun begin. They will growl ferociously and will pull back and forth, alternating with

225

vicious shaking of their heads as if to kill the beast in their clutches. This is great fun for your terrier and is good for teeth cleaning as well. The cotton acts as a dental cleaner, and the pulling action gives your dog's jaws a healthy round of exercise. Couple this with some rounds of fetch with the sock, and you can wear your JRT out in no time or at least get it a little tired. When the sock or shirt gets too ratty around the edges, simply throw it away and tie up a new one.

Bet You Didn't Know

Jack Russells love toys of all sizes and shapes—especially noisy ones—but they also can be satisfied for hours with an old sock or a rope tug.

Jogging, Jet Setting and Other Amusements

Although your Jack Russell Terrier is small, it is blessed with a huge heart in its chest, not to mention a huge lung capacity. Remember that these dogs were bred to go on the hunt and to run with the hounds in search of their prey. Not only do they have a virtually boundless energy supply, their potential for extreme physical fitness also is very strong.

If you are an outgoing family by nature, and hopefully you are if you've chosen to own a JRT, you should have no problem finding ways to exercise and enjoy your terrier. Likewise, your terrier should have no problem keeping up with your busy lifestyle and is likely to thrive in such a bustling, active environment.

Don't feel as if you will wear out your terrier. This really isn't likely. Instead, take your canine friend with you as much as possible, and you will learn to love its company and the attention you get when your terrier steps out on the town with you. Because of their size, JRTs are easy to take along in a car, and they love to watch and smell anything and everything around them.

Any outdoor jaunt can prove interesting for your terrier and fun for you, provided you have spent some time teaching your dog the basics of good doggy citizenship and are prepared to pick up after it should nature call while you are out and about. Introduce your JRT to new people and dogs slowly to make sure the meeting goes well and keep your dog on a leash if it is outside your car and in an unenclosed area.

On the Run

Jogging is a wonderful pastime for both you and your JRT. Unless you are a world-class runner, however, you will probably find that your terrier can outlast you even on your best days. Not only will your JRT keep up with you, you might find yourself pushing a little harder or a little farther to see if you actually can wear the little bugger out!

As an added bonus, people will love your terrier's bouncy, energetic nature. You will find that bringing your pooch along enables you to meet all sorts of new and fun people.

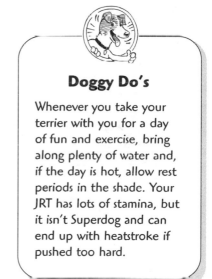

Doggy Do's

Whenever you take your terrier with you for a day of fun and exercise, bring along plenty of water and, if the day is hot, allow rest periods in the shade. Your JRT has lots of stamina, but it isn't Superdog and can end up with heatstroke if pushed too hard.

And if somewhere down the line you do need protection, your canine bodyguard is just the length of a leash away. Don't be fooled by your JRT's happy nature. It can turn into a very effective and protective guard dog if it feels your safety is threatened.

Biking

Biking also can be a good, shared hobby if you take the time to teach your terrier the rules of the road and if you aren't going on a marathon ride. Be sure your dog is totally comfortable on a leash and is well schooled in the heel command. When this is accomplished, begin taking it out for short jaunts with your bike and keep your speed slow should your terrier mistakenly dart out in front of you. As your terrier begins to understand what is expected of it, it will stay next to you as you bike along. Keep in mind, however, that your terrier is running much farther than if you were simply jogging, so keep your distances within reason for your dog.

Horsing Around

JRTs and horses seem to go together like birds of a feather. A JRT can be a wonderful help around the barn. It will keep it free of the rats and mice that love to chew holes in feed sacks and leather tack, and most horses seem to accept the presence of these terriers with remarkable ease. Even grumpy horses that don't particularly care for dogs are tolerant of these zippy white streaks that go running through their stalls.

The number of Jack Russell Terriers purchased by horse owners across the United States has grown dramatically in the past several years. Many horse owners are accustomed to having these little dogs around and welcome their company, provided they behave themselves and are not unruly or destructive. Our JRTs accompany us on trail rides with several of our horses, keeping up easily with our mounts and always uncannily knowing where the horses' feet will land. If you do decide to take your JRT out to visit a ranch, make sure dogs are allowed on the property and watch your dog closely to be sure it doesn't get itself into trouble.

When to Call the Vet

If your dog suddenly starts limping, check all four legs and paws for obvious causes such as a torn toenail or a fox tail between its toes. If you can find nothing of this sort and the lameness doesn't resolve itself within a day, call your vet and schedule an appointment. It could be that your dog tore a ligament or received a kick from a horse that you are unaware of.

The biggest danger you will face with your terrier and horses is the unintentional kick by a horse and the damage it can cause. Horses have several visual blind spots and sometimes are taken unaware by a dashing white terrier. Kicks usually will occur around feeding time or when the horse is in a large area at play, so special care should be taken at these times to protect your dog. Make sure your JRT understands that it should not enter an arena or pasture area and that it should stay safely outside the fence. If your terrier won't obey this rule, keep it on a leash when horses are out running around or trying to eat. This will help protect your dog from harm and you from an unnecessary vet bill.

228

Dog Parks

A trip to the park can be a great outlet for both your family and your dog. Because parks offer lots of the wide-open space usually unavailable in a backyard, they provide your terrier with a super opportunity to run and play. Parks are great for playing ball and Frisbee or even for a good game of chase.

Many suburban neighborhoods are now building enclosed areas within their local parks specifically for doggy exercise. These safe, fenced runs are quite large, and they allow for either solitary play or introduction to other dogs using the facility, depending on the wishes of the individual dog owners. Because the areas are safely fenced, you can let your dog run and be secure in the knowledge that it can't get into trouble, You can focus your energy on getting the most play and exercise for your dog.

These parks are a wonderful way to socialize your potentially antisocial Jack Russell because you can introduce it to one or two new dogs at a time. You also are in a confined area where you can easily reach your dog

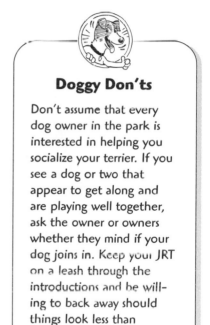

Doggy Don'ts

Don't assume that every dog owner in the park is interested in helping you socialize your terrier. If you see a dog or two that appear to get along and are playing well together, ask the owner or owners whether they mind if your dog joins in. Keep your JRT on a leash through the introductions and be willing to back away should things look less than promising.

and can pull it out of trouble if necessary. Not only that, parks take some of the exercise burden off your shoulders by allowing your dog to romp and run with other dogs, minimizing your constant involvement. By staying close by, your JRT can check on you periodically yet can still enjoy the company and roughhousing of other energetic doggy playmates.

Nature at Its Best

If hiking or camping is more your speed, you will find that your Jack Russell Terrier is just as at home in the great outdoors as it is on the beach or in the park. Terriers love to hunt and explore; being able to do so while accompanying you on a walk will only add to its pleasure. Be careful, though, that you have done all your basic obedience work at home and have thoroughly schooled both the heel and come commands.

Doggy Do's

Check your dog for nicks and ticks after a walk in the woods. Ticks can harbor diseases and can cause irritations in your dog's skin, and nicks should be treated promptly.

Because JRTs are natural hunters, the call of the wild will be stronger here than at home or in a park. Your terrier can easily get itself into trouble by running off after a squirrel or by poking its head down the wrong hole. The safest bet is to explore an area with your terrier safely in tow before ever letting it off the leash. Be sure there are no busy roads around the next bend or a swift running river at the bottom of the hill.

Keep in mind that a terrier's hunting instincts are very strong. The main thing on its mind will be to find a squirrel or another enticing rodent to chase. This could lead your dog right into the clutches of a poisonous snake or some other hidden peril, and it might not respond quickly enough to your calls if it is in the heat of a hunt. Your dog also could stumble over an embankment or fall into an unseen hole while running after some small animal. If this were to happen, it would be hard to find your dog without some serious searching and a whole lot of luck.

It is best to avoid any thickly wooded areas or spaces with abundant small game unless you have your terrier on a leash. This will prevent it from running off after a rustling in the brush that is sure to lead to another rustling in the brush. Eventually, your dog will be far away from camp with no idea how it got there or how to find its way back. By the time your JRT wakes up and realizes it has traveled too far afield, it might be out of shouting distance.

Winter Wonderland

Jack Russells are more water and warm-weather dogs than they are snow bunnies, but they can enjoy the sticky white stuff as well. All it takes is a few extra precautions to ensure your dog's comfort and some common sense about how long to expose your terrier to the elements.

Take your terrier out to the park—playing with other dogs is a good way to increase your JRT's social skills.

The Jack Russell Terrier's coat was meant to protect it from the elements; therefore, it has some natural water-wicking properties. Although England is hardly like Southern California when it comes to weather, terriers were found by the hearth during inclement weather more often than they were found hunting foxes in the snow. Because its coat is thinner than its snow-loving canine counterparts, your JRT should be equipped with a warm sweater or a doggy coat to help keep its body heat up when out in snow or very cold weather. If you plan to play in the snow for a long period of time (such as an hour or two), you also should provide some type of protection for your terrier's paws to prevent freezing and cracking caused by ice crystals.

Doggy Do's

Remember that your terrier is not a Husky or St. Bernard. If you intend to take it into the snow or ice, provide plenty of protection to keep it warm and keep it moving to keep its body temperature up.

If your terrier starts shaking, even with a sweater or coat on, it is probably too cold outside for it. If you have been standing still for a period of time, increase your terrier's activity level to get its muscles moving and its heart pumping. This will raise its core temperature and might be enough to keep it warm. If your terrier keeps shivering in spite of these efforts, do the humane thing and bring it in out of the cold.

Take Your Terrier Along

Whatever your favorite outdoor activity, try to include your JRT. Not only will you enjoy its company on the trip, your terrier will enjoy spending time with you and exercising at the same time. This will lead to a stronger bond between your dog and your family, and it will give you lots of fond memories of your trips. It has the added bonus of relieving much of your dog's pent-up energy, and it is likely to provide a happier, more relaxed terrier at home as well.

The Least You Need to Know

➤ Balls of all types are fascinating to JRTs and make excellent toys to keep them amused.

➤ Choose soft balls for throwing and catching; choose hard balls for chewing and chasing. Make sure all balls are made specifically for dogs.

➤ JRTs love anything that flies, and they are natural jumpers for games of Frisbee.

➤ Many toys on the market will allow you to play with your JRT indoors when an outdoor romp is out of the question.

➤ Be creative when choosing your toys, but realize that your terrier will be just as happy with an old sock as it will be with an expensive, high-tech toy.

➤ With their high energy level, JRTs love exercise. You both will have fun if you take your terrier with you when you go jogging or biking.

➤ Horses and Jack Russells make good companions, provided your dog is mannerly and controllable.

➤ JRTs also like camping and hiking and will gladly accompany you on these trips. Keep your dog on a leash, however, until you have carefully explored the surroundings. Avoid off-leash work in heavily wooded areas or in places where there are many small animals.

➤ If you are going to take your JRT out into snow, be sure to provide a sweater for its comfort and limit the amount of time spent outside.

Chapter 19

Fun, Fun and More Fun

In This Chapter

➤ What is a terrier trial?

➤ Conformation critique

➤ Only obedience

➤ Get down and go to ground!

➤ Russell racing

➤ Agility angles

There is an endless number of ways in which you and your family can enjoy your dog. From playing and swimming in the backyard to beach and mountain excursions, your Jack Russell Terrier is happiest when it is at your heels. But what if you want to meet some other JRT owners to see just how your little white flash stands up to other feisty Jack Russells? The answer is just a trial away.

What Is a Terrier Trial?

Jack Russell Terrier trials are organized activities designed specifically for JRT owners. Some are sanctioned by the JRTCA, some by the AKC, and still others are more like play days and anyone is welcome. The only requirement is that participants have or love Jack Russells.

All JRT trials have one thing in common. They offer a variety of classes for Jack Russell owners to strut their stuff and to see just where their terriers' talents lie.

Bet You Didn't Know

Jack Russell Terrier trials are far more than doggy beauty pageants. Many fast-paced classes also are offered. The most prestigious wins come in the working categories such as go to ground and racing.

Included in most Jack Russell Terrier trials are conformation, obedience, hunting (go to ground), racing and agility competitions. The age, sex, height and ability of the dogs can come into play in a particular type of competition. Regardless of which activity you choose, you are sure to find a classification in which your dog can naturally excel. Let's look at each activity individually, and you can decide which is the most interesting to you.

Conformation Critique

When most people think of dog shows, they think of conformation or "breeding" classes. These beauty-pageant-like classes showcase the terrier that most closely matches the "ideal" for that particular registry or governing body. Much primping and preening goes on before a conformation competition, though perhaps less with JRTs than with other breeds of dogs. Spayed and neutered terriers are not eligible in sanctioned competitions, although they are welcome in play-day classes. The only exceptions are Junior Handler, Veteran and JRTCA Bronze Medallion classes.

The conformation classes are presided over by a judge and a ring steward, much like any other breed conformation class. Occasionally, these two officials are accompanied by an apprentice judge who is working to become a licensed judge. These individuals are responsible for making sure that the terriers are presented in an orderly fashion, that all rules are followed and that the classes proceed in a timely fashion. The announcer provides an update on the classes about to come in and the results of the class in the ring.

Although the judge's view always is subjective, the purpose of the conformation class is to choose the dog that best represents the ideal Jack Russell Terrier, both in physical attributes and in temperament. Physical perfection certainly is the goal, but the terrier also must portray the essence of the working JRT to be considered ideal.

Judging the JRT is a hands-on experience. The judges not only want to view the terrier standing, walking and trotting, they also will "span" the terrier, or check that the circumference of the dogs' rib cages can easily be encircled by normal-sized hands. They do this by placing their hands around the terrier just behind the withers, with their thumbs and little fingers touching. If they can accomplish this, the terrier is said to fit into the breed standard.

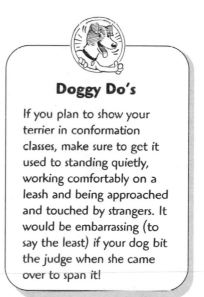

Doggy Do's

If you plan to show your terrier in conformation classes, make sure to get it used to standing quietly, working comfortably on a leash and being approached and touched by strangers. It would be embarrassing (to say the least) if your dog bit the judge when she came over to span it!

To make the class size equitable and manageable, classes traditionally are broken into divisions. These divisions often include puppy, open adult and junior handler, working and miscellaneous classes. Cross entries are not allowed within the open division. These classes often are further divided by height, coat type and experience. Working dogs are required to satisfy hunting requirements before becoming eligible to be shown in that division. In JRTCA competitions, a Bronze Medallion class often is offered for terriers that have earned a JRTCA Bronze Medallion for special accomplishments in field work. Only dogs that satisfy the requirements can enter, and spayed and neutered dogs are allowed.

Preparing to Show Your JRT

Although preparing your terrier for this class isn't quite as training intensive as some of the other trial divisions, you still must do some homework before attempting to compete at a trial. You should practice getting your terrier to walk briskly and dependably on a leash, to stand quietly on a table (though they sometimes are shown on the ground) and to allow itself to be checked and handled (including its teeth, ears and tail). You should also make sure your terrier will act in an acceptable social manner when in the presence of other terriers.

Bet You Didn't Know

If a judge also is a breeder and has produced a terrier that is currently showing, the judge is prohibited from ever judging that dog in the conformation classes.

Remember that your JRT should be in good physical shape when competing in conformation classes. This will enhance its physical appearance and will make spanning it much easier. You want to present your dog in the best light possible, so don't scold or reprimand your terrier in the class if you can possibly help it. Scolding will make your dog tuck or drop its tail, giving the appearance of a timid or unhappy dog. Keep ample space between yourself and the next dog and always be a good sport regardless of the judging results. Most of all, remember that you are doing this for fun. Winning a ribbon is never a life-or-death matter.

Only Obedience

Obedience trials are a great way to show off how well you've trained your terrier. These classes require the terrier to perform several tests of obedience, and the dog and handler with the most points at the end of the class are declared the winners. The tests required depend on the sanctioning body under which you are competing.

Classes are divided by skill level, and there are separate divisions for juniors and adults. All dogs are required to perform a sequence of tests based on their training levels. A score is given for each element or test that reflects not only how well the dog performs the exercise but also its attitude in doing so. Unlike conformation classes, physical appearance is not a factor in judging this division. It only matters whether the terrier correctly completes the test and whether it displays a willing attitude towards the handler. Class size usually is limited so that the dogs are more apt to focus on their handlers than on the hubbub surrounding them.

In novice or beginner classes, terriers are asked to perform heel, heel in a pattern (usually a figure eight), stand for examination and come. All these are performed on a leash at least 6 feet long. Usually, the dogs also are asked to sit and stay and to down and stay for a specified period of time. They also might be asked to heel off the leash and to come off the leash depending on the class requirements and the preferences of the judge. All these skills are fundamentals discussed in Chapter 11, and they easily can be accomplished with some practice and diligence at home.

As the divisions increase, so does the skill level required. At higher levels, handlers might be asked to show that their dogs can heel while not on a leash, can perform a figure eight, can release a toy or dumbbell when asked, can retrieve an object and retrieve while performing jumps and long sits and downs.

As the dogs move into the utility division, they are asked to display their understanding of hand signals, scent discrimination and jumping and retrieving skills. These skills require substantial training and considerable expertise. If you are interested in competing at these levels, you should look for books specifically geared toward advanced obedience training to help you prepare for these competitions.

Get Down and Go to Ground!

The go to ground competition is unique to hunting dogs and can be an exciting competition to watch and participate in. It also can be extremely loud, so bring either a big dose of tolerance or earplugs for this event. Those very voices that make the dogs easy to find underground can be skull-splitting when used in chorus in anticipation of the hunt.

The Jack Russell Terrier was bred to be the perfect subterranean hunting machine, and this competition puts these qualities to the test. The dog that will be most successful in this event is compact with balanced proportions, strong limbs and a small chest that enables it

237

to enter the squirrel or fox hole. Wherever the fox can go, the JRT must be able to follow. The terrier must be flexible enough to maneuver the twists and turns of the tunnels leading to the quarry's den and must be willing and able to bark loudly until found.

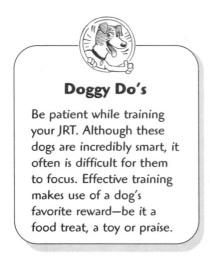

Doggy Do's

Be patient while training your JRT. Although these dogs are incredibly smart, it often is difficult for them to focus. Effective training makes use of a dog's favorite reward—be it a food treat, a toy or praise.

The go to ground trial event was developed to test these skills. Its sole purpose is to test the skills necessary for a JRT to successfully go down into the tunnel, to scent out its prey, to choose the correct paths to find the quarry and to work the quarry as would be needed during a real hunt.

As with other skill competitions, go to ground trials are divided into classes based on the age, size and skill of the terriers competing, and the courses are designed with these class specifications in mind. The most common divisions are novice, puppy, open, advanced, championships and size-split classes.

The courses consist of underground tunnels that have been designed specifically for this use. The more difficult the division, the more turns and dead-ends the terrier will have to navigate to reach its prey. The tunnels also get longer as the dogs move up into higher levels of competition. The quarry can be a squirrel, a rat or another suitable rodent. All these animals are caged to prevent injury.

The go to ground competition has a set course of events that the promoters of the trial must follow. The terrier is placed at the opening of the tunnel with all four feet on the ground. The starter tells the handler to release the dog, and a stopwatch is started. It is the JRT's job to navigate the twists and turns of the tunnel and to locate the quarry as fast as it can. After it reaches the rodent, the terrier must bark, whine, scratch or otherwise "mark" the quarry for a specific amount of time. After this is accomplished, the time is recorded and the next JRT is set loose on the course.

The JRT with the best time wins. If the terrier fails to find the quarry, doesn't mark it once it has found it or leaves the tunnel more than

Go to ground competitions test a dog's ability to maneuver through tunnels and to scent out its quarry. This is where a JRT's instincts really shine. (photo by Catherine Romaine Brown and the JRTCA)

once, the dog is disqualified (except in novice classes). The judge for the event is stationed at the finish line and makes sure the terrier works the prey for the allotted time before deeming the time as official. The ruling of the course judge is final.

Bet You Didn't Know

Schooling on the day of a go to ground trial is not permitted. Any terrier, regardless of registration, that has scored 100 percent on a previous novice or open test is ineligible to compete in the go to ground competition at a JRTCA or an AWTA trial.

This is a fun competition that requires very little preparation on your part, and it allows you to view your terrier in a situation that shows its remarkable natural hunting ability. It will certainly give you a newfound respect for your JRT's hunting skills and, perhaps, a new understanding of why barking and digging are so much a part of your Jack Russell's makeup.

Russell Racing

Perhaps one of the most exciting events at the JRT trial is the racing competition. Like the go to ground event, it can get very loud as the dogs bark in anticipation of running their race. Be prepared for this.

As a new Jack Russell Terrier owner, you probably were surprised at how fast your dog can fetch a ball or chase a cat. If you really want to see your dog in action, put your terrier into one of the racing competitions. You will be amazed at just how fast several JRTs racing against one another can go.

Two types of races usually are offered at the trials: flat races and races over hurdles (steeplechase). As with the other competitions, races are divided in the standard ways by height, age, skill and sex. Because speed is a factor and taller dogs have much longer legs than shorter dogs, all divisions usually are split by height.

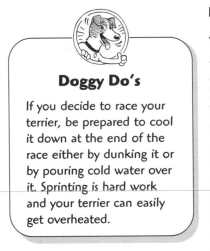

Doggy Do's

If you decide to race your terrier, be prepared to cool it down at the end of the race either by dunking it or by pouring cold water over it. Sprinting is hard work and your terrier can easily get overheated.

Racing Particulars

The course is 150 to 225 feet long and has a starting box at one end and a finish line at the other. The finish line usually is made from several bales of straw or hay with a hole in the middle. This provides a soft wall should several careening JRTs make it to the end at the same time. A piece of fur or a squirrel's tail is used as a lure to get things going, and it is attached to a piece of rope or a string to be pulled along in front of the pack. This keeps the terriers' attention on the chase rather than on fighting one another. The first terrier through the hole at the end wins.

As an added safety precaution, the dogs' mouths are fitted with muzzles. This protects not only the other dogs but the handlers and catchers as well. The muzzles must be made from either a plastic basket or from a soft material, and they should not be of the figure-eight variety. In sanctioned events, a muzzle is mandatory.

The course is designed without any turns, and the running area should be about 10 feet wide. The perimeter of the track is defined either by bales of hay or by some type of plastic fencing. The starting box is big enough for six fully-grown JRTs and is made from wood, plastic or another flexible material. After the dogs are loaded, a wire or plastic barrier is placed in front of the starting gate and is attached to a release mechanism. The race should be run on either dirt or turf that provides plenty of traction without injuring the pads of the dogs' feet. The hole at the end is about 8 to 10 inches wide, which is adequate for a normal-sized JRT to rocket through.

The official judge stands at the finish line to record the order of finish and to make sure the run was legal. The judge's decision always is final. The racing steward assigns collars, checks all equipment to be sure it is safe and legal, oversees the starting gate and polices aggressive or fighting terriers. The starter makes sure all dogs are properly positioned in the box, opens the gate and signals the start of the lure by the lure handler. The catchers remove the terriers promptly from the end box at the finish line to prevent impromptu fights from breaking out.

The Steeplechase

Steeplechase races add the difficulty of jumping hurdles to the excitement of the standard race. The jumps are placed at least 20 feet apart, with the final jump being at least 30 feet from the finish line. The terriers must negotiate a minimum of four jumps that are no higher than 8 inches for puppies and 16 inches for grown dogs. Competitions usually request that the dogs be fitted with colored collars to help distinguish order of finish and to prevent confusion.

Getting Ready to Race

If you think your dog would enjoy participating in this activity, you will need a few pieces of training equipment and some time to work with your JRT. It takes a bit of planning, training and conditioning to be successful, and rarely will a terrier do well in its first few starts.

Your dog first must be introduced to the lure before any actual race training begins. This is important because your dog needs to get excited about chasing this piece of fur before you can expect it to run

When hurdles are included in the race, the action really heats up! (photo by Catherine Romaine Brown and the JRTCA)

its little heart out. Let your terrier catch the lure several times and make it a fun game of tug-of-war so your dog looks forward to playing with the lure. You can use a sock, a piece of fur, a fuzzy toy or any other such item that you can safely attach to a 20-foot piece of string and that resembles a fox or squirrel's tail.

Doggy Don'ts

Don't start training your puppy using any type of jump until it is at least 5 months old. Puppies' bones are still forming at this age, and they can't take the pressure jumping puts on their joints. When you do begin, start low and gradually work up to higher obstacles.

You also need to get your terrier accustomed to wearing a muzzle. Be sure to ask for a plastic basket or "softie" muzzle rather than the figure-eight variety. Tease your terrier with the lure and then run from your JRT while pulling the lure behind you. Your dog still can catch the lure in spite of the muzzle, and you should let it do so from time to time. School your dog several times until it knows that chasing and catching the lure is fun.

If you are planning to show in the steeplechase division, you need to get your JRT used to following the lure over jumps. You can use something as simple as hay bales or PVC pipe structures, or you can build more elaborate hurdles from wood. Whatever you use, make sure it is safe for your dog and that any solid structures angle away from your terrier as it jumps. Drag the lure over the top of the jump several times to encourage your JRT to jump the hurdle to get the lure. After a brief time, it should be leaping like a pro.

All this training is invaluable, but none of it takes the place of actual racing experience. Although your Jack Russell might perform famously at home, it might turn into a blathering idiot at the trial itself and might freeze in the starting gate or even run in the wrong direction. With real experience, your dog's racing skills will improve.

Racing Etiquette

Be patient with your dog's performance. It can take a significant
amount of time for your terrier to
become proficient and comfortable in
a race situation. Always remember
that you are at a competition and are
being helped by many club volun-
teers. The more courteous and appre-
ciative you are of their help, the more
likely you are to be welcomed back.

Agility Angles

Chapter 20 covers all-breed agility
competitions, but they also are

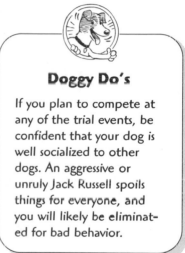

Doggy Do's

If you plan to compete at any of the trial events, be confident that your dog is well socialized to other dogs. An aggressive or unruly Jack Russell spoils things for everyone, and you will likely be eliminated for bad behavior.

offered specifically for Jack Russell Terriers. In fact, the JRT clubs have made it easy for first-time competitors to try their hands at agility training and competition by offering a special division for on-lead competitors. This special class is unique to the Jack Russell breed.

By allowing competitors to keep their terriers on lead, the clubs decrease the feelings of intimidation that often accompany many newcomers to such a complex and difficult sport. It also keeps interest high by providing a controlled and structured environment. By staying on lead to negotiate the course, both terriers and owners can concentrate on the task at hand rather than worrying about an overzealous dog running off and getting into trouble.

Agility competitions are the Olympics of dog training, and hours upon hours of schooling go into a successful agility dog. Because few dog owners have the equipment necessary to train for agility competitions, they often are limited to the time spent at trials to practice working with the required obstacles. On-lead course work gets both the dog and the owner comfortable with the intricacies of each obstacle and provides a means to keep a frustrated JRT under control.

Bet You Didn't Know

Three scores of 170 or better (out of 200) are required for the terrier to receive its on-lead Agility Certificate. This means that the terrier completed all the obstacles and received an adequate proficiency score.

Patience is the most valuable training tool in agility work. Dogs are asked to jump through tires, to run through tunnels of all shapes and configurations, to maneuver teeter-totters, to walk on a narrow, tightrope-like bridge, to swerve through closely spaced poles and to climb up and over a tall A-frame. Not only must they accomplish each and every obstacle successfully, they are timed as well, so they must perform with a high degree of speed.

On-lead courses are offered in both novice and advanced levels. The dogs competing in novice classes are true beginners that literally are just learning the ins and outs of the sport. The advanced dogs are a bit more skilled but are not ready to make the jump to the true, off-lead agility classes. After an on-lead Agility Certificate is earned, the terrier must advance to the off-lead agility competitions. Once a dog competes in off-lead classes, it is ineligible to return to on-lead competition.

When a dog refuses an obstacle, avoids an obstacle, completes an obstacle out of sequence, knocks down a hurdle, pushes off a rail, anticipates the beginning of the course, runs under an obstacle or jumps off and then back on an obstacle, points are deducted from the team's score. The use of food or toys by the handler, verbal or physical abuse of the dog, the handler touching the dog or the equipment on the course or the dog eliminating on the course are all grounds for disqualification.

Agility for Kids

In the children's division, more emphasis is placed on the child's interaction with her terrier and the child's attitude toward the competition and suggestions made from the judges or coaches. The child also must know the dog's number, the expected course and how to safely negotiate the obstacles. The judges are far more interested in how the child/terrier team mentally approaches the course than in the actual performance on the course.

Teamwork at Its Best

If you are interested in training for this complex sport, you first should master all the basic training discussed in Chapter 11 as well as the more advanced commands found in most obedience training books. Agility is a sport that requires extreme concentration and focus from both you and your JRT, and you must spend long hours working together until you are working as a team. Because of this, dogs under 1 year of age are not eligible to compete in agility classes. Attend as many agility trials as possible to introduce your terrier to the required elements and to perfect its skills on each one.

Bet You Didn't Know

Agility courses are perfect for terriers that have a high drive to please their owners. As long as you keep the training fun, JRTs will thrive on the mental challenges necessary to negotiate the obstacles, and they will use their natural proclivity for speed to whiz through the courses. Not only that, they also are wicked fun to watch!

Remember that you cannot use the leash as a crutch. The organizers will not allow you to drag your dog through the obstacles, nor can you use fear or intimidation to coerce your dog into submission. You cannot navigate the obstacles yourself to show your terrier how it's done, nor can you chase your dog through an obstacle. In other words, you must willingly work as a team to be successful in this sport!

How to Get Involved

Now that you've seen the possibilities that abound at Jack Russell Terrier trials, you can contact several of your local clubs to find out when the next trials will be held and where the closest ones are to your home. Chapter 23 lists innumerable resources available to help you track down this information. Even if you're not sure you are interested, go to one and see what it's all about. You might find that it is just the challenge you've been looking for!

The Least You Need to Know

➤ Jack Russell Terrier trials are more than just doggy beauty pageants. They offer classes to test your terrier's training, speed and hunting skills.

➤ Make sure that you spend time socializing your dog before attempting to compete at a terrier trial.

➤ Conformation classes focus on the physical characteristics and temperament of your terrier but are judged with hunting specifications in mind.

➤ Obedience classes are offered with a wide variety of skills required. This is a good place to show off your terrier's basic training.

➤ Go to ground competitions test your terrier's ability to track and to work underground quarry.

➤ JRT races are some of the most exciting events at the trials. If you choose to race your terrier, you will have to do some schooling at home to get your terrier used to chasing a lure and to navigating jumps.

➤ Agility requires intense training, concentration and teamwork from you and your JRT. If you want a challenge, look into this division of JRT trials.

It's Doggy Boot Camp

Most people are content to simply enjoy their dogs as part of the family. They let the dogs play happily around their neighborhood parks and are unconcerned about keeping up with the Joneses. For some families, however, bigger, faster and smarter is better. These people are drawn to agility competitions in which speed, accuracy and a little luck all play a part in determining the final outcome of the competition.

Agility Answers

The sport of dog agility originally was developed in the late 1970s as an exhibition sport in Great Britain, and it was patterned after the jumping events seen in the equestrian world. The sport is open to all dog breeds, regardless of registration status or mixed ancestry, and it combines agility, speed, control and accuracy. All dogs compete using the same set of obstacles, although height allowances are made for jumps and for times on the course. Some obstacles favor larger dogs; others are easier for smaller dogs. Dogs in the middle range of both weight and size usually have a slight advantage, but the sport is proud of the fact that no one breed is more successful than another. Representatives of many breeds have won national titles.

Bet You Didn't Know

Agility is one of the few sports in the dog world in which all breeds compete together. With the exception of obstacle height and allowable time, no distinction is made for the differences in the dogs' sizes. All dogs competing must navigate the same set of obstacles.

Since the sport's inception, its popularity has grown steadily. The United States Agility Association was founded in 1986 to promote the sport in the United States. The following year, the National Club for Dog Agility was formed (now administered by the United Kennel Club). Since this early interest, many smaller clubs have been created across the United States. More recently, the AKC has joined in and has developed its own set of rules for this increasingly popular sport.

Regardless of the individual clubs, courses or rules, the basic fundamental elements of the sport remain the same. In a nutshell, the dogs must jump over, maneuver through and traverse a wide variety of obstacles in the fastest time possible without missing an element or falling off a piece of equipment. The dog that completes the course in the shortest amount of time with the fewest faults wins the competition. Sounds simple, right? Think again. The courses are mind-boggling for first-time agility competitors. After you understand the concepts and philosophy behind the sport, however, it becomes a fascinating display of talent and teamwork.

The benefit to you, the Jack Russell owner, is that it gives your zippy little dog with a big brain the opportunity to put its skills to work in a positive way instead of sitting at home trying to decide which piece of furniture it wants to destroy next. It also is a wonderful aggression outlet because many JRTs attack the course with the same ferociousness they would use on the neighbor's dog. Needless to say, the former display is a bit more socially acceptable.

One of the biggest benefits your terrier will receive from agility training is the capability to focus its attention and to direct its energy in a positive way. It also gives both you and your JRT a wonderful physical outlet for energy and keeps your dog in peak physical condition.

Ornery Obstacles

Now that you have an idea of what's required on an agility course, let's look at some of the specific obstacles you might find and explore some of their subtle variations. At first glance, this eclectic mixture of obstacles might look like a giant doggy playground, but closer inspection will show that each and every obstacle is geared toward testing a specific skill and the dog's confidence level.

The obstacles are divided into several categories including hurdles or jumps, tire or window jumps, contact obstacles, pause obstacles, tunnels and weave poles. The most common dimensions for each obstacle are pro-

Doggy Do's

Success at agility trials requires a dog and its trainer to work together. This is a great way to build a cooperative relationship based on trust and mutual respect. A terrier that is this tuned in to its owner is less likely to do something to displease her, thus creating a less destructive Jack Russell Terrier.

vided in this chapter to allow you to build your own, should you decide you want to become further involved in the sport. If you really get involved, you can turn your own backyard into a JRT playpen!

Jumping Jacks

Jumps or hurdles make up a large portion of the agility course. Because these are one of the only obstacles in which an allowance is given for dogs of different heights and because there are several different types of jumps, we'll take a look at these first.

The variance in jump heights differs from organization to organization, and you should check with the trial's sponsoring club to see what the specific jump heights will be for a given competition. As a rule, dogs 12 inches and shorter will be asked to jump hurdles that are no more than 12 inches high. Dogs in the 12- to 16-inch range jump hurdles that are no more than 16 inches high. Dogs in the 16- to 21-inch range jump hurdles that are no more than 24 inches high. Dogs taller than 21 inches jump hurdles that are no more than 30 inches high.

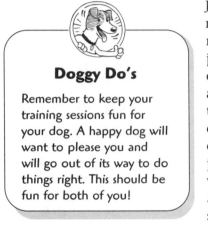

Doggy Do's

Remember to keep your training sessions fun for your dog. A happy dog will want to please you and will go out of its way to do things right. This should be fun for both of you!

Jumps are made from a variety of materials and are seen in a wide range of configurations. Single-bar jumps are commonly seen on agility courses because they are easy to build and set up, and they effectively test the dog's jumping ability. These hurdles actually consist of two square or cylindrical bars placed across two side jump standards. Usually made of wood or plastic, the bars must be 4 to 5 feet long and must be painted with stripes so the dogs can see them. The dog must jump in the direction specified by the course designer or judge and must clear the hurdle to avoid penalty.

Panel jumps also are seen on the course and consist of several cross boards placed one on top of the other to give the appearance of a solid wall jump. The boards are 3 to 4 inches wide, are 4 to 5 feet long and can be no thicker than 1 inch. They are set on the supports in such a manner that, although they look solid, the top rails can easily be knocked off. The dog must clear the top board without knocking it off for the jump to be considered successful.

A double-bar jump, or a double oxer, requires that a dog not only jump up but clear a span as well. It can be either one special jump or a combination of two single jumps placed 4 and 12 inches apart. The top back bar usually is higher than the front bar, giving the appearance of a slanted jump. The dogs must clear both bars for the jump to count.

Agility trials require the dog to negotiate a variety of obstacles such as hurdles. (photo by Catherine Romaine Brown)

The triple-bar jump is a step more difficult than the oxer. It requires the dog to clear a jump consisting of three ascending jumps, for a total height of between 8 inches and 24 inches and a total width of between 8 and 24 inches. This can be quite an imposing jump and usually is seen in the more advanced levels of agility.

Bet You Didn't Know

In most agility divisions, you need to successfully complete three qualifying runs under two different judges in that particular division for your dog to earn a title.

The broad jump requires the widest jump by the dog and is arranged either as a standard broad jump (ascending order) or as a hogback (ascending for half and then descending for half to create a round-top jump) that is 12 to 32 inches wide. The length of the jump is twice as long as the height. Corner markers, when used, usually are

251

painted a different color for visibility. The dog must successfully jump the entire hurdle without touching it for the effort to be considered successful.

Two specialty jumps might be used in a course as well, and they are very similar to one another. These are the circle or tire jump and the window jump. The circle jump consists of a circular opening, often a tire, that is suspended from a frame. The dog is required to jump through the opening. The inner width of the opening is about 24 inches, and there must be at least 8 inches between the outside of the tire and the sides of the frame. It also must be adjustable to the five different jump heights required.

The window jump is similar except that, instead of a tire, the jump has either a round or square opening. It usually is made of some type of cloth and is shaped like a window. Like the tire jump, the opening is approximately 24 inches across, and it must be adjustable for the different height requirements. If either of these jumps is used in agility courses specifically for JRTs, the opening must be between 17 and 20 inches.

Contact Sport?

Contact obstacles actually are pieces of equipment on which a safety or contact zone has been painted. The zones act as a safety feature because the dog must touch all the required zones, preventing it from jumping off too early and possibly injuring itself. Forcing the dog to stay on the obstacle for the full length ensures that the dog completes the entire test of the obstacle. It also positions the dog in the safest place to dismount at the end of the obstacle.

Contact obstacles consist of the see-saw or teeter-totter, the A-frame and the dog walk. Zones are painted at the beginning and at the end of each obstacle, forcing the dog to touch each zone to avoid faults. The only contact obstacle that allows the dog to miss a zone is the A-frame, though all dogs must touch the down-side contact zone for the obstacle to be counted.

The see-saw is exactly what it sounds like—a plank of wood supported in the center that drops down as the dog mounts and dismounts. The plank is 12 inches wide and 8 to 12 feet long. The pivot point should be 16 to 27 inches above the ground. The contact zones are

36 to 42 inches long and are located on each end of the see-saw. The top of the plank should be treated with some type of nonskid surface. The purpose of the obstacle is to show control and lack of fear during the movement of the equipment and to test the dog's patience while waiting for the plank to touch the ground prior to the dismount.

Bet You Didn't Know

To keep things interesting, course designers rarely place two contact obstacles side by side on a course, they never begin or end a run with either the weave poles or a contact obstacle.

The A-frame is made of two panels leaning together at the top to form an A-shaped obstacle. This piece of equipment usually is made of wood, and the panels are between 35 and 50 inches wide and between 8 and 9 feet long. The bottom 42 inches of each panel are painted with a contact zone, and the coating on the A-frame should be a rough, nonskid surface. Slats are affixed to each side of the frame to provide a toe-hold for the dogs and are 6 to 15 inches apart. The dog must climb up one side of the A-frame and down the other, and usually only the down-side contact zone must be touched to be a legal run. The A-frame ranges from 4 feet, 11 inches to 6 feet, 3 inches at its tallest point.

The dog walk is the canine equivalent to the balance beam in gymnastics. The dogs are asked to climb up a ramp, run across a 12-inch walk and descend the other side. The walk is either 8 or 12 feet long and is 36 to 48 inches off the ground at the highest point. As with all the contact obstacles, a nonslip surface is provided for the dogs' safety. Slats also are provided for safety and are located at 12-inch intervals. Contact zones are painted on the lower 36 to 42 inches of each ramp, and the dog must touch both zones to avoid penalty. Although the obstacle is called a dog walk, the dogs actually run up, over and down this obstacle. With their small feet, JRTs are able to traverse this obstacle more quickly than most larger dogs.

The Paws Pause

The pause table is a test of how much patience your dog really has. In the midst of all this running, jumping and navigating, the pause table requires the dog to jump onto a table, to either sit or lie down for five seconds and then to jump off. The table is 36 inches square and is covered with carpeting or another nonskid surface. The height of the table ranges from 8 to 24 inches, depending on the height division in which it is required.

Terrier Tunnels

No obstacle on the agility course is more suited to JRTs than the tunnels, and Jack Russells usually excel on this obstacle. Two types of tunnels are found on the course. One tests the dog's ability to enter and exit dark spaces quickly and its willingness to navigate turns; the other is collapsible and tests whether the dog can push its way through to the other side. Both tunnels test the confidence of the dog.

The open tunnel is a flexible tube made of material bent into turns and shapes. The openings are either round or rectangular and are 24 inches wide. The length can vary between 10 and 20 feet. The tunnel must be secured to the ground for safety, and the dog should not be able to see the end of the tunnel when it enters.

Bet You Didn't Know

Agility courses are made more difficult with the use of "traps," in which two obstacles are placed in close proximity to one another. The dog must watch the handler closely to see which route is the correct one and must quickly act accordingly.

The closed tunnel is much more difficult. The first 2 to 3 feet of the tunnel are rigid, but the rest of the tunnel collapses in around the dog. The material is a heavy cloth, and the only way out is through the exit, which is totally obscured by the weight of the tunnel. The overall length that the dog must traverse is 12 to 13 feet.

This obstacle puts the dog in an almost claustrophobic situation, and only dogs confident in their abilities will make it through without effort. If you've ever seen your JRT tunnel its way under the covers of your bed and out the foot end, however, you've seen why they do so well in this event! On the flip side, some closed tunnels favor bigger dogs because of the weight of the material used. It's harder for a little dog to muscle its way through.

Zippy Zig-Zags

I have seen many agility trials in my day, and I still am amazed by the speed and accuracy of a dog successfully completing the weave pole section. Weave poles consist of six to twelve upright poles placed 20 to 24 inches apart. The poles must be flexible to allow them to bend around larger dogs, and they should be painted with stripes for easier visibility. The dogs must weave through the poles, never missing one, for the length of the obstacle. If the dog misses a pole, the handler has the option of restarting just before the missed pole or completing the entire sequence over again. The weave poles test flexibility and speed, and the judges are looking for a fluid run through the poles. It truly is a fascinating obstacle to watch!

Now on Course . . .

Now that you're familiar the obstacles in an agility course, let's see how these obstacles are arranged to make a challenging run for both dog and handler. You'll also examine them through a judge's eyes to see how these courses are judged.

Each course has a maximum time limit assigned to it based on the number of obstacles and the difficulty of the division. The time allowed for the entire course also varies depending on the height division and is determined on a yards-per-second allotment (ranging from 2 yards-per-second to

Doggy Do's

If you think you might want to participate in agility trials, go watch a few to see whether you truly have what it takes to train your dog for these events. You might find that it's too much work for you to participate and that you enjoy the spectator seat better than the trainer's corner.

2¾ yards-per-second). The resulting time without penalties is called the Standard Course Time (SCT), and the dog must have a clean run for the time to be counted. The number of obstacles also varies depending on the skill level and the sponsoring association, and it ranges from twelve to twenty pieces of equipment.

All courses are completed with dogs off of their leashes. The handler can use verbal commands and hand signals, but food, toys and other devices are not allowed on the course. The handler can work in any position she prefers and can stand any distance away, but the course designer might lay out a course that limits the access of the handler to the dog. Collars are not allowed in any agility competition except those trials sponsored by the AKC and the JRTCA on-leash competitions. If a collar is used, it must be a simple flat-buckle collar without tags or attachments. Weave poles usually are not introduced in the novice division.

The judge's job is to make sure all obstacles are negotiated and all contact zones are touched and with no handler interference. Deductions are taken for refusals, for running out of an obstacle, for moving from the pause table, for beginning before the start is initiated, for working the course out of sequence and for any illegal outside assistance. Missing a contact zone, knocking down an obstacle, running an incorrect course without correction, excessive refusals, leaving the see-saw too early, excessive handling or coaching, harsh commands or corrections, eliminating on the course, exceeding the maximum course time and failure to perform all are grounds for mandatory disqualification.

Bet You Didn't Know

Like a trap, a "call-off" is used by the course designer to make the run more challenging. An incorrect obstacle is located directly in the dog's path, and the handler must call the dog off that path and onto the correct one prior to the dog committing itself to the incorrect obstacle.

Designers know how to make a course easier or more difficult depending on the skill level of the handler and the dog. They use the approach angles, the order of the obstacles and the positions of the obstacles to create a challenge within the given division. Each course designer tries to keep his courses interesting by varying both the pace and the intricacies of the obstacles. They keep handlers and dogs on their toes through call-offs, traps and options. He can further throw a wrench into the competition by placing restrictions on the handlers at various places throughout the course. At the novice level, however, no restrictions can be used.

Sizing It Up

Are you beginning to see just how challenging this sport can be? Let's look further at some of the difficulties a small dog such as a JRT can have with agility competitions as well as at some of the advantages their size might provide.

Perhaps the biggest disadvantage a Jack Russell Terrier has compared to a Border Collie or similar dog is that the obstacles often are over the JRT's head. It often spends much of its time looking up to see which obstacle is coming up next. A large A-frame might look like a mountain to a JRT but not be nearly as intimidating to a German Shepherd. Likewise, it takes more energy and effort for a JRT to push through a heavy closed tunnel than for a larger dog to accomplish the same activity.

Navigating a course is more difficult for the JRT handler as well. Because smaller dogs must get closer to the obstacles to effectively traverse them, the handler has less time to position herself around the course and might distract the dog by moving from side to side. It is easier to tell where a large dog is inside a tunnel, and the handler has the benefit of knowing when the dog will emerge.

On the flip side, the Jack Russell Terrier is very sure on its feet and is lightning fast on the sprints over and between obstacles. Narrow obstacles such as the dog walk and burrowing obstacles such as the tunnel work pose few problems for your agile little terrier. And because JRTs love to jump, the hurdles encountered on the course rarely appear daunting to the JRT. It also is easier to keep a small dog in shape during inclement weather. In the end, however, you need to judge for yourself whether your terrier has what it takes to be an agility star.

Training Tips

Complete training of the agility dog is far beyond the scope of this book let alone this chapter, but I will give you some helpful hints to start you on your way, should you decide you'd like to give agility training a try. If, after trying some of the techniques and attending some agility competitions as a spectator, you decide you'd like to give it a serious go, find some good books geared specifically toward agility training and start mapping out your schooling strategy. Remember that agility training takes a serious time commitment and lots of patience. Make sure you are up for it before you invest too much time and money into the sport.

Doggy Do's

Train your JRT without excessively bending over the obstacles. Not only is it harder for you to keep up with your JRT if you constantly are down at the obstacle's level, you will look silly crawling around the course after your terrier.

Jack Russell Schwarzenegger

Conditioning and training your dog for agility work go firmly hand in hand. Don't kid yourself. Agility is a physical sport for both the handler and the dog. Your terrier must be in peak physical condition to navigate the courses at top speeds, and you have to be equally physically fit to keep up with it. Plan to spend lots of time working on strength and cardiovascular fitness prior to starting serious obstacle training.

Start Off Slowly

After you and your terrier have reached an acceptable a level of fitness, start introducing some of the required obstacles. A low dog walk and small jumps often are some of the easiest obstacles for your JRT to master. If you keep the obstacles close to the ground at first, your terrier is less likely to be intimidated should it take a fall or misjudge a jump. As its confidence grows, you can increase the heights of the obstacles and can introduce some of the more difficult equipment such as the A-frame and weave poles.

Keep Practice Fun

The easiest way to coax a terrier over, around and through an obstacle is to make a game of it. Terriers love to play and love to eat. Use both of these interests to make your training sessions into one long play session, and your JRT will amaze you at how quickly it can pick things up. If you fall into the trap of getting too serious too quickly, however, your JRT will easily know the difference and will become surly and reluctant.

Doggy Don'ts

Don't push your puppy into agility work right away. Not only are its focus and concentration levels not fully developed, neither are its bones and joints. Let your puppy grow up first before committing it to agility training.

Remember that agility competitions are supposed to be fun for both you and your JRT. You can't, no matter how hard you try, coerce your JRT into learning through intimidation or force. It might work briefly, but in the long run, your terrier will always outsmart you and will put its efforts into evasion rather than cooperation.

A good agility team is based on trust, commitment and teamwork. Without these fundamentals, success will be fleeting at best and a distant dream at worse. There should be no pressure to perform and no punishment for hesitancy. There should be only pure joy at a job well done when you and your terrier successfully navigate your first agility course!

Bet You Didn't Know

Many dog trainers eventually substitute a clicker for food or treats while training. At first, the two are used interchangeably to let the dog know it has performed correctly. As the dog progresses, however, the clicker is used more often as a training reinforcement.

The Least You Need to Know

➤ Agility has become an increasingly popular sport that requires dogs and their handlers to navigate a complex course of obstacles.

➤ In agility contests, all breeds compete together using fundamentally the same course.

➤ The obstacles used in agility are designed to test your dog's specific skills and training.

➤ The dog must complete the course within the standard course time to avoid a penalty.

➤ It's the course designer's job to make the course tough. That's what keeps it fun!

➤ Some JRTs take to agility training more readily than others. You need to be honest about your individual terrier's strengths and weaknesses when deciding whether it might be successful.

➤ Wait until your puppy is old enough to concentrate and until its bones have matured before beginning agility work.

➤ If you make agility training fun for your JRT, you will have a much more cooperative terrier.

Part 6

Educate Yourself

With so many resources available in today's marketplace, only an idiot would refuse to use relevant information that could help him make the best decisions possible. Since you're reading this book, this obviously excludes you.

There is so much information to be learned that even a book as wonderful as this will still leave questions in your mind about specific subjects, training techniques and health concerns. This part provides a multitude of other places to look for any information you need, from how to find the right club to training your dog not to eat your couch. If you are looking to expand your mental horizons, you've come to the right place. Let's see what we can find!

The American Kennel Club

The AKC—History and Programs

The American Kennel Club was established as a nonprofit organization in 1884, and it is the oldest registry of purebred dogs in the United States. Its services include registering individual dogs and litters, sanctioning dog events and promoting responsible breeding and dog ownership. Last year alone, the AKC registered more than one million dogs and more than 500,000 litters. This proliferation has occurred despite caveats about indiscriminate and irresponsible breeding brought about by backyard breeders intent on making a fast buck.

Many such breeders claim to be affiliated with a registry similar to the AKC to sell their puppies. An AKC puppy purchased from such a breeder, however, cannot compare in quality with an AKC puppy from a reputable, reliable breeder. AKC registry alone does not ensure quality because neither the puppy or dog being registered nor its parents are examined to determine their suitability for registration. In addition, the AKC does not require blood-typing or other proof to verify that the resulting litter is indeed the product of the claimed parents. But reputable breeders involved with the AKC and its registration strive to ensure that their stock closely conforms to the quality of perfection demanded by their particular breed standard, and they work hard to maintain accurate breeding and registration records.

Bet You Didn't Know

The American Kennel Club (AKC) does not provide registration services for dogs acquired from places such as the Humane Society or other protective leagues. It also will not register dogs donated as prizes for raffles or auctions or those purchased at sheriff's sales.

The offspring of dogs registered with the AKC automatically are eligible for registration. Dogs with only limited registration, usually dogs from one registered parent and one unregistered parent, can compete in all AKC events except conformation competitions and have access to all AKC educational and informational services. Fully registered dogs can compete in all AKC-sanctioned activities.

If a dog is sold as AKC registerable, it means the puppy or dog is eligible to be registered but the registration papers have not yet been sent in. The buyer should receive a registration application form, which the seller fills out first. He should then give it to the buyer, who will complete it and send it on to the AKC with the appropriate registration fee. All required signatures should accompany the registration application. Upon receipt and process of this registration—and provided all information furnished is complete and correct—the new owner will receive an AKC registration certificate.

The buyer should obtain all the necessary registration papers from the seller prior to purchasing the dog. If the papers still are not available when you take possession of your puppy or dog, this is a warning sign to proceed with caution with the sale or to cease and desist altogether. At the very least, call the AKC to verify that the dog can be registered and get the breeder to commit in writing to his claims. Also ask for a signed letter from the breeder stating why the papers currently are not available and stating his intent to furnish them to you as soon as they are available.

If an AKC registration application is not available to you as the buyer, you should receive a bill of sale or a written statement signed by the breeder. The document should provide full breeding information such as the dog's breed, sex, color and date of birth, and the name of the breeder and the registered names of the sire and the dam (and, hopefully, their registration numbers). If you are unable to obtain the dog's complete pedigree or if the identification you receive does not exactly match the puppy in question, you should not buy it.

Don't be afraid to trust your instincts. If you sense that something doesn't ring true or if something the breeder says makes you uncomfortable, tell the breeder you will get back to him and then do some research on your own. If the breeder claims to have AKC dogs, call the AKC directly and ask whether this breeder has stock registered with the American Kennel Club. While you have the AKC on the phone, verify that the offspring of these dogs would be eligible for registry through AKC. If the answer is no, you've saved yourself some money and heartache.

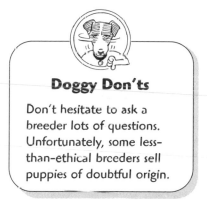

Doggy Don'ts

Don't hesitate to ask a breeder lots of questions. Unfortunately, some less-than-ethical breeders sell puppies of doubtful origin.

Who's My Family?

A female dog can mate with several males if facilities are not property regulated and controlled, thus making the dam's offspring of doubtful origin. Remember that female dogs ovulate each and every time they are bred. It is very possible for a bitch to produce puppies from more than one sire. Thus, it is possible that the sire listed on a puppy's registration papers is not the true father of the pup.

Although the AKC has taken steps to prevent this type of registration misuse, it unfortunately still occurs. You, as a buyer, should be aware of these practices and should protect yourself from this type of fraud whenever possible. The AKC will often investigate and even revoke the registration of a litter if research reveals that the inspected puppies or adult dogs do not resemble the breed under which they are registered or if the puppies have traits that could not possibly have occurred as a result of mating the two claimed dogs.

Bet You Didn't Know

The AKC employs regional field inspectors who verify the breeder's records, verify his identification and examine kennel conditions. Inspectors have the right to withdraw registration privileges if kennel conditions appear to threaten the dogs' health and well-being.

Ownership Issues

The AKC has stringent rules regarding ownership, change of ownership, ownership of dogs by commercial organizations or corporations, naming of dogs, contracts to spay or neuter and stud and dam breeding contracts. In the case of a stud contract, the AKC strongly suggests that these agreements be in writing, be clear in nature regarding the duties and responsibilities on both sides and be signed by both parties. A copy should be kept by both persons. It is incumbent upon the owner of the stud to set the stud fee. Payment can be made in cash, although the owner of the stud might request the "pick of the litter" instead. The AKC also can help with ownership problems stemming from divorce.

If a dog with AKC papers is sold or given away to a shelter or a rescue organization, the documentation must be marked "void" and returned to the AKC. It cannot be given along with the dog. Likewise, if you buy a puppy or an adult dog from a pet store, the AKC requires that the store have transfer forms available for

If a breeder claims his puppies can be registered with the AKC, you can call the club for verification.

AKC-registerable puppies purchased from private owners or breeders. These transfer forms must accompany the puppy at the time of the sale. If they are not available, it is the pet store's responsibility to supply the buyer with the puppy's breed, sex, color, correct markings, date of birth, litter number (if available), sale date and the names of the sire, dam and breeder. Such puppies cannot be registered in the store or kennel's name. Only individuals can own dogs, and the dog's ownership chain must be traceable.

Ingenious Identifications

Among its many services, the AKC sponsors a Companion Animal Recovery program that operates twenty-four hours a day. The program provides identification and recovery services by utilizing a central database that records identification numbers for dog owners that choose to use a permanent form of identification. Anyone trying to locate a dog identified with a microchip or tattoo can contact the AKC's Companion Animal Recovery program and give them the dog's identification number.

Doggy Do's

Ask lots of questions when purchasing a puppy without papers already in hand. Although you can't possibly head off every problem that might arise, you need to realize that, without already completed and processed papers, you are taking a chance that you might never end up with papers on this puppy.

Any animal shelter or participating veterinarian that retrieves a dog can scan it to see if a microchip has been implanted. As of September 1998, more than 280,000 dogs have been enrolled in this program and more than 10,000 lost animals have been reunited with their owners, representing a 100 percent success rate of recovery.

Microchips and tattoos don't guarantee that your dog won't get lost or be stolen, but it gives you an advantage in the recovery department. Permanent identification is important and should be seriously considered, especially given the amount of money invested in a registered dog compared to the very modest cost of the procedure. Note that microchip identification is not required by AKC for either registration or participation in AKC events.

Another form of identification is a tattoo. Although tattooing also offers the advantage of permanent identification, it can be less effective than a microchip over time. Tattoos can become blurred (especially if the dog grows and the tattoo stretches) and can be difficult to find on a dog's body.

Bet You Didn't Know

The AKC's Companion Animal Recovery program, a twenty-four-hour-a-day pet ID and recovery service, has successfully reunited thousands of lost pets with their owners.

The best way to have your dog tattooed or implanted with a microchip is to consult your veterinarian and have him perform the procedure. If you decide to use a microchip, an AKC Companion Animal Recovery enrollment form and collar tag will be provided. The form should be filled out and sent to the AKC immediately. If your dog already is identified with a microchip implant other than the one used by the AKC, you can call the AKC's toll-free number to ask for an enrollment form. This also can be done over the Internet, and the fee is reasonable. There is no enrollment fee for an assistance dog.

Special AKC Programs

In addition to providing registration and identification services, the AKC provides dog lovers with a wealth of information and activities.

Research Resources

One of the most widely used AKC services is its library—one of the largest libraries devoted to dogs worldwide. The library was established in April 1934, and it presently contains around 16,000 volumes. It includes bound periodicals, foreign and domestic stud books, art, literature, juvenile books, videos, stamps and bookplates. A collection of *AKC Gazettes*, the official AKC publication, and stud books are available to people involved in research.

The AKC library is an archive for anything about purebred dogs, and it covers topics ranging from origins and breeding to practically any dog-related item of interest to dog owners. It provides assistance, guidance and direction to anyone interested in advancing the welfare and understanding of purebred dogs.

Its main categories include individual breeds, training, breeding and care. The library subscribes to more than 250 periodicals and newspapers worldwide that provide information about sporting, hound, working, terrier, toy, nonsporting and herding breeds.

The library's primary function is to respond to requests for information not available from other AKC departments. Its staff attempts to obtain the necessary information to enable dog owners to make selective and informed choices regarding their specific area of inquiry.

Won't You Be My Neighbor?

The AKC also sponsors the American Kennel Club Canine Good Citizen program. This is a certification program that tests a dog's behavior in daily situations in a relaxed and positive atmosphere. Dogs demonstrating that they are reliable members of the family and are members of the community in good standing receive an AKC certificate.

Bet You Didn't Know

The AKC's Canine Good Citizen program urges everyone who owns a dog to participate in its certification. The program focuses on the training that makes meeting a dog a pleasant event. Remember, a well-behaved dog is a joy rather than a nuisance and, as a rule, is welcomed everywhere.

The program is fun as well as beneficial and is not competitive in nature. In addition to creating a new bond with your dog, it also represents a test of your dog's good manners and its desire to please you. Both purebred and mixed-breed dogs are accepted. Tests include acceptance of strangers in a friendly situation, sitting quietly and allowing petting in the presence of its owner, appearance and grooming and walking on a loose leash or through a crowd. Other tests involve the "sit" and "down" commands, coming when called, reaction to strange dogs or other distractions that cross its path and the ability to be left alone if necessary.

Bet You Didn't Know

The AKC's Obedience Department focuses on training your dog and offers puppy classes and basic classes for other dogs. It also offers Canine Good Citizen, novice, advanced novice (which prepares your dog to enter obedience trials) and training-for-tracking classes that develop your dog's ability to track humans.

The Canine Good Citizen test is administered at a variety of locations including kennel clubs, obedience clubs, training facilities, parks, recreation centers or community colleges. Anyone interested in this program can obtain forms and kits directly from the AKC if your group, club or interested organization of dog owners wants to coordinate an event.

Health Watch

The AKC's Canine Health Foundation was established in 1995 and was started with a $1 million endowment. Its purpose is to support and encourage research to foster healthy dogs, particularly in the area of genetics. The AKC and its Canine Health Foundation have been leaders in funding research to identify and solve genetic problems currently affecting dogs worldwide. The AKC Canine Health Foundation has enabled researchers to create vaccines such as the one developed for the parvovirus, a disease which kills puppies and young dogs of all breeds.

Dogs can suffer a variety of ailments that lead to severe health problems and even death. Although some diseases, such as arthritis or cancer, are similar to those found in humans, others are breed-specific. The work of researchers such as Dr. George Brewer of the University of Michigan, for example, has resulted in the identification of a gene that causes copper toxicosis in Bedlington Terriers. This discovery has the potential to completely eliminate this particular disease. A recent infusion of Foundation funds has been earmarked for identifying genetic markers for various doggy diseases. Work currently is in progress in the hope that such research will help prevent potentially fatal diseases from being passed on to future dog generations.

The AKC's Research Planning Department serves its membership and addresses issues of importance to future generations of dogs. It conducts surveys over the Internet, collects data to glean the public's view and perception of the AKC, examines dog-show participants' attitudes and focuses on other issues dealing with how the public views purebred dogs.

Smart Starts

The AKC awards scholarships to outstanding college students who have in some way substantially contributed to the world of purebred dogs. In 1998, forty-seven such scholarships were awarded to deserving students based on financial need, academic performance, future potential and the student's involvement with purebred dogs. Students must be enrolled full time in an accredited college of veterinary medicine.

271

An Educational Services Division booth was created in 1996 and serves as an information center to answer questions and to supply information about breeder referral, show rules and dog registration. This booth travels all over the country to show sites. In 1997, it visited twenty-five shows attended by more than 500,000 people.

The goal of the club's Public Education Department is to promote responsible dog ownership to the public and to advance the sport of purebred dogs. Some of its programs also are geared to children. This department holds public seminars twice a year. The seminars are open to all AKC members, and they offer dog owners an opportunity to network and to discuss issues of mutual interest.

The AKC employs the services of a consultant specializing in government relations to represent its interests in Washington, D.C. This person's responsibilities are to coordinate with other animal-related organizations and to generate federal legislation of importance to dog fanciers. State legislation is monitored through the efforts of more than forty AKC clubs statewide. Many state laws have been enacted as a result of these efforts to ensure the safety, health and protection of dogs, dog buyers and kennel owners.

Bet You Didn't Know

Many of the AKC's pamphlets and much of its information on the Internet includes everyday, practical tips such as where to board your dog, what to look for in a boarding kennel (security, comfort, composition of the runs and how often the facilities are cleaned) and other concerns.

The AKC's online service provides quick and accurate information about the club, its services and just about any area of interest or inquiry. The email address is info@akc.org. It is a good idea to supply your dog's name and registration number for a faster and more accurate response and to assist the AKC staff if you are seeking an answer to a specific question about your dog.

AKC vis-à-vis Jack Russell Terriers

The Jack Russell Terrier Breeders Association (JRTBA), now the Jack Russell Terrier Association of America, is cooperating with the AKC in registering Jack Russell Terriers. In 1987, the organization began restructuring itself to meet the AKC's guidelines. In 1992, it also incorporated the AKC's structure and layout. Their by-laws also follow the AKC format.

Although the AKC officially recognized the Jack Russell Terrier as of November 1, 1998, the AKC's secretary advised that, effective March 1998, the AKC has decided to no longer accept open registrations for Jack Russell Terriers. The AKC also stated that all future dogs wanting to become AKC registered must come from AKC-registered parents, and the breeder must register the litter with the AKC. In other words, if you want an AKC-registered puppy, you must purchase a puppy with previously registered AKC parents or from an AKC-registered litter.

The Least You Need to Know

➤ The AKC is the oldest dog registry in the United States.

➤ When purchasing an AKC-registered dog, make sure you have all the proper registration forms, a bill of sale and your dog's vital statistics prior to concluding the purchase.

➤ It is important for your dog to wear a permanent ID such as a tattoo or a microchip in addition to a tag on its collar. This increases its chances of being promptly reunited with you if it is lost or stolen.

➤ The AKC provides information that covers many areas of interest to dog owners.

➤ The AKC can be reached via the Internet by emailing info@akc.org. Don't forget to have your dog's name and registration number handy if you are seeking specific information about your dog.

➤ The AKC currently is not accepting registration of Jack Russell Terriers unless the puppy comes from a registered litter or from an AKC-registered parent.

The Jack Russell Terrier Club of America (JRTCA)

The Other Alternative

The Jack Russell Terrier Club of America (JRTCA) was founded in 1976 to maintain and preserve the characteristics that make the Jack Russell so special. It is the national breed club and registry for Jack Russell Terriers in the United States, and its main focus is to retain the integrity and physical structure of the breed as it was established in England. This means the JRTCA wants to preserve the characteristics and instincts needed to perform as working and hunting dogs rather than merely as show pieces.

The original JRTs developed by Parson Jack in England possessed a strong sense of confidence, loyalty, intelligence and tenacity—characteristics crucial for a dog asked to flush a fox from its den. They also possessed the conformation traits of small chests, angulated shoulders, powerful hindquarters and strong forepaws that made it easy for them to go to ground after their prey. Add to this a natural desire to dig and explore subterranean dens, and you have the perfect fox-hunting terrier.

Thoughts and Ideals

Working in concert with the Jack Russell Terrier Club of Great Britain (JRTCGB) and the Jack Russell Terrier United World Federation (JRTUWF), which is a worldwide organization, the JRTCA opposes registration of Jack Russell Terriers with the American Kennel Club or any other all-breed registry. The JRTCA fears that, should the breed be registered by these organizations, the history and purpose of the dog will be sacrificed for show-ring appeal. The organization does not want Jack Russells to fall victim to the fate of other purebred breeds and succumb to genetic and mental defects and the effects of inbreeding.

Likewise, the JRTCA opposes registration with the United Kennel Club (UKC). The UKC, like the AKC, registers a variety of breeds. The UKC began accepting Jack Russell Terriers for registration in 1992 against JRTCA's advice and wishes, but many owners supported the move. As JRTs become increasingly popular, it is inevitable that additional registries will spring up to offer even more registry choices to JRT owners. It is important to keep in mind, however, that you are the final judge and jury when it comes to deciding what registry and clubs are right for you. Everyone is likely to have an opinion, but you are the one who has to live with your decision.

The JRTCA believes Jack Russell Terriers have maintained their integrity of form and function by avoiding inbreeding and by keeping out serious faults since the late 1800s. Many other breeds either no longer resemble their ancestors or the resemblance has considerably faded. Opponents, however, cite the ever-increasing physical problems within the breed as proof that these standards simply aren't working.

Like JRTs, JRTCA proponents are a tenacious group and are devoted to preserving their opinion of what the breed should be. Another of the group's goals is to demand the highest standards from Jack Russell breeders. The organization also seeks to inform and educate the public about the breed, and it urges newcomers to investigate the

JRT's idiosyncrasies *before* buying one. Again, it cannot be emphasized enough that you are not buying a Wishbone or an Eddie. You've read it repeatedly throughout this book but it cannot be overemphasized—Jack Russell Terriers are not for everyone.

JRTCA Breed Registry

The JRTCA's breed registry is unique in that each application for registration is judged on the dog's own merits. The registration of the dog's parents does not automatically ensure that the offspring will be accepted for registry. A JRT cannot be registered until it is 1 year old so that its teeth, height and other aspects of its growth and maturity can be evaluated. The terrier then is either accepted or denied based on its own unique merits or faults.

To register a dog with the JRTCA, certain documents must be obtained. First, an original veterinarian's certificate (do not accept a copy) designed specifically for Jack Russell Terriers should be issued by a licensed vet and should be signed within thirty days of application. The certificate must state that the dog has been examined and that it is free of genetic defects such as hip dysplasia or epilepsy. If your dog has been neutered or spayed, an appropriate certificate attesting to this fact from an accredited veterinarian can be accepted in lieu of a vet certificate.

Bet You Didn't Know

Unlike other registries, the JRTCA will not register entire litters at birth. Each dog must be registered individually, provided it meets the registry's stringent requirements after it reaches 1 year of age.

As of January 1, 1997, a full four-generation pedigree issued by the breeder (with five generations preferred) also must accompany the application for registry. Any dog that shows significant inbreeding will not be accepted for registration. A three-generation pedigree is required to register a spayed or neutered dog. The owner of the sire also must supply a stud certificate that verifies the breeding of the stud to the dam of the dog to be registered.

Clear photographs of the dog (front, back and side views) must be submitted to evaluate its conformity to breed standards. The photos should be taken on level ground and should clearly show the dog's body, legs and feet. The front photo should clearly show the ears, head and legs to evaluate conformation. Each photo must be signed by your veterinarian as truly representing the dog examined. A new veterinarian certificate form was implemented in January 1996, and the registry no longer accepts registrations submitted on forms older than January 1995.

If your Jack Russell Terrier was purchased from a breeder that has a kennel registered with the JRTCA, the kennel name can precede your chosen terrier's name. If the breeder is not JRTCA registered, the kennel name cannot be included as part of your dog's registered name. The club recommends that breeding stock be registered prior to being bred. Although the JRTCA cannot endorse or recommend a specific breeder to prospective buyers, it will supply a JRTCA informational packet containing an extensive breeders' directory that lists more than ninety breeders throughout the United States. The listings include a picture and a description of the JRTCA breeders, all of whom must subscribe to the Breeders' Code of Ethics.

Any dogs not accepted into the registry are certified, which means the owner receives a certificate and the dog is listed in the registry files as certified but not registered. The JRTCA prides itself on turning down dogs unsuitable for registry due to genetic defects and other physical flaws, thus attempting to protect the Jack Russell's future and physical integrity by keeping serious faults from being propagated within the breed. Many critics, however, claim that these faults are creeping in regardless of the registration policy and feel that the AKC is as discriminating in their stock, thus fueling the controversy between these registries.

Russell Rescue

One of the most important and valuable services the JRTCA offers is its Russell Rescue's placement service for abandoned or displaced JRTs. This labor of love is supported by people who care and are concerned about all Jack Russell Terriers and their welfare. Many people make the mistake of purchasing a Jack Russell because their kids think they're cute and want "a funny little dog like the one on TV," only to discover that the dog's personality and traits don't fit in with the family's lifestyle. Many of these dogs end up in a rescue placement service, some living with several families before finding a permanent home.

The donations received by Russell Rescue are used for spaying and neutering, vet services, vaccinations, temporary housing and other needs of abandoned terriers. Russell Rescue cautions potential adoptive owners that many rescue dogs have special problems that must be recognized and addressed *prior* to making a commitment to a rescued Jack Russell.

Doggy Don'ts

Don't buy a Jack Russell Terrier with your heart rather than your head. This little dog and its funny antics might not be for you, despite its wide appeal. Rescue placement services are filled with "owners' mistakes," in which families didn't take the time to make sure a Jack Russell Terrier was the right dog for them.

Applying for a Rescue Dog

Not everyone applying for a Russell Rescue dog is approved. Applicants must first answer some tough questions about why they are interested in a JRT, and they must demonstrate that they are fully aware of the responsibility they are accepting.

It is important to Russell Rescue that rescued dogs not go through yet another traumatic experience and end up with the wrong family again. Some dogs have been abused or left alone for extended periods of time, or they are simply unwanted because they didn't live up to their owners' expectations. They are not bad dogs; they

Doggy Do's

If you are unsure whether a JRT is right for you, consider becoming a foster parent to a rescued terrier. Applications for both adoption and foster parenting are available from the JRTCA office. This might be a good way for you to decide whether you want to become an adoptive parent to a rescued JRT.

An important arm of the JRTCA is Russell Rescue, a group that finds new homes for abandoned Jack Russells.

are just typical terriers. It takes a special home and family to give them the love and care they need so they won't be adopted over and over.

If you have the patience and the time to devote to such a dog, you might find that owning a rescue dog can be a fulfilling and rewarding experience for you while giving the dog a second chance at a good home. Keep in mind that these dogs have been through a difficult period in their lives, and they need perhaps even more love and attention than a puppy purchased from a breeder who has been pampered from the start and knows it belongs with its family.

Rescue dogs are like older adopted children who aren't sure whether they will fit in and who often feel insecure about their status in the family. Most make wonderful pets if given the chance and if their owners recognize and accept that they have adopted a Jack Russell Terrier, not a Poodle or a Labrador Retriever. If you do decide to adopt such a dog, you might want to join the JRTCA and find a group of JRTCA owners with whom you can exchange information and vent frustrations if necessary.

Rescue Requirements

Russell Rescue has requirements that prospective adoptive families must meet prior to being accepted into the program. A fence or a contained area is a must, as is a home without children under 6 years old. Adoptive homes should be cat-free because older JRTs don't usually share their space well with cats. Apartments also are discouraged as homes for adopted JRTs, particularly if the family members are away for extended periods during the day because of work and school obligations.

Bet You Didn't Know

Jack Russell Terriers require firm and consistent discipline. Their intelligence will test the limits of your patience, and a JRT will often train you rather than the other way around. Be sure to learn about JRTs in advance to make sure their personalities and quirks won't clash with your own.

Unfortunately, but understandably, many applications for a Russell Rescue dog are not approved. Each is looked over carefully to determine whether the family, home and lifestyle are suited to adopting a rescued JRT, and it must be understood from the outset that application does not guarantee acceptance. As soon as the application is approved or denied, the applicant is contacted and given the information. If you apply and are declined, remember that Russell Rescue workers want to place the rescue dog in the most appropriate home possible, and they strive to ensure wise and permanent placement for their wards.

Even if you find that this type of dog isn't for you, all Russell Rescue homes need the support of the general public to continue their work. The public can help by.

➤ Making donations of dog supplies

➤ Offering free veterinary services for spaying and neutering

➤ Paying for costs involved in shipping a dog to its new home

➤ Providing advertising services

➤ Providing dog-grooming assistance

➤ Contributing funds for educational programs to instruct the public about the personality of the Jack Russell Terrier

Surfing Sources

The JRTCA's Bad Dog Talk Web page is particularly valuable to prospective JRT owners in that it illustrates many of the worst-case scenarios of owning a Jack Russell. It enables people to see situations in which the dogs are acting as normal terriers. If a family cannot cope with these typical JRT behaviors, it should look to buy another more placid breed that is better suited to the family's temperament.

Among other things listed on the Web page are reminders of the typical JRT personality—JRTs are very active, they often can be aggressive with other animals and pets, they fare better in a home with a yard and they must be kept busy and exercised. Most of all, they are social little creatures who do not do well if left alone all day or if ignored for extended periods of time. Both experienced and novice JRT owners can become overwhelmed by the demands a Jack Russell makes on their lives and time, which often is why they give up the terrier that will ultimately end up in rescue placement.

Numerous JRTCA Web pages address subjects ranging from training equipment to crate training, deafness, housetraining, separation anxiety, play equipment and inherited defects. *True Grit*, the official JRTCA Web site, offers picture galleries, video clips, funny stories and many links to JRT Web pages and sources of videos and books.

Bet You Didn't Know

The JRTCA's official publication is *True Grit* magazine, named after the feisty nature of the dog. It contains many articles of interest to Jack Russell Terrier owners. A subscription is offered free of charge with each JRTCA membership.

True Grit also lists trial schedules, terrier trial events and affiliated clubs. If you plan to show your Jack Russell in obedience or working competitions, the JRTCA offers Web sites devoted solely to conformation and obedience training as well as training tips for showing and working events.

The Jack Talk Forum offers a long list of valuable topics, problems and anecdotes from Jack Russell owners who then have the opportunity to read the questions and answers from other JRT owners worldwide. The forum can help people understand that the specific activity, trait or strange behavior demonstrated by their JRT often is typical of the breed and that they are not alone in their frustrations. The forum covers a range of topics from the use of electric fences to behavior problems to housetraining or excessive barking. Some of these questions and answers are humorous, some are informative and all are valuable. You are bound to find a topic that parallels your own experience with your individual terrorist, and you might even get the answer to a question or concern that you've wondered about.

The JRTCA training tips Web page (http://www.terrier.com/puptrain.htm) lists valuable tips for training your dog and advises on a variety of topics ranging from training equipment to housetraining, submissive urination, aggression and training a deaf terrier.

Bet You Didn't Know

All judges of go to ground trial events must be sanctioned by the JRTCA. It is a matter of opinion whether a good go to ground terrier also makes a good hunting terrier or vice versa.

Another valuable feature offered by the JRTCA Web page is the Tips, Advice and Training section that covers topics ranging from how to join JRTCA to a question-and-answer section addressing the most frequently asked questions of Jack Russell owners. Keep in mind, however, that these resources reflect the JRTCA's viewpoint and do not represent the views of other registries. Ultimately, only you can make the decision as to which registry you want to join. It is up to you, and only you, to use all the information available from a variety of sources to make your own, personal, educated decision.

Jack Russell Terrier mania has spread worldwide. Many JRTs now can be found on the Jack Russell Friends Web page that covers more than 175 areas all over the world including Malaysia, Australia, Canada, Japan, the Cayman Islands, Singapore, Europe and the Philippines. In addition, the JRTCA's Affiliated Clubs Web page contains a list of nationwide clubs for JRT enthusiasts in one geographic area who want to communicate amongst themselves and to share their affinity for the breed. It is suggested that any club wanting to affiliate with the JRTCA should e-mail or write for an application. State representatives are readily available for help and information.

The External Links section contains links to Web sites maintained outside the control of the JRTCA by individual Webmasters. The opinions reflected in these links do not necessarily reflect those of the JRTCA. The external links include performance-related links, publication links about dogs on the Web and in print (Howell Book House and Amazon) and miscellaneous links covering a range of topics from traveling with your dog to "bad dog" anecdotes.

Doggy Do's

Take advantage of all the Web pages, informational sites and books that exist about Jack Russell Terriers and the activities unique to the breed. You'll be surprised and amazed at the amount of valuable information available at very little expense to you, and you'll encounter innumerable ideas that will make living with your terrorist a bit easier.

JRTCA Members Only is a section that provides JRTCA members with up-to-date information about the organization. There also is a section in which JRT owners or prospective owners can read more than 400 stories and anecdotes written by Jack Russell owners.

The JRTCA go to ground Web page is devoted to anything and everything JRT owners might want to know about equipment, rules and classes. It even provides diagrams to help people understand the events and to give owners wanting to enroll their dogs in trial events a thorough understanding of what to expect.

The medical information Web page addresses inherited diseases in JRTs as well as other health problems your terrier might encounter. It offers articles and information about ear and eye testing, the ASPCA and

National Animal Poison Control, heart disease and many other health concerns. This information, however, should not be considered a substitute for seeking your vet's advice in the case of your own JRT's illness or injury.

Yet another service of the JRTCA is a list of affiliated clubs throughout the United States. JRT enthusiasts can keep in touch and can participate in JRT activities in their local areas. You might want to check the Web site http://www.terrier.com/clubs.htm to determine whether there is a nearby club to join. Or you might want to inquire about forming your own club by contacting the JRTCA office via e-mail at JRTCA@worldnet.att.net. You also can find out how to affiliate with the JRTCA if you have already formed a club of your own.

The Least You Need to Know

➤ The JRTCA was founded to preserve and maintain the special characteristics of the Jack Russell Terrier, particularly its integrity as a fox hunter rather than as a show dog.

➤ The JRTCA registers each dog based on its own merits and does not register entire litters at birth.

➤ Do not buy a JRT puppy or dog unless you have the complete documentation from the breeder. This documentation is required to register your dog.

➤ Russell Rescue is one of the many services the JRTCA offers to displaced, rejected or unwanted dogs whose owners didn't take the time to find out that a JRT wasn't the right breed for them.

➤ The JRTCA has a Web site that provides answers to just about any questions a JRT owner might have on a multitude of subjects.

➤ Ultimately, the decision to join the AKC, the JRTCA or any other dog registry rests with you. Be sure to check out all the registries to form your own opinion to decide which one is best for you.

Chapter 23

Jack Russells Online

A Family of Friends

Although just a few years ago the Jack Russell Terrier was virtually unknown to all but its enthusiasts, the use of JRTs on television and in films has boosted their popularity dramatically. Currently, thousands of Jack Russell Terrier owners can be found both in the United States and overseas. Obviously, all these folks have something in common—a love for the funny little dog that owns them and a desire to be in touch with people who share their enthusiasm and affection for the breed. If nothing else, it's nice to know other people out there are as crazy as you are for owning one or more of these little terrorists.

With the increase in popularity of the World Wide Web and the growing number of Jack Russell Terrier enthusiasts, many new Web sites are dedicated to locating and informing Jack Russell Terrier owners about specific activities, areas of interest and clubs to bring together JRT lovers and enthusiasts, owners or prospective owners.

Many of these sites also offer information, training tips and other useful ideas about how to entertain your dog and how to meet other Jack Russell Terrier owners.

Doggy Don'ts

Don't join a club just because it is close and handy. Find a club in which dog owners are compatible, are friendly and like to share their experiences with their own JRTs.

Both nationally and internationally, there are many JRT breed registries such as the American Kennel Club (AKC), the Kennel Club (KC) in the United Kingdom and the Canadian Kennel Club (CKC). Most of these registries contain links to every breed and every interest such as obedience trials, agility trials and the like. World Class Dogs has an extensive Web site that lists many domestic and foreign clubs. Its home page is located at **www.worldclassdogs.com/** WCD-DogClubs.html, where you can search for a JRT club near you.

With the recent introduction of the Jack Russell Terrier into the ranks of the American Kennel Club's accepted breeds, many JRT owners are curious as to the standards required of this new registering entity and the benefits and drawbacks of this registry versus those that have been in place for a long time. As of this writing, the AKC currently is not accepting any outside registrations (those of dogs produced from non–AKC-registered parents). It is, however, still accepting inquiries about the AKC in general and about JRTs specifically. The AKC can be reached on the Internet at **info@akc.org.**

If you prefer to use less technical means to contact the AKC, it can be reached as follows:

American Kennel Club
260 Madison Avenue
New York, NY 10016
(919) 233-9767 (Information and Registration)
(212) 696-8200 (General Information)
(212) 696-8300 (Events)
(212) 696-8299 (Fax)

Bet You Didn't Know

Whether you are interested in entering your dog in an obedience trial, an agility trial or a working class, you should have no problem finding a club for your dog to compete in its chosen activity.

The Jack Russell Terrier Club of America (JRTCA) is the oldest and largest of the registries recognizing the Jack Russell Terrier in the United States. It is geared solely to JRTs (see Chapter 22 for more information) and is focused less on the show ring than on hunting and working terriers. Its home page at **www.terrier.com** contains a wealth of links and information about the breed ranging from how to decide whether a JRT is right for you to video clips and worldwide JRT links. It also contains a multitude of stories from other Jack Russell owners about their dogs' antics and odd behaviors. This is a good place to go if you are feeling overwhelmed by your terrier's personality and need to know whether others are having the same problems you are.

The JRTCA Affiliated Clubs list can be found at the preceding home page under "JRTCA Menu." This page currently lists recognized clubs by geographical areas, and clubs can be found all over the country. The JRTCA can be reached via e-mail at **JRTCA@worldnet.att.net** if you are looking to form a club or just want to find one in your area. The organization always is seeking information about JRTs all over the world, and it always is looking for new ways to reach Jack Russell owners and enthusiasts.

If you prefer to write or phone, you can use the following information:

JRTCA
P.O. Box 4527
Lutherville, MD 21094-4527
(410) 561-3655 (Phone)
(410) 560-2563 (Fax)

The Dirt-Dog.com Web page also lists JRT clubs in certain areas of the country and in some foreign countries. This page can be found at **www.dirt-dog.com/clubs/index.html.** It is a good source for local, regional and national terrier clubs, and it often lists schedules and planned events for these clubs.

The Dog Zone currently lists JRT clubs in Arizona, Georgia, Ohio, Virginia and British Columbia. You can access its Web page at **www.dogzone.com/clubs/jackruss.htm** for more information and for a list of contact persons' names, addresses and e-mail addresses.

The Canine Connections Web site at **www.cheta.net/connect/ canine/clubs/bystate.htm** features U.S. breeds and kennel clubs by state and by breed as well as an index of information about clubs, pet products, recipes, breeders and so on. This is a good all-around site for people in search of additional information about dogs in general.

The English Jack Russell Terrier Club of America, Inc. is the newly formed official registry for the short-legged Jack Russell Terrier. This club is dedicated to establishing recognition as a division of the breed. Because this type of JRT is not preferred by the other registries, this new registry provides recognition and registration possibilities that were previously unavailable to these dog owners. With the increased popularity of this smaller, more compact Jack Russell, this is the place to meet and talk with other small JRT owners. Anyone who owns or is contemplating purchasing a short-legged JRT might want to contact this organization for its list of clubs and trial schedules at **http://ejrtca.com.** Its e-mail address is jks4me@earthlink.net.

Bet You Didn't Know

Although short-legged Jack Russell Terriers are considered "incorrect" by AKC and JRTCA standards, they make excellent pets and now even have their own official registry, the English Jack Russell Terrier Club of America, Inc.

Jack Russell Terriers are so lovable that they've generated a mind-boggling number of organizations and Web sites devoted just to them.

The following are other organizations devoted to Jack Russell Terriers:

The Jack Russell Terrier Breeders' Association
P.O. Box 115
Winchester Center, CT 06094
(203) 379-3282

The Jack Russell Terrier Club of Canada
242 Henrietta St.
Fort Erie, Ontario
Canada L2A 2K7
(905) 871-8691

The Jack Russell Terrier Club of Great Britain
Aston Heath Farm
Sudbury, Derbyshire
England DEGS88

The American Working Terrier Association
P.O. Box QQ
East Quogue, NY 11942

The Least You Need to Know

➤ Although living with a Jack Russell Terrier often can be overwhelming, remember the many resources on magazine shelves, at the book store and on the Internet that can answer just about any question you might have.

➤ With a little time and effort, you can find a local club where you can share your experiences (both good and bad) with other JRT owners and know you're not alone.

➤ Many Internet resources are available to help you locate a club for almost any interest. Ask another JRT owner for suggestions of clubs near you or go surfing on the Internet to see what you can find. If you are not comfortable with your choice, keep looking.

Recommended Reading and Resources

In addition to the many Internet sites provided in Chapter 23, numerous books and magazines are aimed at Jack Russell lovers.

Magazines

True Grit magazine, the official publication of the JRTCA, is included with any JRTCA membership. It lists new clubs and activities and keeps members abreast of issues and information that affect them and their dogs. It is published in January, March, May, July, September and November.

Down to Earth, the official publication of the AWTA.

Parson's Nook, the official publication of the JRTBA.

Books

The Barnes & Noble and Amazon Web sites contain extensive listings of books that pertain to specific breeds or training, medical reference, genetics or any specific activity such as obedience trials, hunting and working. In addition to books specifically about the Jack Russell breed, general books can help when training, grooming and trying to decide whether you are interested in breeding your JRT. Many of the medical-care books provide helpful information that dog owners can use when their own veterinarians are unavailable or when immediate attention is necessary on the way to the vet's office.

The following are just a few of the books on the market that specifically target Jack Russell Terriers:

Atter, Sheila. *Jack Russell Terriers Today.* New York: Howell Book House, 1995.

Chapman, Eddie. *The Working Jack Russell Terrier.* Dorchester, Dorset, England: The Dorset Press, 1985.

Coile, Caroline D. *Jack Russell Terriers: Everything About Purchase, Care, Nutrition, Behavior and Training.* Hauppauge, NY: Barron's Educational Series, Inc., 1996.

Jackson, Jean and Frank Jackson. *Parson Jack Russell Terriers: An Owner's Companion.* Crowood Press, 1991.

James, Ken. *Working Jack Russell Terriers.* Bedford, PA: Hunter House Press, 1995.

Kosloff, George and Raymond S. Vena. *Guide to Owning a Jack Russell Terrier: Puppy Care, Grooming, Training, History, Health-Breed Standard.* Neptune, NJ: TFH Publications, 1996.

Nicholas, Anna Katherine. *Jack Russell Terriers.* Neptune, NJ: TFH Publications, 1996.

Plummer, D. Brian. *The Complete Jack Russell Terrier.* New York: Howell Book House, 1980.

Romaine Brown, Catherine. *The Jack Russell Terrier: An Owner's Guide to a Happy Healthy Pet.* New York: Howell Book House, 1996.

Romaine Brown, Catherine. *The Jack Russell Terrier: Courageous Companion.* New York: Howell Book House, 1998.

Valentine, John. *Pet Owner's Guide to the Jack Russell Terrier.* Seven Hills Book Distributors, 1997.

Index